ERIC GILL'S

MASTERPIECES OF WOOD ENGRAVING

OVER 250 ILLUSTRATIONS

EDITED AND WITH AN INTRODUCTION BY

DAVID A. BERONÄ

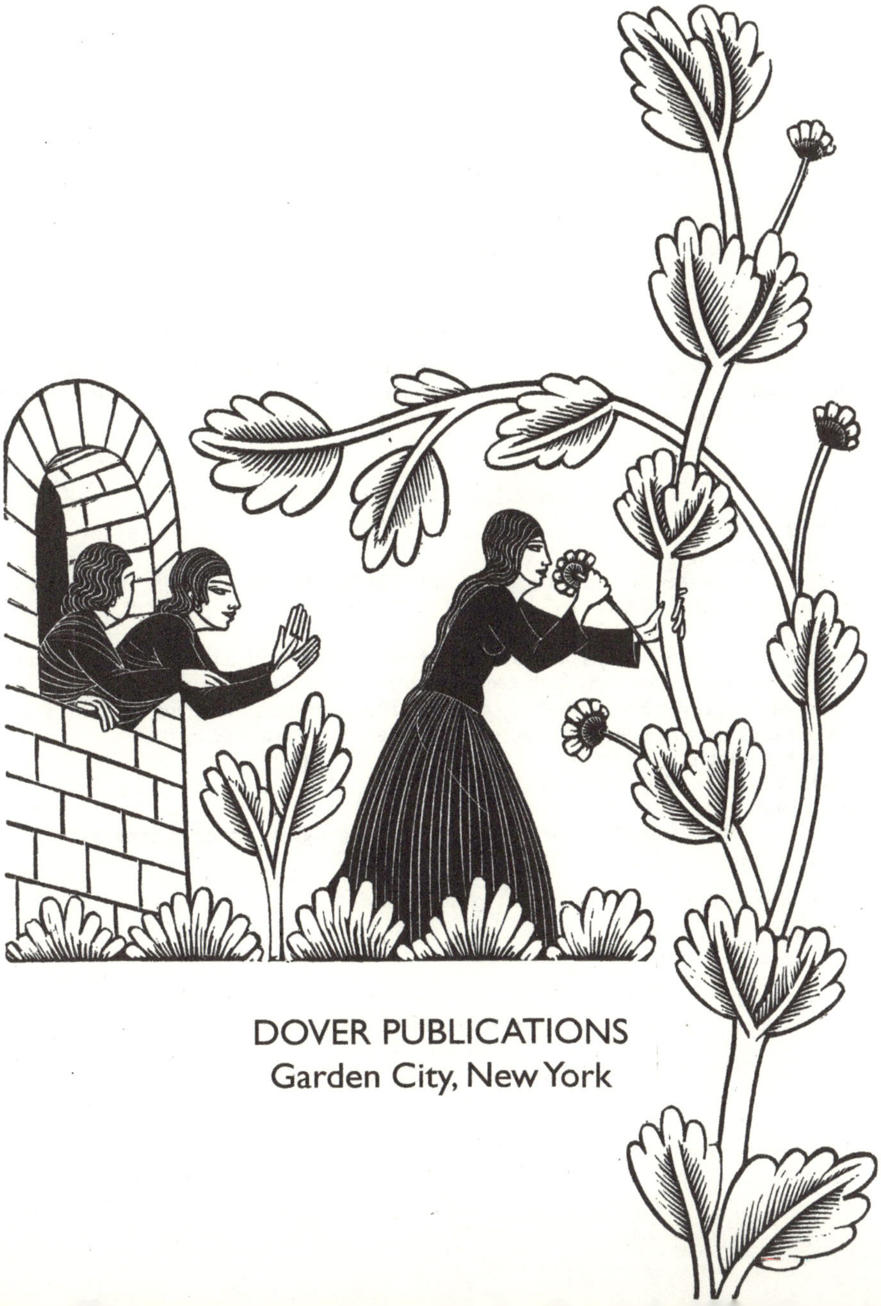

DOVER PUBLICATIONS
Garden City, New York

Sources

Andrews, Martin J. *The Life and Work of Robert Gibbings*. Bicester, England: Primrose Hill Press, 2003.

Cribb, Ruth and Joe Cribb. *Eric Gill: Lust for Letter and Line*. London: The British Museum Press, 2011.

Dreyfus, John. *A Typographical Masterpiece*. San Francisco: The Book Club of California, 1990.

Furst, John. *The Modern Woodcut*. London: John Lane The Bodley Head Limited, 1924.

Gill, Eric. *Autobiography*. London: Jonathan Cape, 1940.

—. *Engravings 1928-1933*. London: Faber & Faber Ltd, 1934.

—. *Letters of Eric Gill*. Ed. Walter Shewring. New York: The Devin-Adair Company, 1948.

—. *Twenty-Five Nudes Engraved by Eric Gill*. New York: The Devin-Adair Company, 1950.

MacCarthy, Fiona. *Eric Gill: A Lover's Quest for Art and God*. New York: E.P. Dutton, 1989.

Salaman, Malcolm C. *The Art of the Woodcut: Masterworks from the 1920s*. Mineola, New York: Dover Publications, 2010.

Skelton, Christopher. *The Engravings of Eric Gill*. Wellingborough, England: Skelton's Press, 1983.

Copyright

Bibliographical Note

Eric Gill's Masterpieces of Wood Engraving, first published by Dover Publications in 2013, is a new compilation of wood engraving plates from various sources. David A. Beronä has selected the plates and provided an Introduction specially for the Dover edition.

Library of Congress Cataloging-in-Publication Data

Gill, Eric, 1882–1940.
[Works. Selections]
Eric Gill's masterpieces of wood engraving : over 250 illustrations / Eric Gill ; edited and with an introduction by David A. Beronä
p. cm.
Summary: "This original collection gathers the finest woodcuts of one of the most creative and prolific English artists of the early 20th century. Ranging from the religious to the erotic, featured designs include images inspired by The Song of Songs, The Canterbury Tales, and The Four Gospels. A feast for the eyes and an important and accessible reference." — Provided by publisher.
Includes bibliographical references.
ISBN-13: 978-0-486-48205-7 (pbk.)
ISBN-10: 0-486-48205-7
1. Gill, Eric, 1882–1940—Themes, motives. I. Beronä, David A., editor of compilation, writer of added text. II. Title.

NE1147.6.G55A4 2012
769.92—dc23

2012030154

Manufactured in the United States of America
48205703
www.doverpublications.com

INTRODUCTION

DAVID A. BERONÄ

Gill was a most extraordinary person, and it is very strange how his immediacy lingers.

—Fiona MacCarthy

Eric Gill (1882–1940) was a noted letter cutter, typographer, sculptor, wood engraver, and writer of the twentieth century—as well as a man of contradictions, as Fiona MacCarthy claims in her revealing 1989 biography, the first to clearly disclose the sexual transgressions (including incest and numerous affairs) documented by Gill in his diaries and *Autobiography* but glossed over by previous biographers. His wood engravings present Gill's opposing religious and secular themes and represent a pinnacle of the wood engraving revival that dominated book illustration in the early twentieth century.

Gill originally pursued work as an apprentice draughtsman for a London architect. He also attended classes in stonemasonry at Westminster Technical College and enrolled in calligraphy courses at the Central School of Arts and Crafts. There he met Edward Johnson, who is recognized, along with the German type designer Rudolf Koch, as the founders of modern calligraphy. Gill left his apprenticeship and, through the encouragement of Johnson, started a business as a letterer and memorial mason. In 1904 he married Ethel (Mary) Moore; in 1905 he joined Johnson in an Arts and Crafts community in Hammersmith. Here he became interested in the ideals and traditions of the Arts and Crafts movement, which opposed industrialization and capitalism. This focus on hand-crafted products and the code of a medieval lifestyle appealed to Gill, who created his own commune at Ditchling in Sussex in 1907. Douglas (Hilary) Pepler, who shared Gill's ideas, joined him in Ditchling and helped establish St. Dominic's Press, which followed the artistic and socialist ideals of William Morris. Gill and Mary, as well as Pepler, converted to Catholicism in 1913 and established the Guild of St. Joseph and St. Dominic from 1916 through 1924. The Guild attracted Catholic craftsmen with its clear message of moving away from industrialism to a more devotional and structured manner of living. Gill also was influenced by the Catholic priest Father Vincent McNabb, who was a proponent of "distributism," which Ruth and Joe Cribb defined as "a form of Catholic socialism known as the 'back-to-the-land' movement" and was highly endorsed by noted British Catholic writers G. K. Chesterton and Hilaire Belloc.

An association in 1904 with Count Harry Kessler, a German patron of the arts and founder of The Cranach Press, led to Gill's early interest in book illustration. In his *Autobiography*, Gill comments on the importance of Kessler and his future work as a wood engraver:

> He had a Press of his own at Weimar and I used to do engraved title-pages and initial letters for him, in fact it was largely by his encouragement and financial help that I took up the engraving of letters on wood instead of drawing them on paper for photographic reproduction, and this led to pictorial engraving and all my future work for the St. Dominic's Press at Ditchling and the Golden Cockerel Press.

Gill's first wood engravings in 1906 were limited to small jobs, including Christmas cards (Plates 230–234) and bookplates (Plates 203–221). Gill collaborated with Pepler on the book *The Devil's Devices*, printed from a hand press and illustrated by Gill in 1915. This project led to the establishment of St. Dominic's Press, which printed numerous wood engravings by Gill in a variety of books and pamphlets, as well as a magazine, *The Game*, which was published in six volumes from 1916 to 1923. The dimensions of his prints grew more intricate (Plates 187 and 188) in *The Game,* and his lines emblazoned open space, while, in other examples, his focus was on sparing lines against sizable areas of white space (Plates 189 and 190). *The Game,* as well as books such as *Concerning Dragons* (1916; Plates 3–6), demonstrated Gill's growing experimentation with form and narrative style.

Gill's work as a letterer and sculptor grew during these years, and he accepted his first large public sculpture commission, which exempted him from enlistment in the war, to create fourteen *Stations of the Cross* in Westminster Cathedral. Each limestone panel was 5 feet, 8 inches square with an accompanying sheet of wood engravings for devotional use that was printed by Pepler at St. Dominic's Press in 1917 (*The Way of the Cross;* Plates 235–248). Fiona MacCarthy, in her biography, captured the friendship between these two men:

> Gill and Pepler saw each other almost every day. It was an almost schoolboy friendship in their innocent high spirits and delight in one another's company as they worked on the press, planned the issues of *The Game* and roamed around the countryside delivering the headstones and the war memorials which were by now providing Gill with a quite steady source of income.

Gill's early work included prints such as a nude portrait of Petra, Gill's daughter, "Hair Combing" (Plate 193). Gill not only mixed his content but also his technique, shown in his use of white-line engraving depicting provocative nudes, including the previously mentioned Petra (Plate 193), as well as Plates 194 and 195; portraits (Plate 249); and the bold display of a penis in the Crucifix prints (Plates 192 and 225).

In 1920, Gill, along with other artists, including Robert Gibbings, Paul Nash, and Lucien Pissarro, established the Society of Wood Engravers (Plate 226), which revived the woodcut tradition. His personal interest in wood engraving flourished. In *Autumn Midnight* (1923), Gill displayed a wide range of decorated initials, which he developed in greater detail later on with his illustrations for the Golden Cockerel Press. The detail in the small images shows Gill's growing skill as an engraver and his strict focus on the power of his fine line (Plates 7–24).

Christopher Skelton, in *The Engravings of Eric Gill* (1983), notes that Pepler recorded one of the few descriptions of Gill at work:

> The first thing which struck me as an observer of Gill at work was the sureness and steadiness of his hand at minute detail; the assurance and swiftness of a sweep line is one thing (and here he was a part master) but the hairs on an eyelash another—and he liked to play about with hairs and rays which can hardly be distinguished with a magnifying glass (and easily tended to be filled with ink in printing). Then he was always obliging. When I wanted a tail piece to end a chapter or an initial letter with which to begin one, he would tumble to the point at once, probably improve upon my suggestion, supply the block ready for the press within an hour, and come in to see it printed that same afternoon.

Gill resigned from the Guild of St. Joseph and St. Dominic and moved to Capel-y-ffin in the Black Mountains of South Wales following differences with Pepler in 1925. MacCarthy suggests: "It was one of Gill's great errors that in quarrelling with Pepler he rejected the one person who could see him as he was."

In 1925, Gill began work with Gibbings's Golden Cockerel Press, where he illustrated thirteen books, and his wood engravings became celebrated by a larger public. He had, at this point in his career, created a number of sculptures and typefaces and was already noted as a letter cutter. His association with the Golden Cockerel Press triggered his imagination and resulted in noted books of the century such as *The Canterbury Tales* and *The Four Gospels.* It is important to acknowledge that Gill's early work with Johnston, Kessler, and especially Pepler provided the foundation for Gill to extend his steadfast focus on wood engraving and achieve such success.

His increasing depiction of the naked body became a standard for his illustrations in books for the Golden Cockerel Press beginning with *Sonnets and Verses* (Plates 25–27) and *The Song of Songs* (Plates 25–36), which provoked controversy over the extensive nudity and depiction of sex. *Troilus and Criseyde* (Plates 40–50) and *The Canterbury Tales* (Plates 53–72) by Geoffrey Chaucer, published next, captured the whimsical interplay between words and images displayed in medieval illuminated manuscripts. These two books are examples of Gill's admiration for medieval book illustration, shown in his extensive display of decorated initials and border decorations. In *Troilus and Criseyde,* Gill mixed full-page illustrations with a combination of black and white lines and a rich assortment of shapes that presented a sense of motion. He created serpentine flora with simple figures to cushion the distinctive text. These border decorations reflect the narrative stanzas in an unassuming manner. In *The Canterbury Tales*, Gill repeated the decorated borders he displayed in *Troilus and Criseyde* and enhanced decorated initials with striking figures associated with the action in each chapter. The variety of figures in motion suspended in space within an arrangement of flora is amazingly inventive and provokes admiration and surprise (Plate 67). Image and text are sharp and clear against a white background. Visually we enter the pictorial canopy that evolves into a textual narrative that is pleasantly supported with decorations.

In 1928 Gill moved to Pigotts in Buckinghamshire, where he co-founded, with his son-in-law, Rene Hague, The Hague and Gill Press, and where he remained until his death of lung cancer in 1940. During this time, Gill illustrated numerous books for various publishers, including *Canticum Canticorum* for Kessler's Cranach Press with, as Skelton indicates, a "new technique of lightening areas of black with a fine stipple" (Plates 74–83) and *Clothes* for Jonathan Cape (Plates 84–90).

Two of the major critics of the time had differing reactions to Gill's work. Malcolm Salaman refers to "that masterly black line of his is the expressive medium" in "The Crucifixion" (Plate 39) from *Passio Domini Nostri Jesu Christi* and later describes the "exquisite promise" in Gill's decorations of Chaucer's *Troilus and Criseyde*. Herbert Furst found in Gill's design "an ineradicable self-consciousness, a sense of personal value and importance which were objectionable but for the fact that the artist never spares himself; the slightest thing he does is executed with meticulous care and with an intellectual nicety." In the preface to *Engravings 1928-1933*, Gill replied to his critics:

> As to my lack of emotional display I think that the business of wood engraving is very much like the business of typography. I think tenderness and warmth in such things are not to be looked for except in the workmanship. You do not want the designer of printing types to wear his heart on his sleeve—my engravings are, I admit, only a kind of printer's flowers.

One of the important books of the twentieth century, *The Four Gospels* (Plates 91–120), was published in 1931 by Golden Cockerel Press and remains a masterpiece of book design and illustration. The edition was limited to 500 copies and received immediate acclaim from critics. The authoritative account of this book, written by John Dreyfus, is *A Typographical Masterpiece*. Dreyfus quotes Harold Child's fervent praise:

> It would be rash to say that this is the most beautiful book which even the Golden Cockerel Press has produced; but those who approach it with the very natural conviction that somehow and somewhere it is bound to seem unworthy, to jar, or to disappoint, are very likely to find that they are wrong. It is a book, first of all, that can be read. The type is superb . . . Mr. Gill has never done anything finer than these intensely dramatic woodcuts . . . Of the workmanship of the book, printing, paper, binding . . . it is only necessary to say that it is up to the standard of the Golden Cockerel Press.

Gill's skillful—almost acrobatic—arrangement of figures entwined within a scaffold of letters is stunning (Plate 98) and frolicsome (Plate 102). The life of Christ was a common theme for a number of books published during this era, including wordless woodcut novels such as *Das St. Johannis-Evangelium nach Holzschnitten* by the German artist Daniel Greiner, *Die Passion* by the German Otto Pankok, and *The Life of Christ in Woodcuts* by the American James Reid, with distinct portrayals of Christ. Reid also illustrated *The Song of Songs*, a forgotten edition displaying Reid's more powerful woodcut illustrations that have a sensuality equal to Gill.

Gill continued to illustrate for the Golden Cockerel Press with the books *The Constant Mistress* (Plates 147–49); *The Green Ship* (Plates 150–57), with its stunning double title page (Plates 150–51); and *The Travels & Sufferings of Father Jen De Brébeuf* (Plates 180–81). During this time, Gill also illustrated editions of Shakespeare plays for the Limited Editions Club—*Hamlet, Prince of Denmark* (Plates 121–26) and *Henry the Eighth* (Plates 162–64)—with his recognized "spray of leaves" decoration. He did work for J.M. Dent & Sons in *The New Temple Shakespeare* (Plates 128–132); *The Aldine Bible: The New Testament* (Plates 138–146), with an innovative pictorial scroll in various illustrations (Plates 139–143) in contrast to the traditionally regarded scroll with words (Plate 144); and *The Holy Sonnets of John Donne* (Plates 182–85), using some uncharacteristic marbling effects in the prints.

It is fitting that one of Gill's last works, *Twenty-Five Nudes* (Plates 165–179), is not a work with a religious or literary theme but is more closely tied to the focus of his life-long sexual desire—the female figure. In his introduction, Gill summarized his feelings about the nude and drawing:

> The human body is in fact a good joke—let us take it so. The only serious and solemn part of drawing from life is the technique itself. How to draw? That is the serious question. What is drawing? To draw is to drag or pull something along, & in this matter it means dragging or pulling a pencil or brush along the surface of paper. We may agree perhaps that pushing a graver is, by a sort of license, also a kind of drawing—drawing backwards.

According to Fiona MacCarthy, Beatrice Warde (Plate 251), a longtime lover and the model for many of Gill's nudes, "personified the feminist woman Gill so frequently derided: living on her own in a situation of conventionally dubious morality; making her own way in a professional world, the predominantly male world of typography." Gill had his own set of sexual standards presented in his veneration of the penis in "Domestic Hose" (Plate 201), his sexual exploits, and moral transgressions that signify a personality with a hunger to feed a large ego and an insatiable need for power and control.

The drawings of these nudes are provocative in their simplicity and innocence and, perhaps, *Twenty-Five Nudes* and *The Holy Gospels* are the bookends that frame the volume of his work—including 1,000 engravings; 300 books, articles, and pamphlets; six typefaces; 750 pieces of lettering; and over 100 sculptures in stone. In regard to his wood engravings, what continues to provoke interest in Gill is his fine line. Other printmakers with more narrative skill than Gill rarely compete with his prominent straightforward lines, whether in the soft roundness of a breast or in the humble pose of Christ.

David A. Beronä is a historian of the illustrated book and the recognized authority on the woodcut novel. He has published and presented papers widely on this topic and is the author of *Wordless Books: The Original Graphic Novels*—a winner at the New York Book Show and a Harvey Awards nominee. He selected and edited *Alastair Drawings and Illustrations* (2011), which showcases the Decadent works of Baron Hans Henning Voigt. He is the Dean of the Library and Academic Support Services at Plymouth State University, New Hampshire.

Book Illustrations

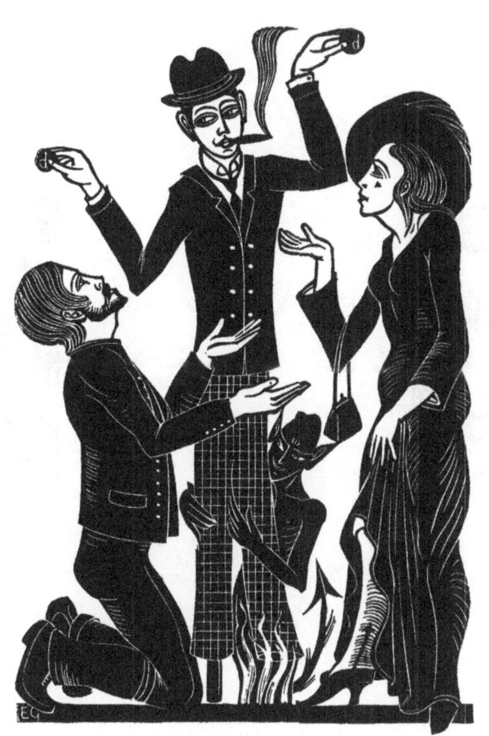

1 The Purchaser
1915
The Devil's Devices

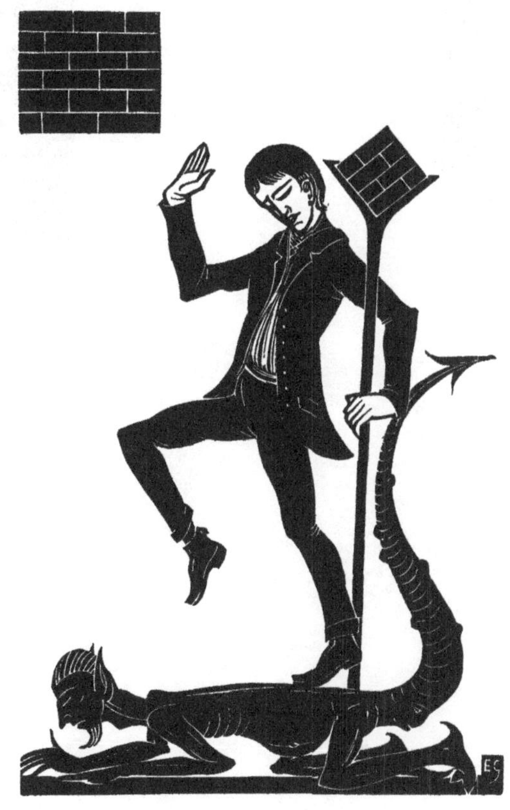

2 The Happy Labourer
1915
The Devil's Devices

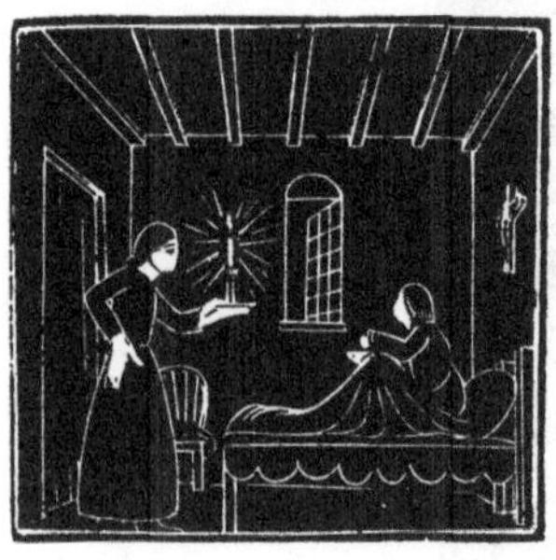

3 Child and Nurse
1916
Concerning Dragons

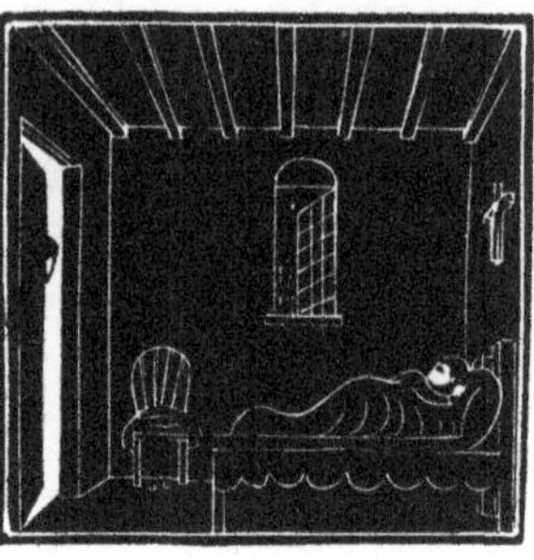

4 Child in Bed
1916
Concerning Dragons

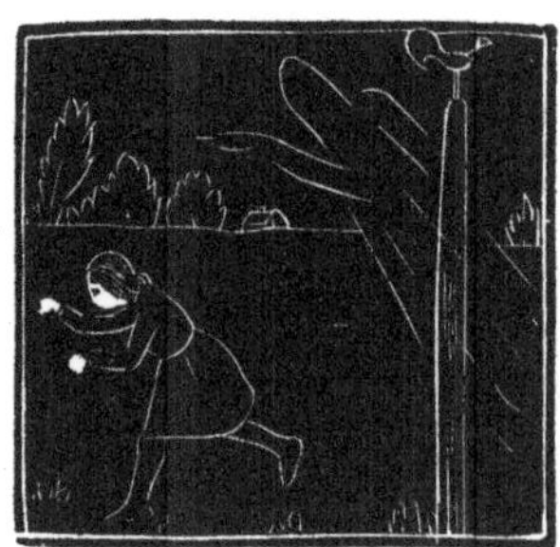

5 Child and Ghost
1916
Concerning Dragons

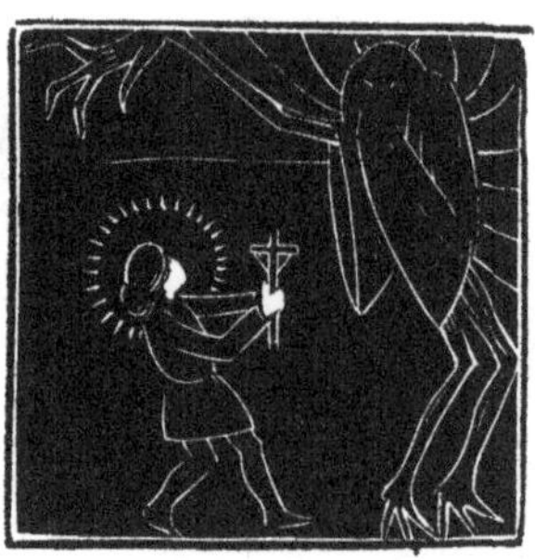

6 Child and Spectre
1916
Concerning Dragons

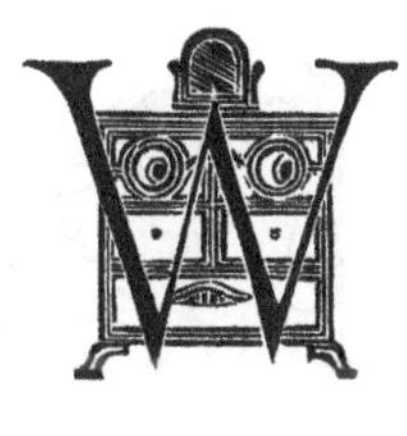

7

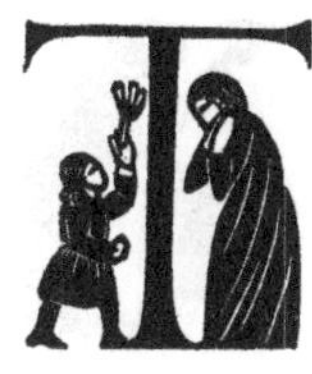

8

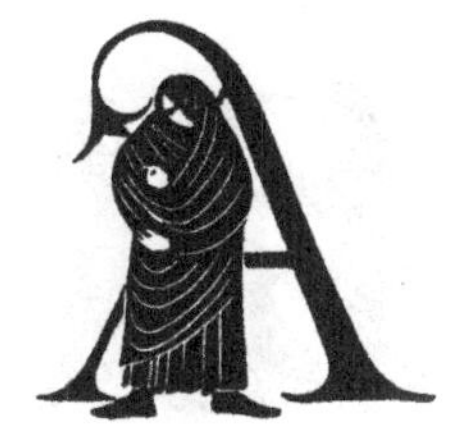

9

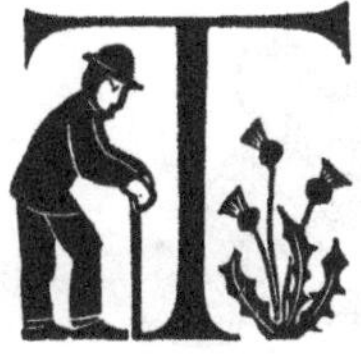

10

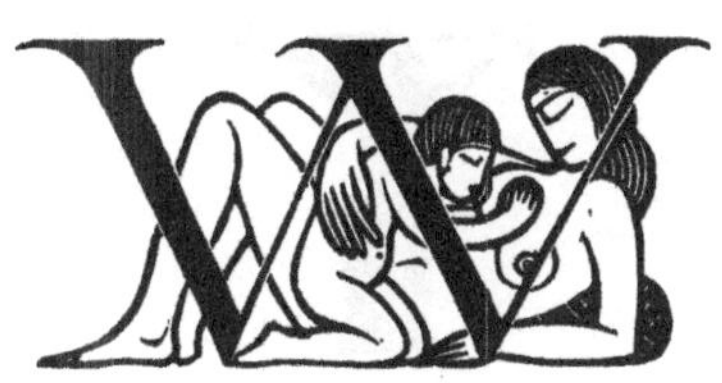

11

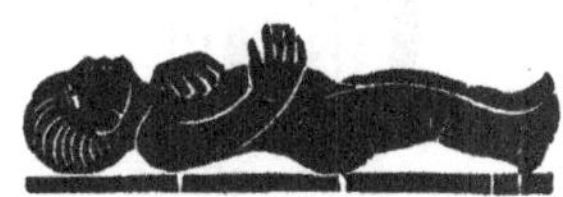

12

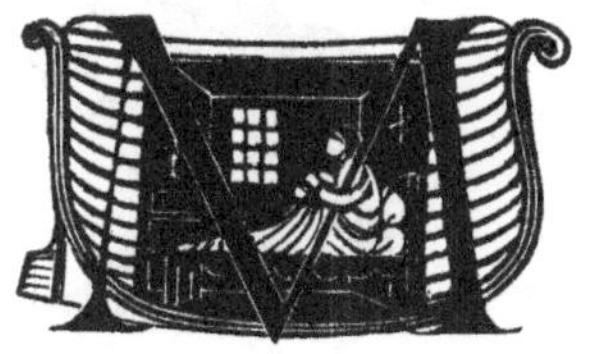

13

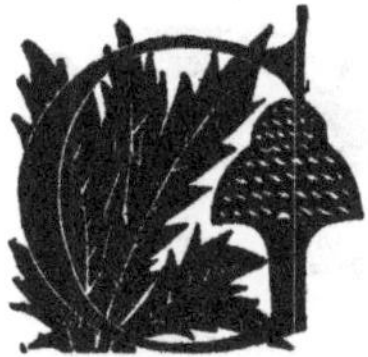

14

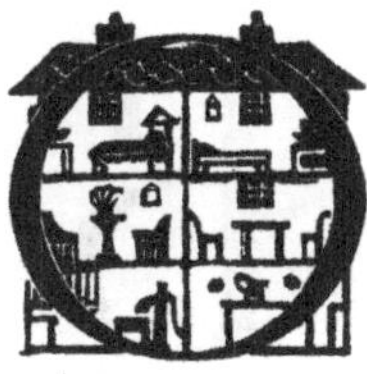

15

Initial Letters
1923
Autumn Midnight

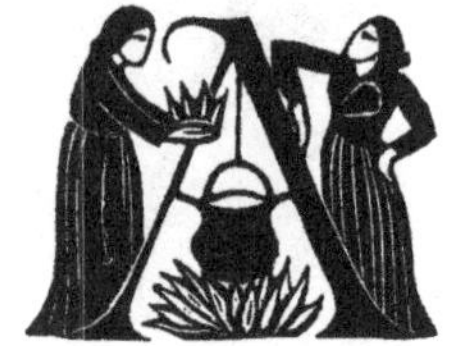

16

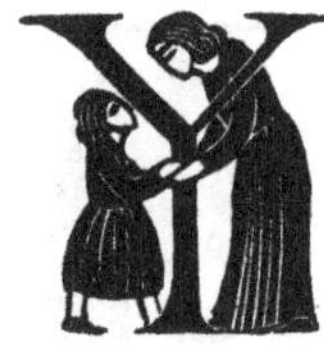

17

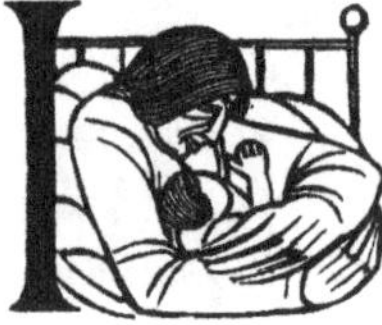

18

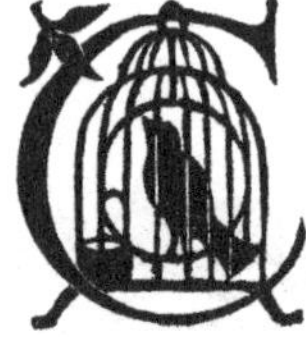

19

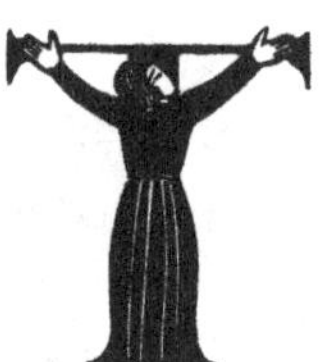

20

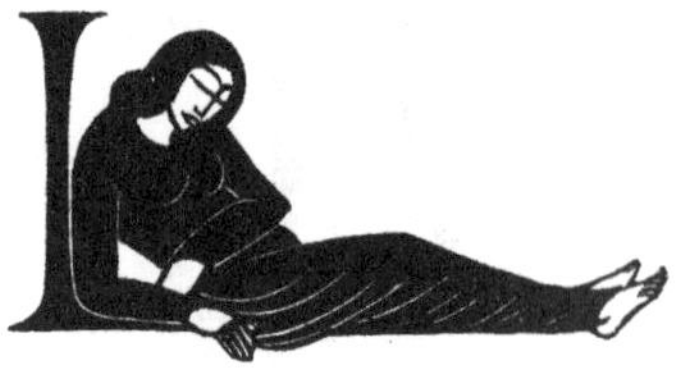

21

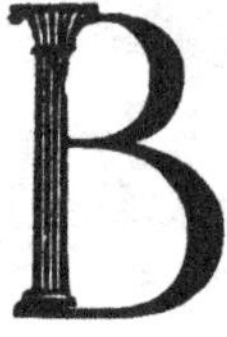

22

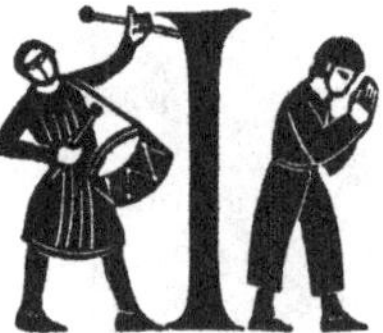

23

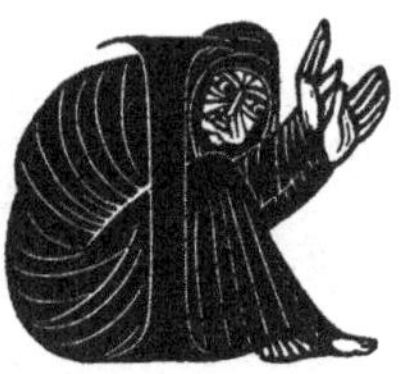

24

Initial Letters
1923
Autumn Midnight

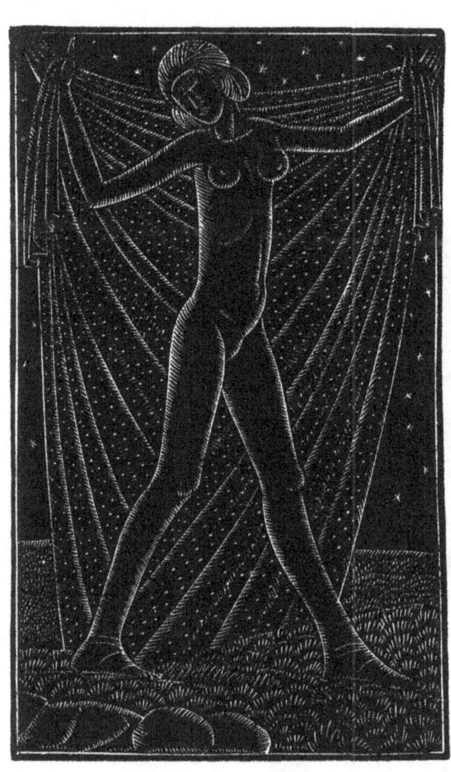

25 Naked Girl with Cloak
1924
Sonnets and Verses

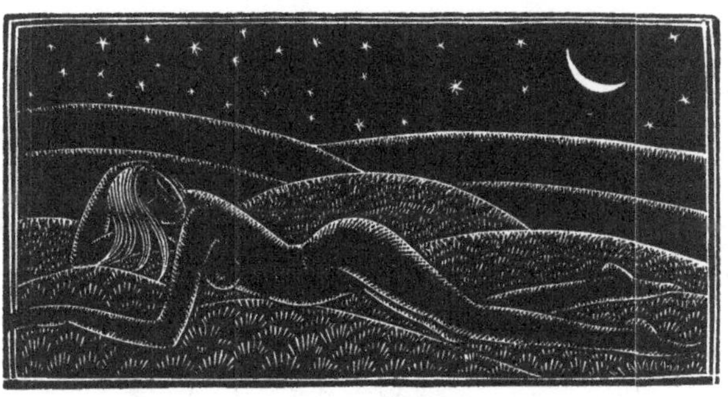

26 Naked Girl Lying on Grass
1924
Sonnets and Verses

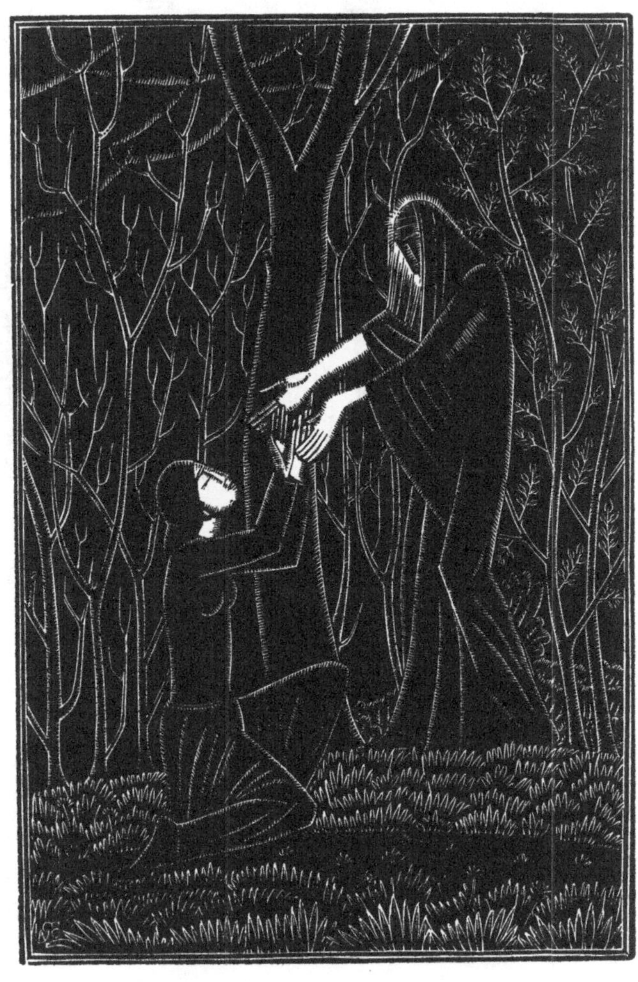

27 Death and the Lady
1924
Sonnets and Verses

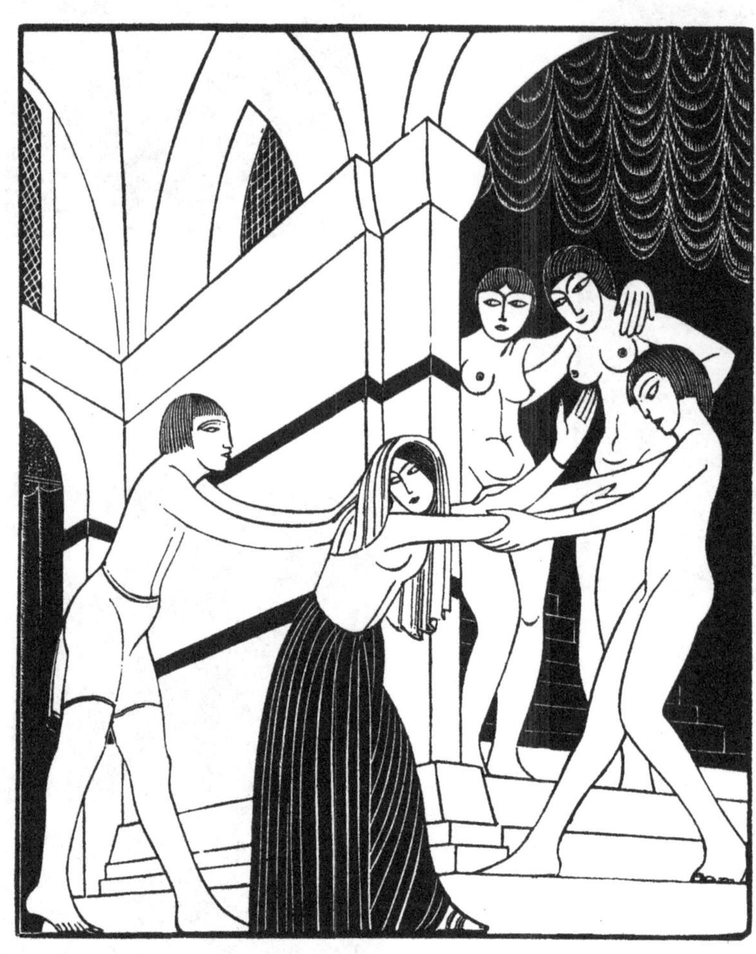

28 The Harem
1925
The Song of Songs

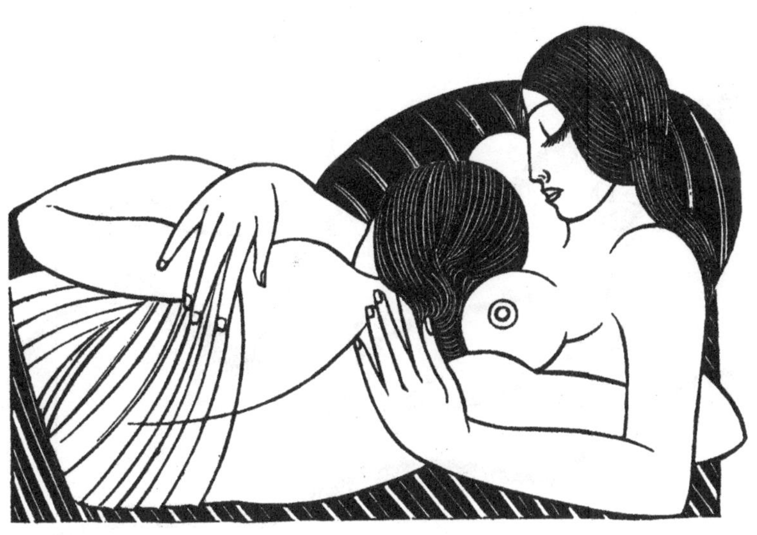

29 Inter Ubera Mea
1925
The Song of Songs

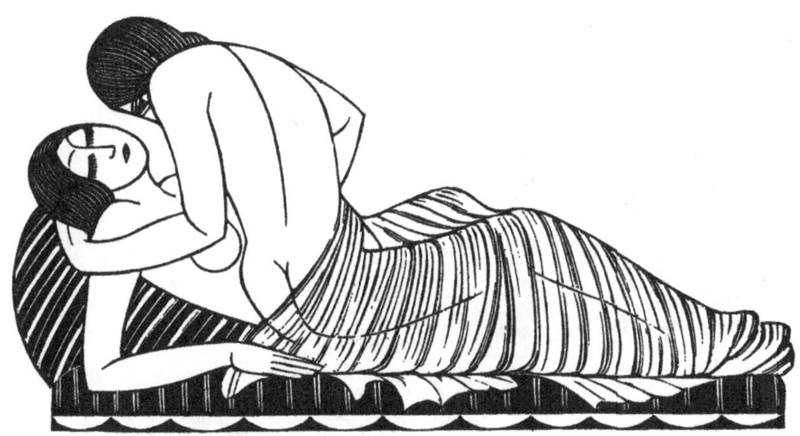

30 His Left Hand Under My Head
1925
The Song of Songs

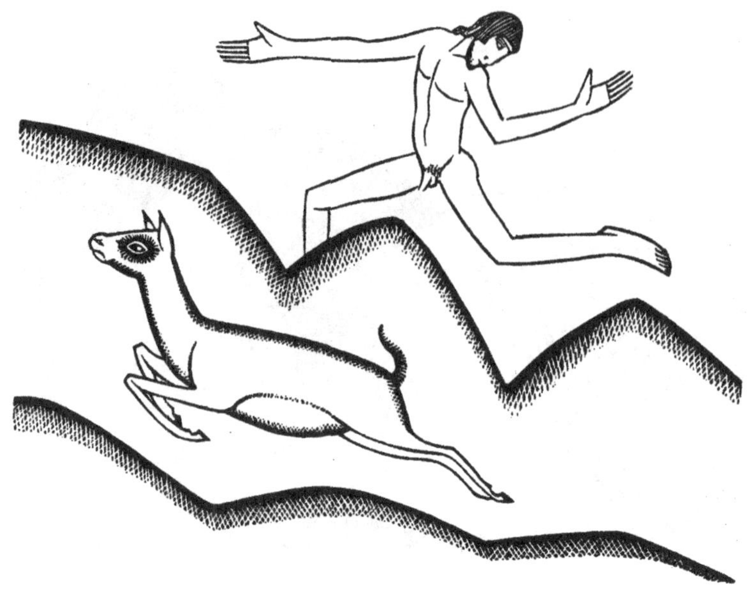

31 Skipping Upon the Mountains
1925
The Song of Songs

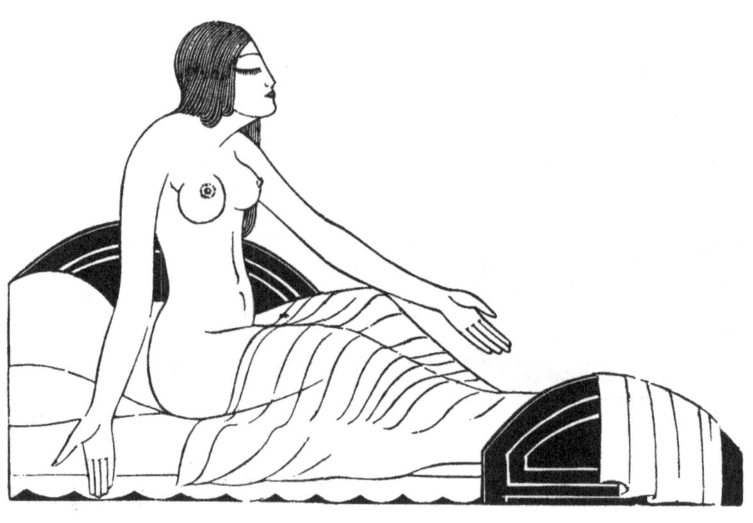

32 On My Bed by Night
1925
The Song of Songs

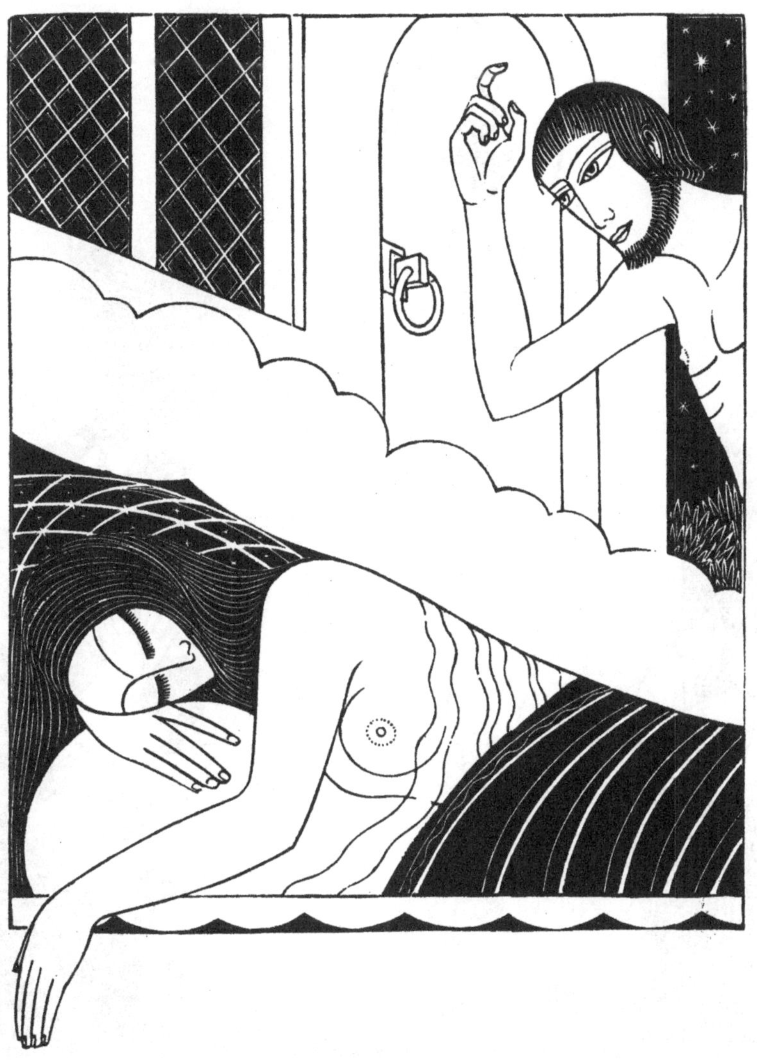

33 The Voice of My Beloved
1925
The Song of Songs

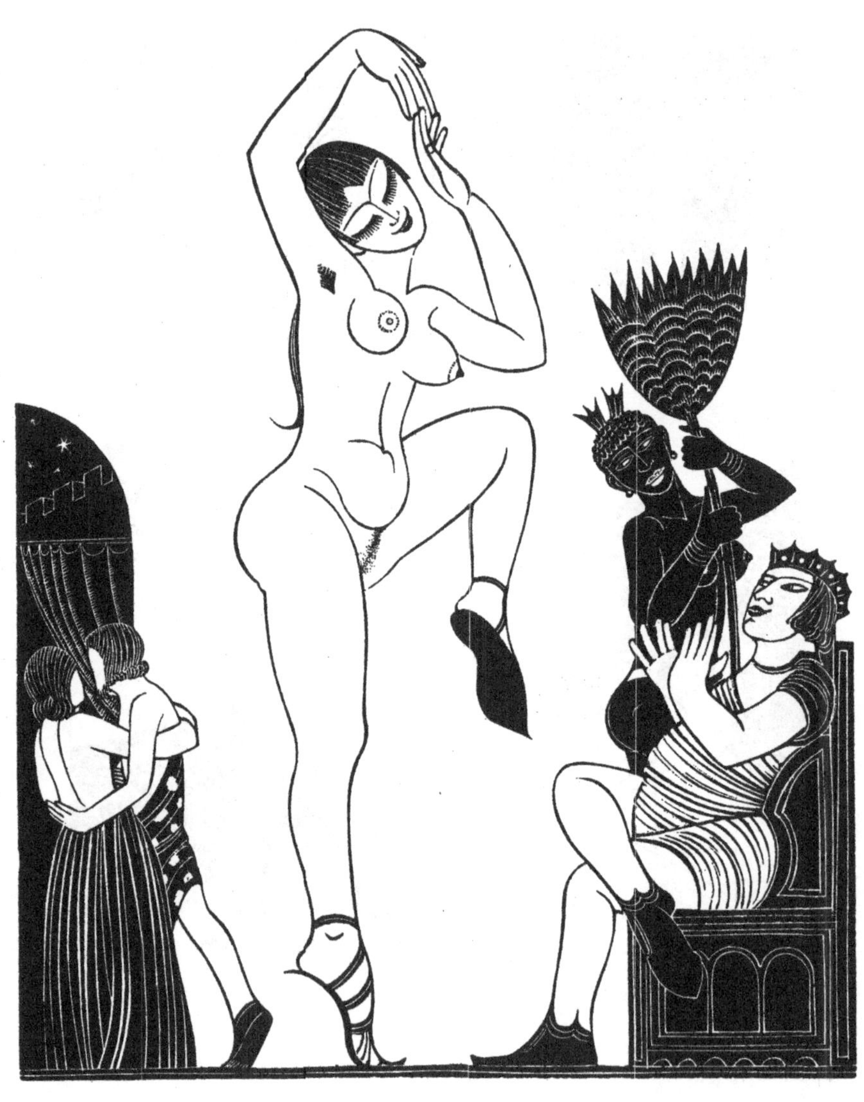

34 The Dancer
1925
The Song of Songs

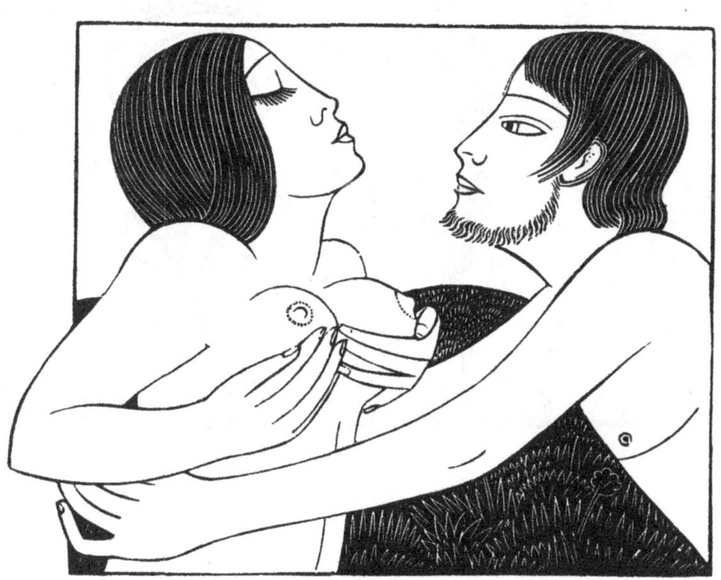

35 Ibi Dabo Tibi
1925
The Song of Songs

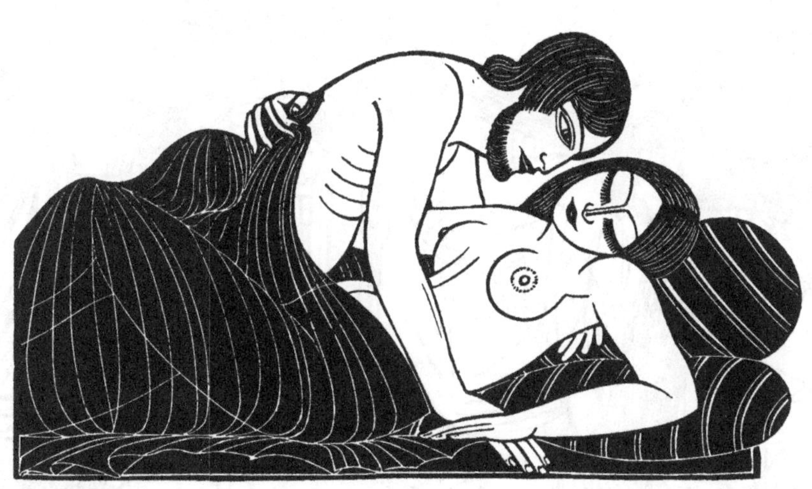

36 The Juice of My Pomegranates
1925
The Song of Songs

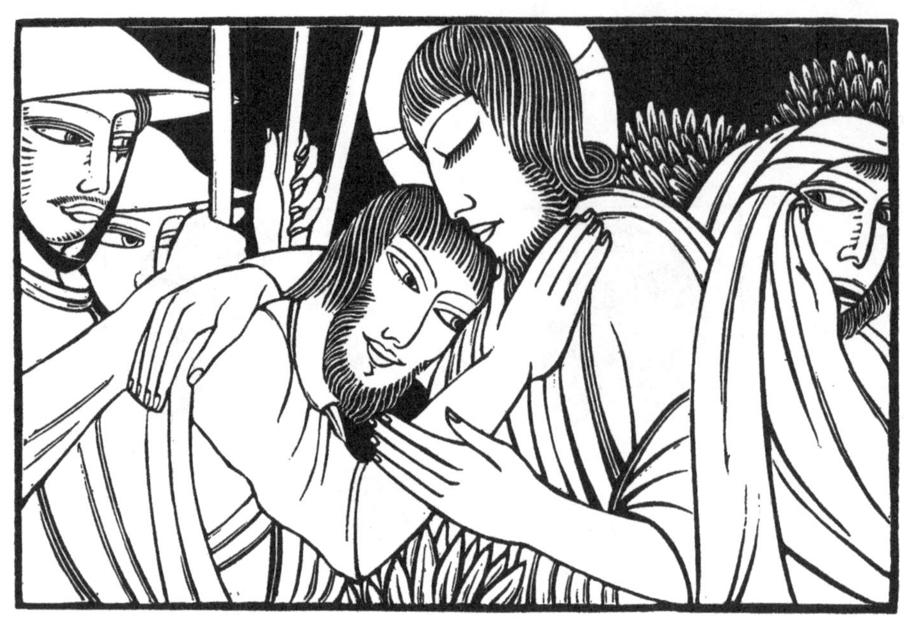

37 The Kiss of Judas
1926
Passio Domini Nostri Jesu Christi

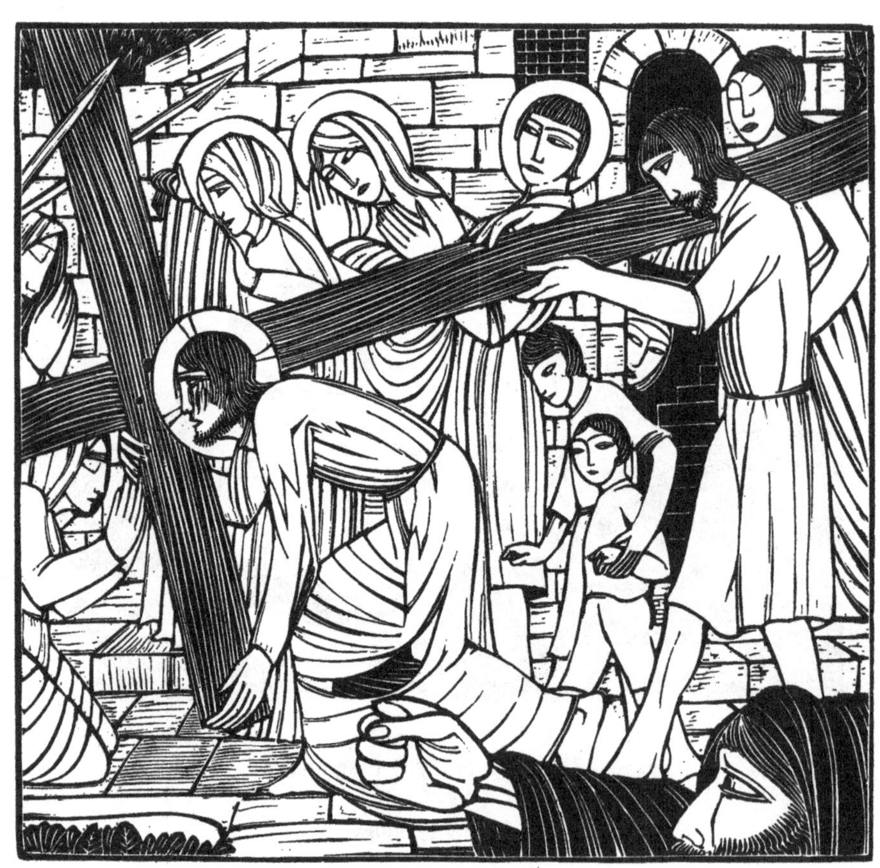

38 The Carrying of the Cross
1926
Passio Domini Nostri Jesu Christi

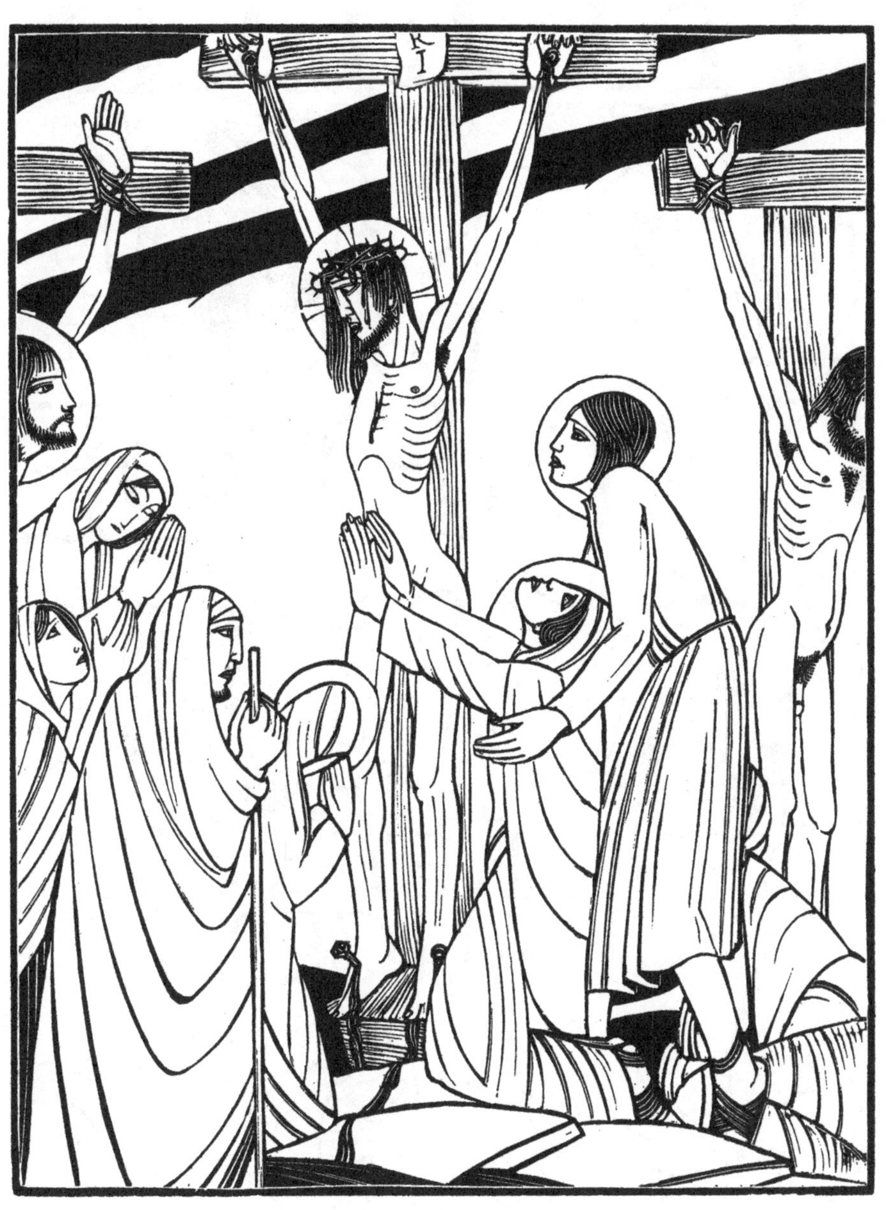

39 The Crucifixion
1926
Passio Domini Nostri Jesu Christi

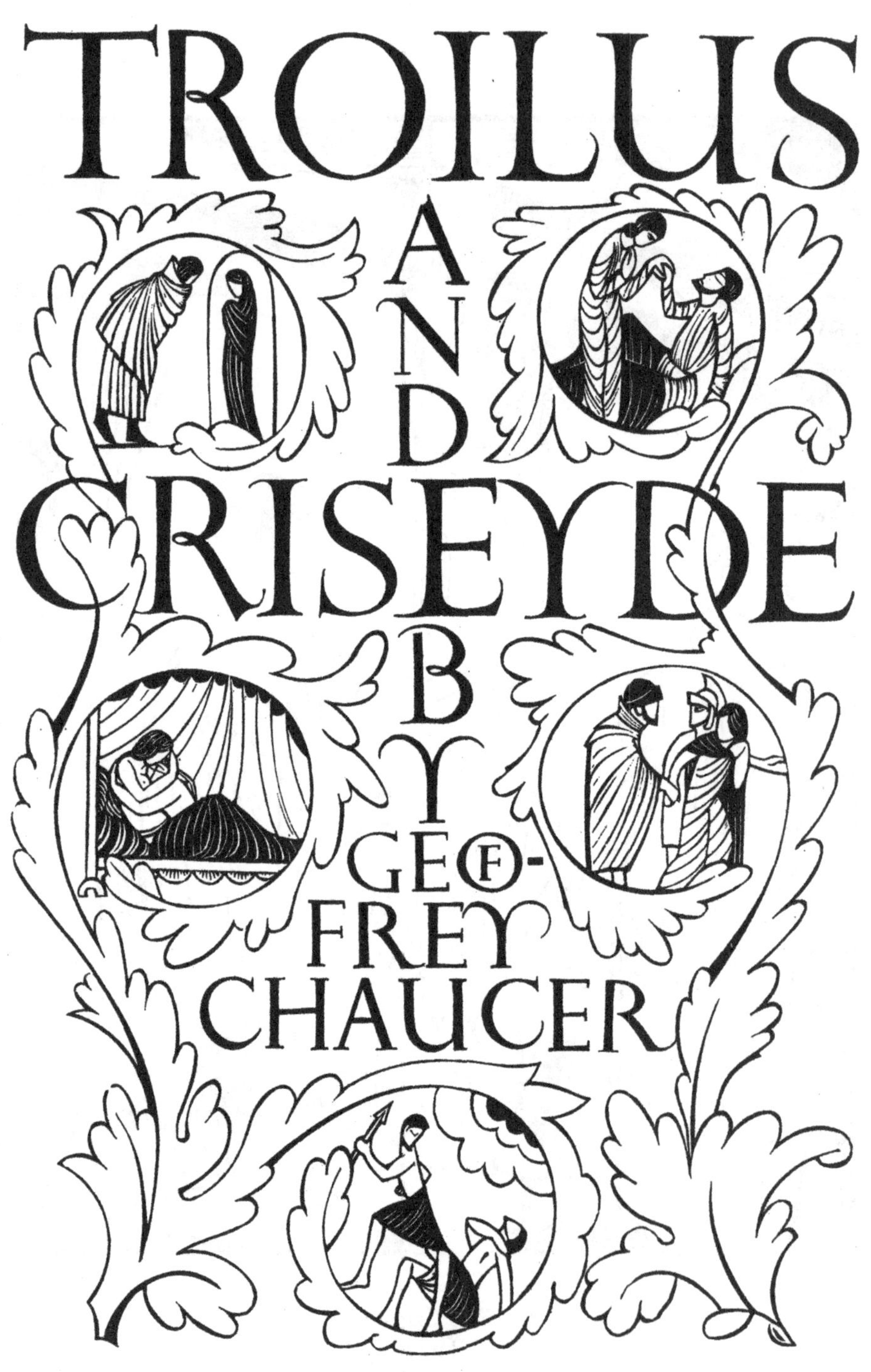

40 Troilus and Criseyde by Geoffrey Chaucer
1927
Troilus and Criseyde

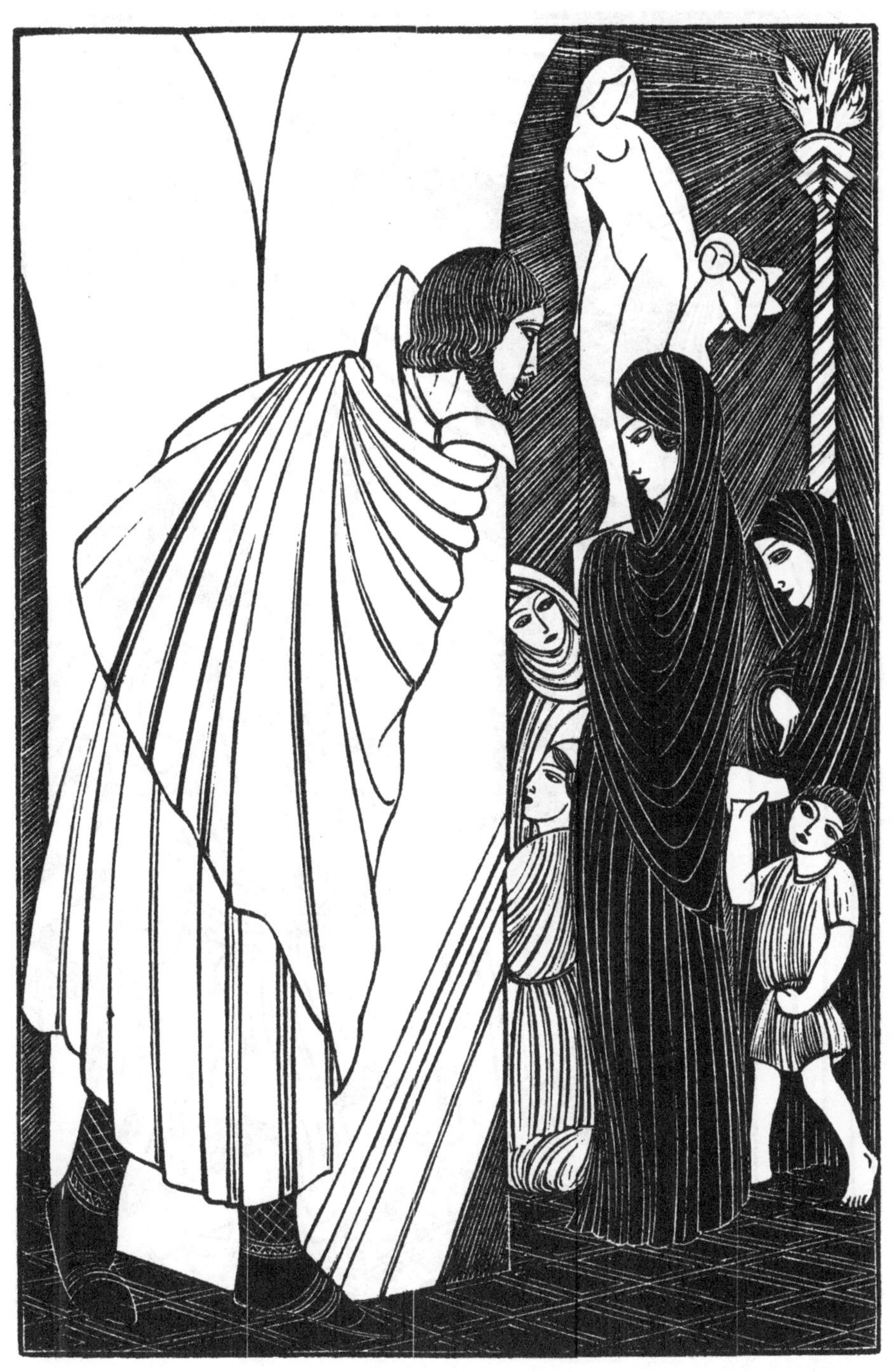

41 Meeting of Troilus and Criseyde
1927
Troilus and Criseyde

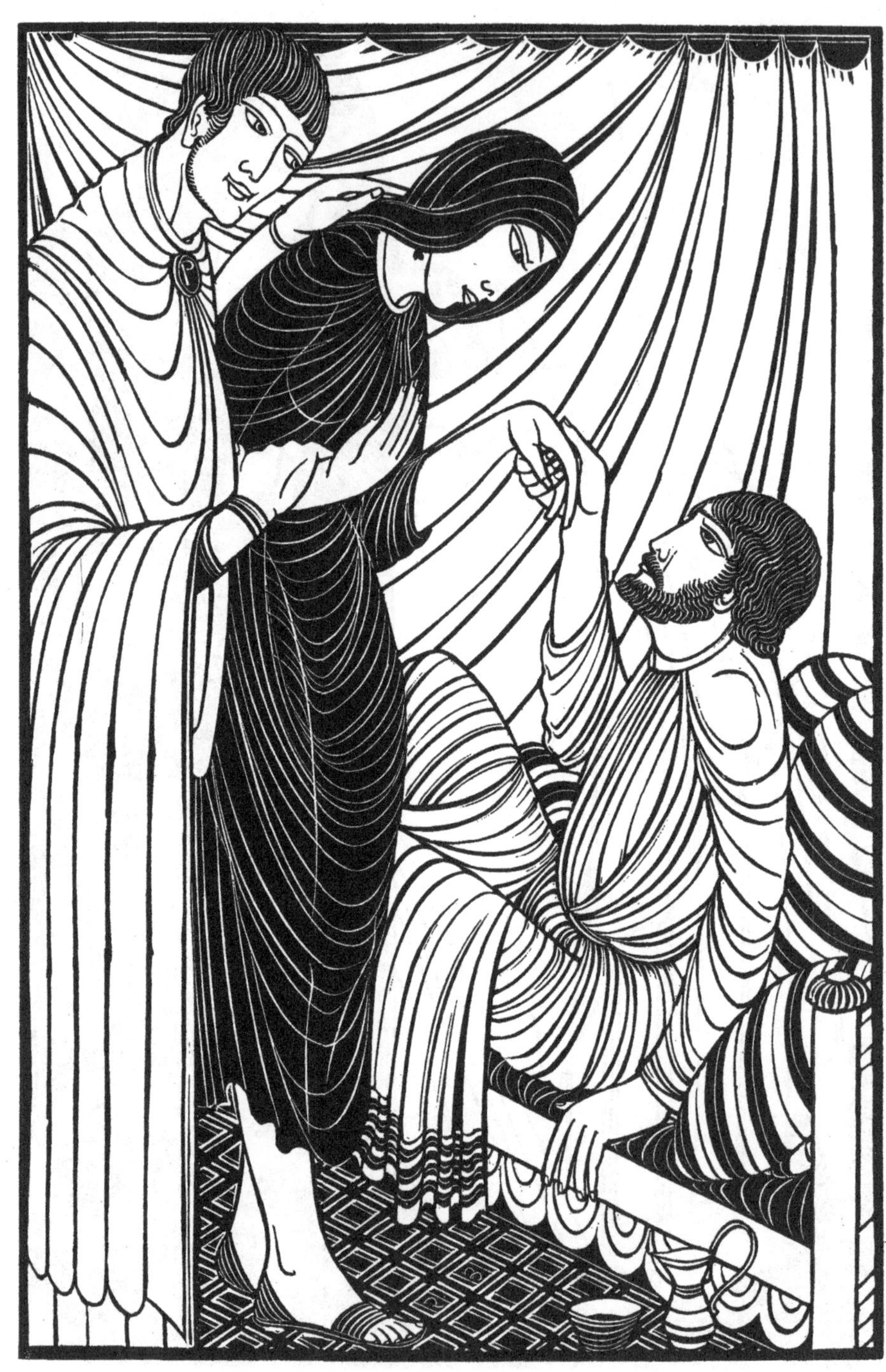

42 Criseyde Visits Troilus
1927
Troilus and Criseyde

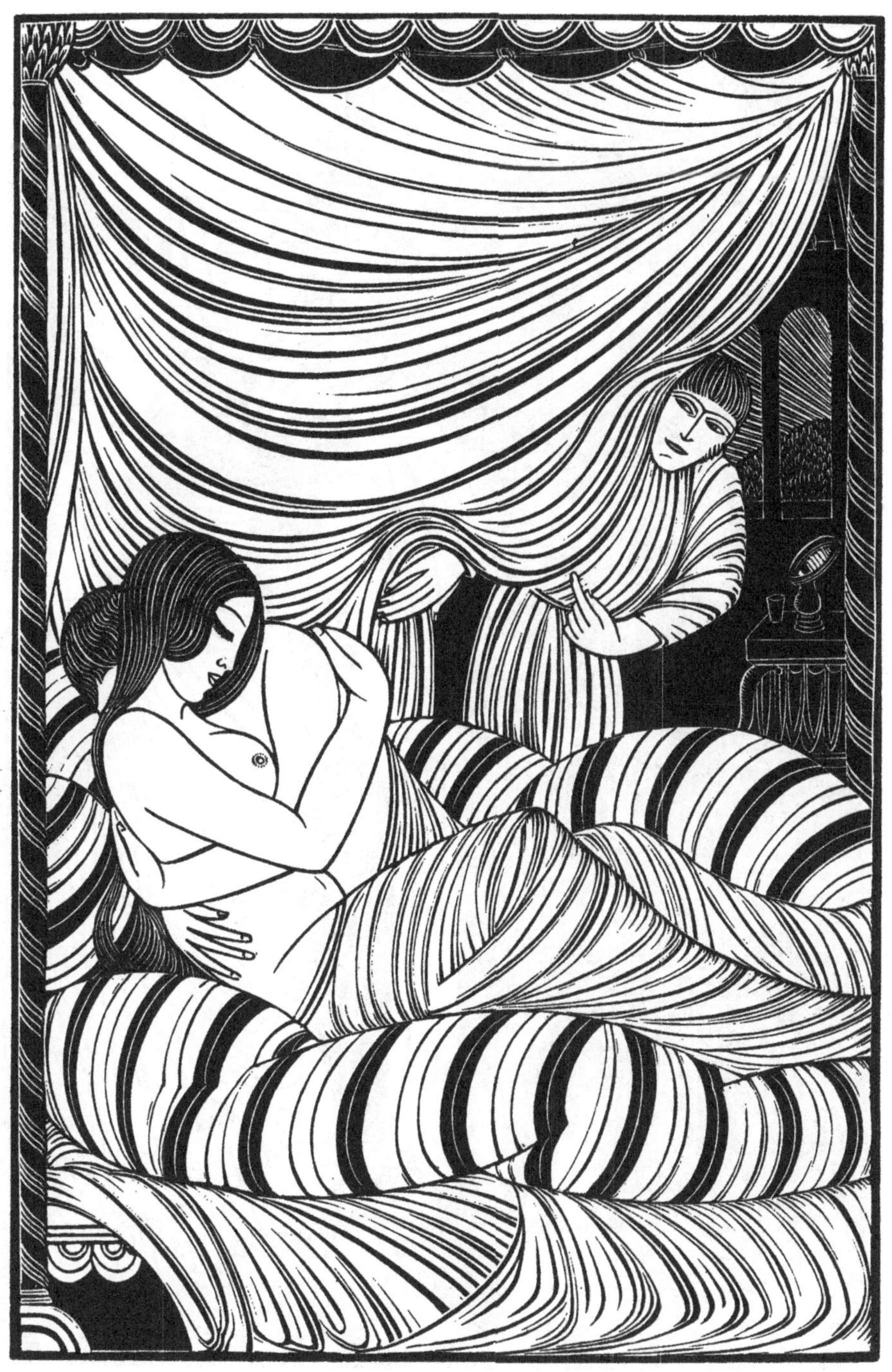

43 Approaching Dawn
1927
Troilus and Criseyde

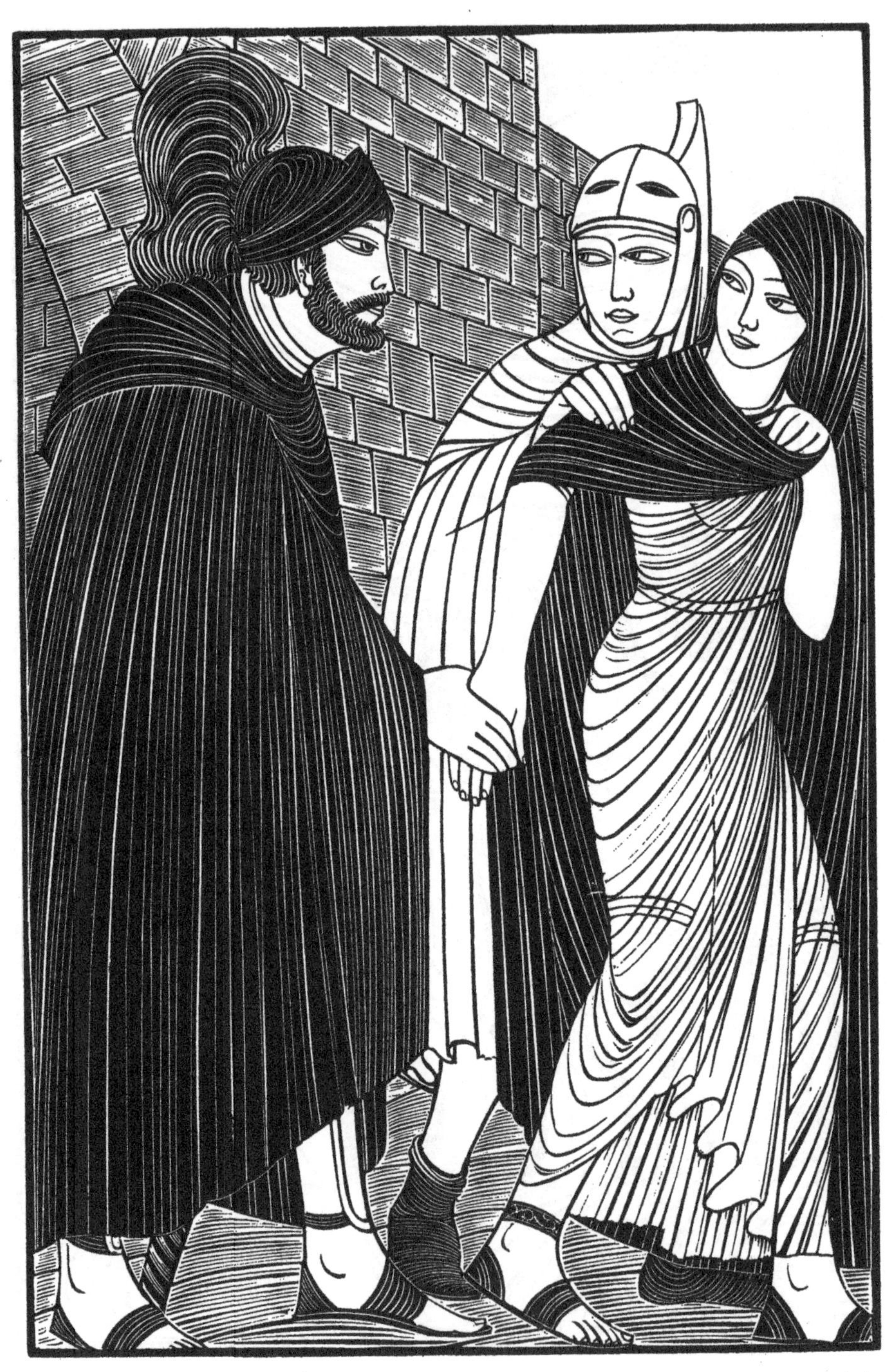

44 The Parting
1927
Troilus and Criseyde

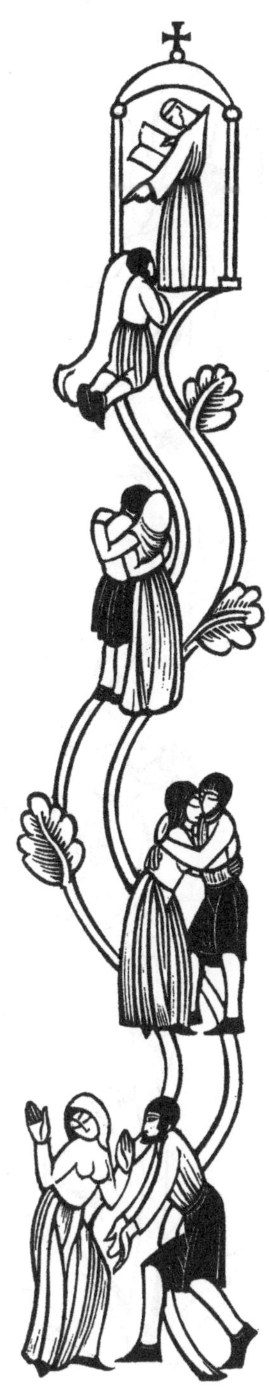

45 Man and Girl on Way to Church
1927
Troilus and Criseyde

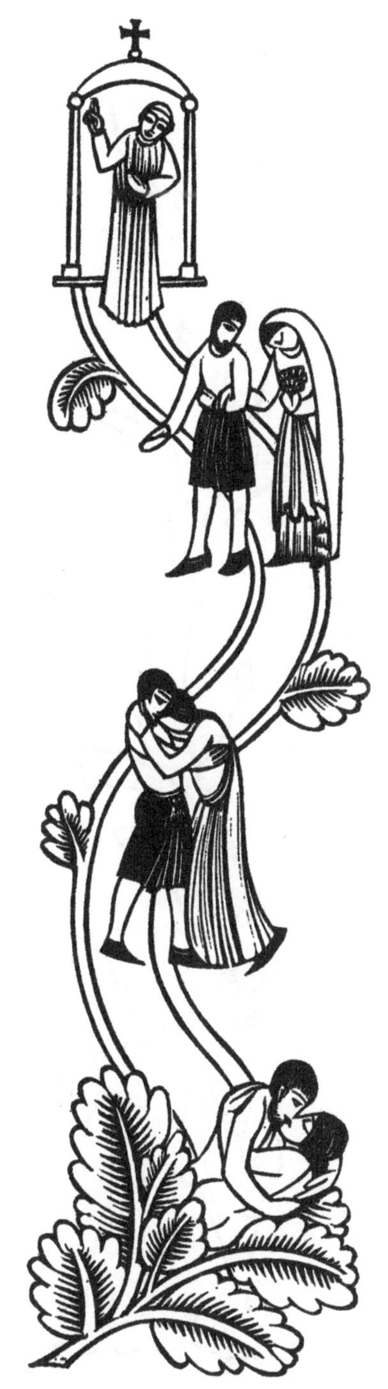

46 Man and Girl on Way from Church
1927
Troilus and Criseyde

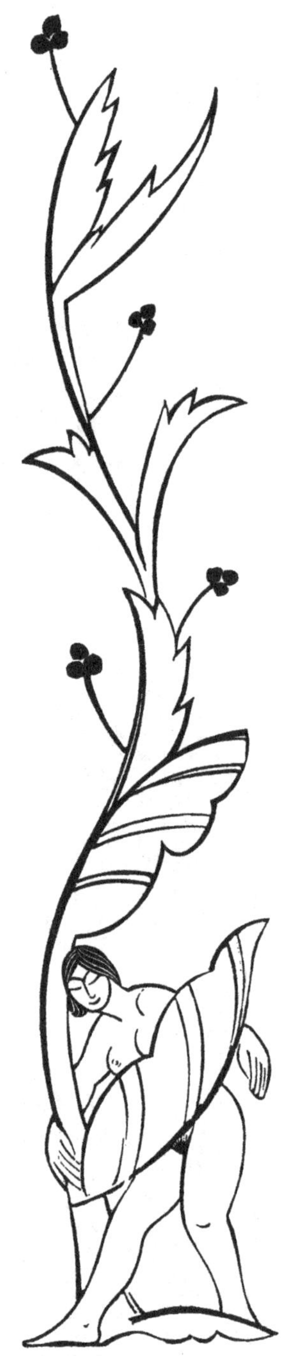

47 Girl Standing
1926
Troilus and Criseyde

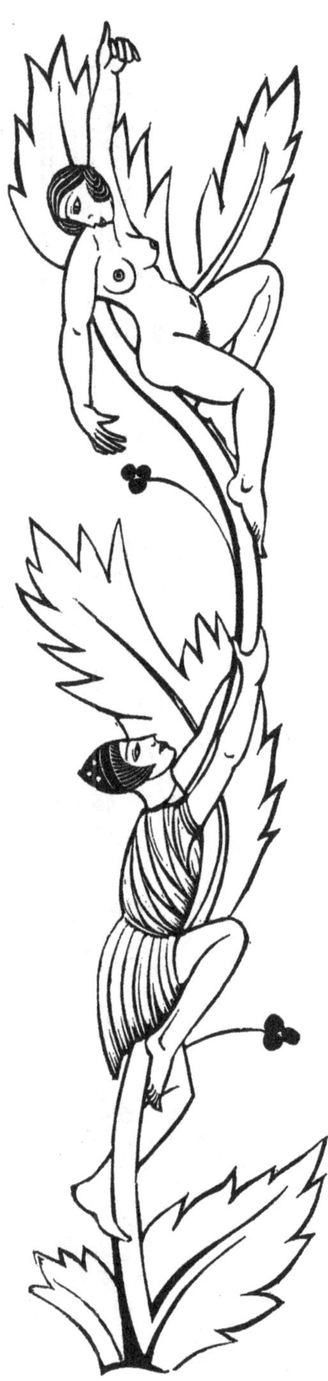

48 Man Climbing to Girl
1926
Troilus and Criseyde

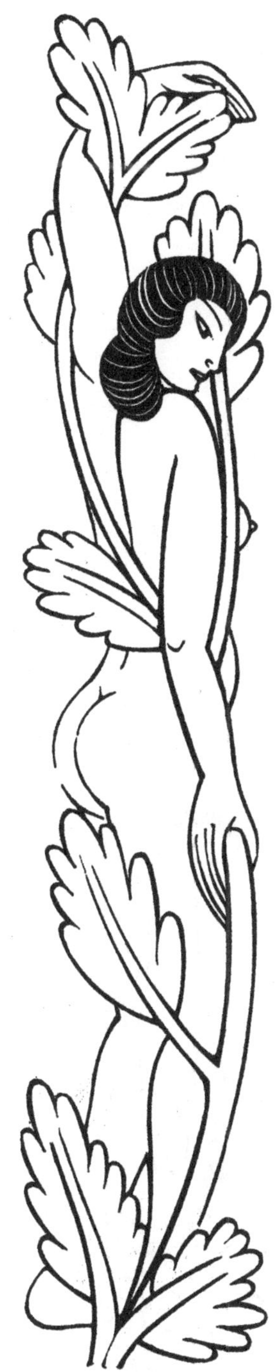

49 Naked Girl Facing Right
1927
Troilus and Criseyde

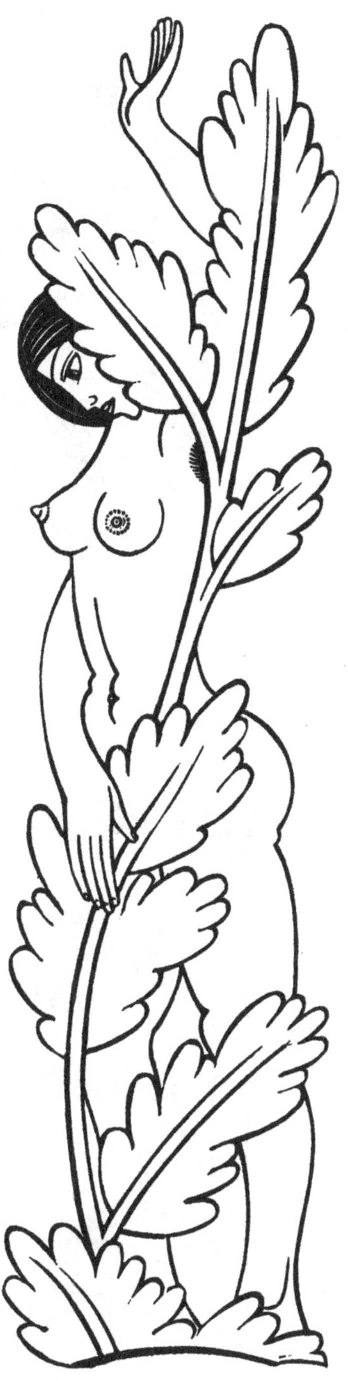

50 Naked Girl Facing Left
1927
Troilus and Criseyde

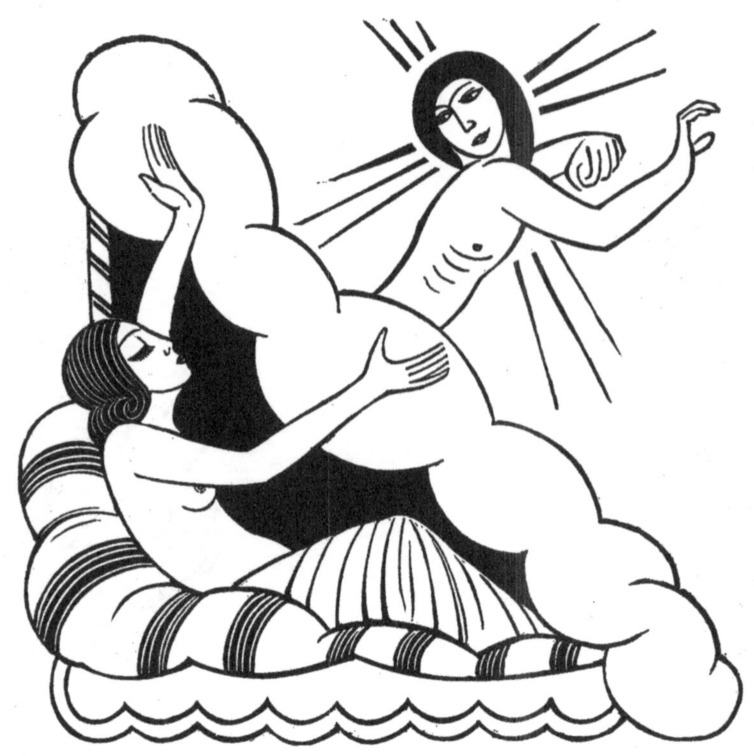

51 The Flight
1927
The Song of the Soul

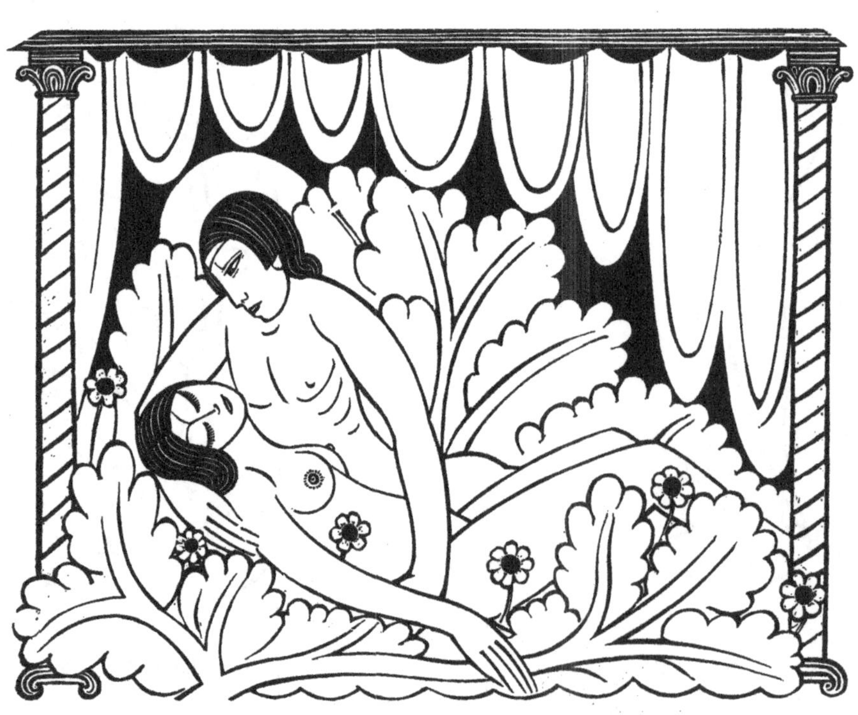

52 Our Bed Is All of Flowers
1927
The Song of the Soul

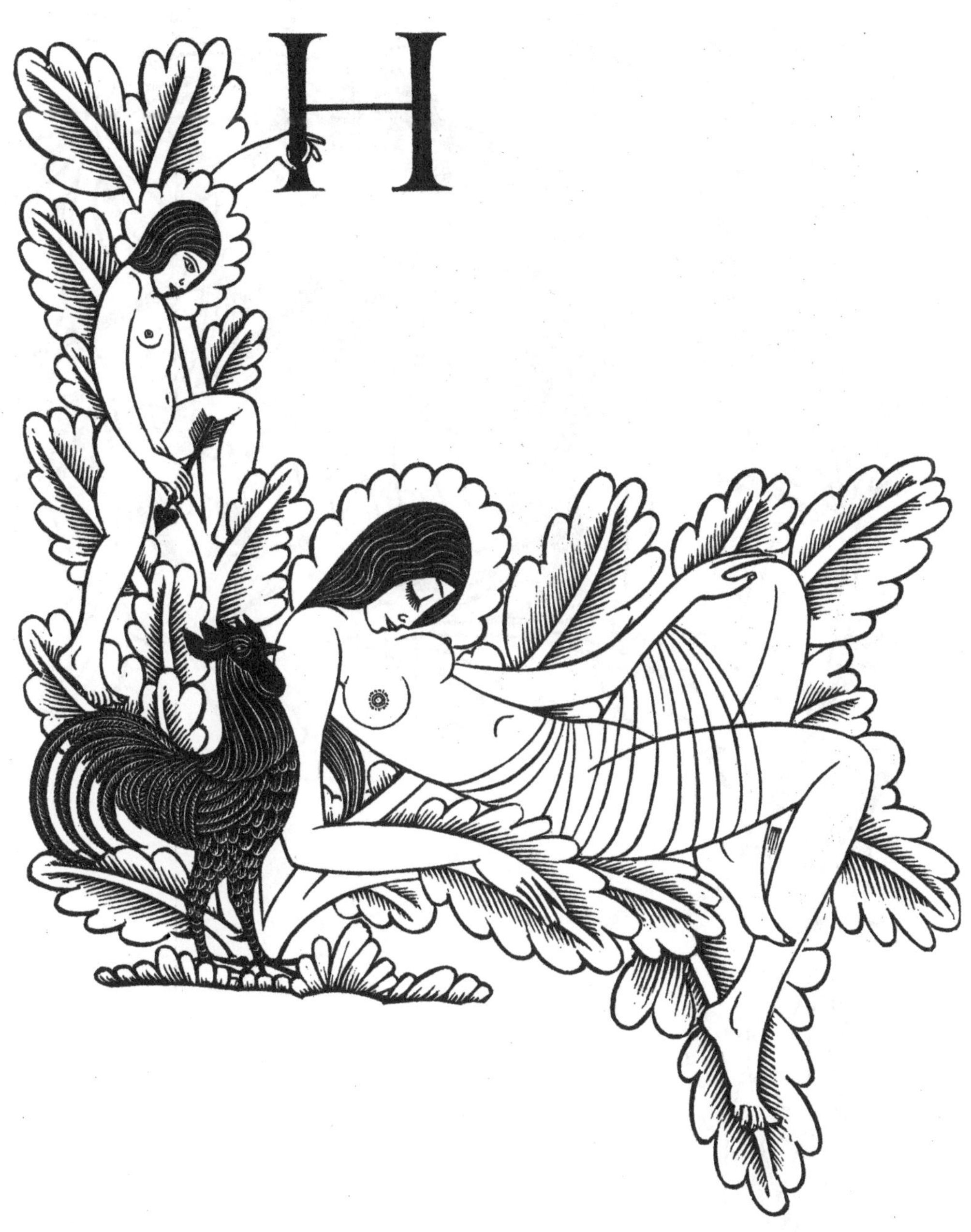

53 Venus and Cupid with the Golden Cockerel, with Letter H
1928
The Canterbury Tales

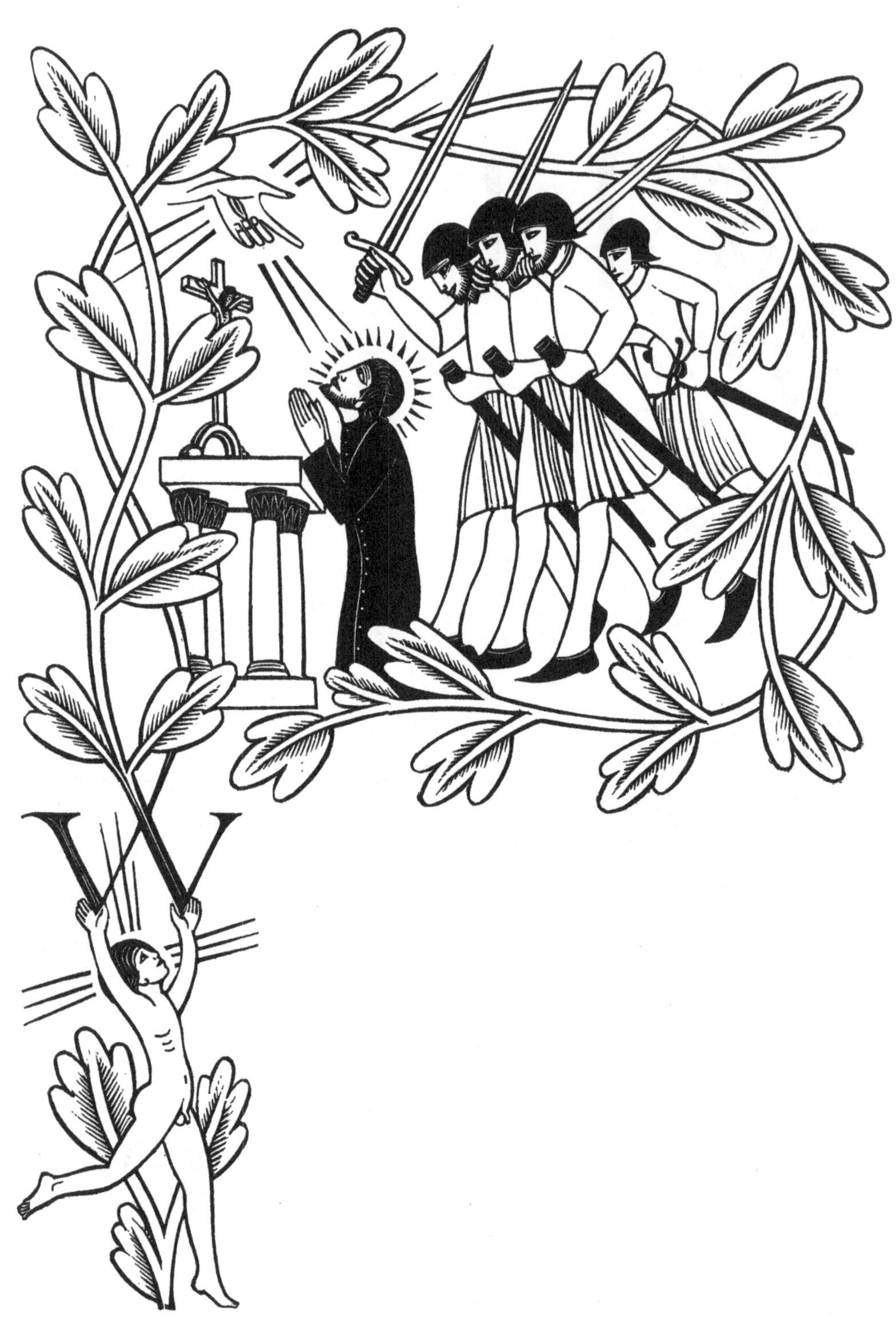

54 The Martyrdom of St Thomas of Canterbury,
with Letter W and Nude Boy
1928
The Canterbury Tales

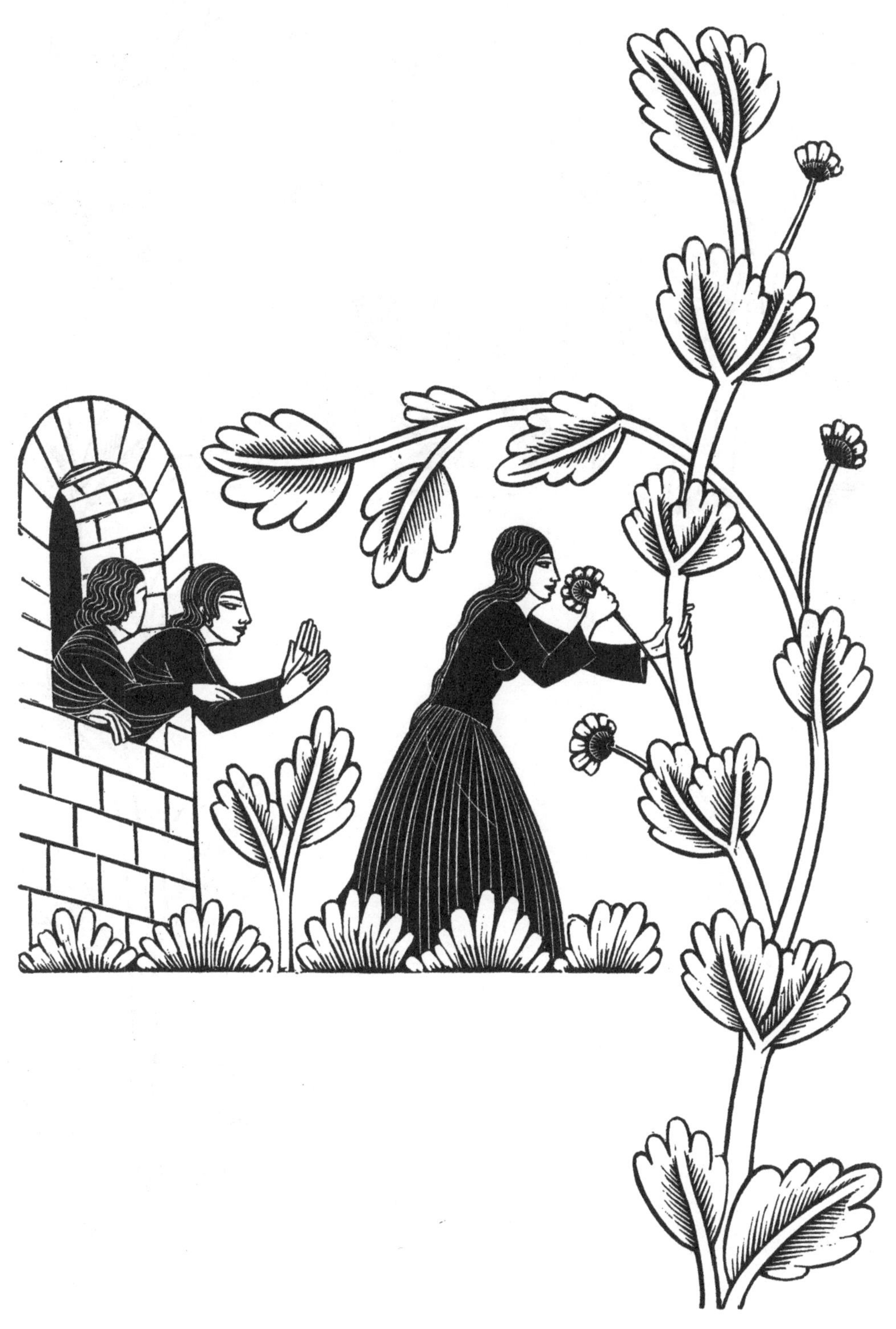

55 The Knight's Tale
1928
The Canterbury Tales

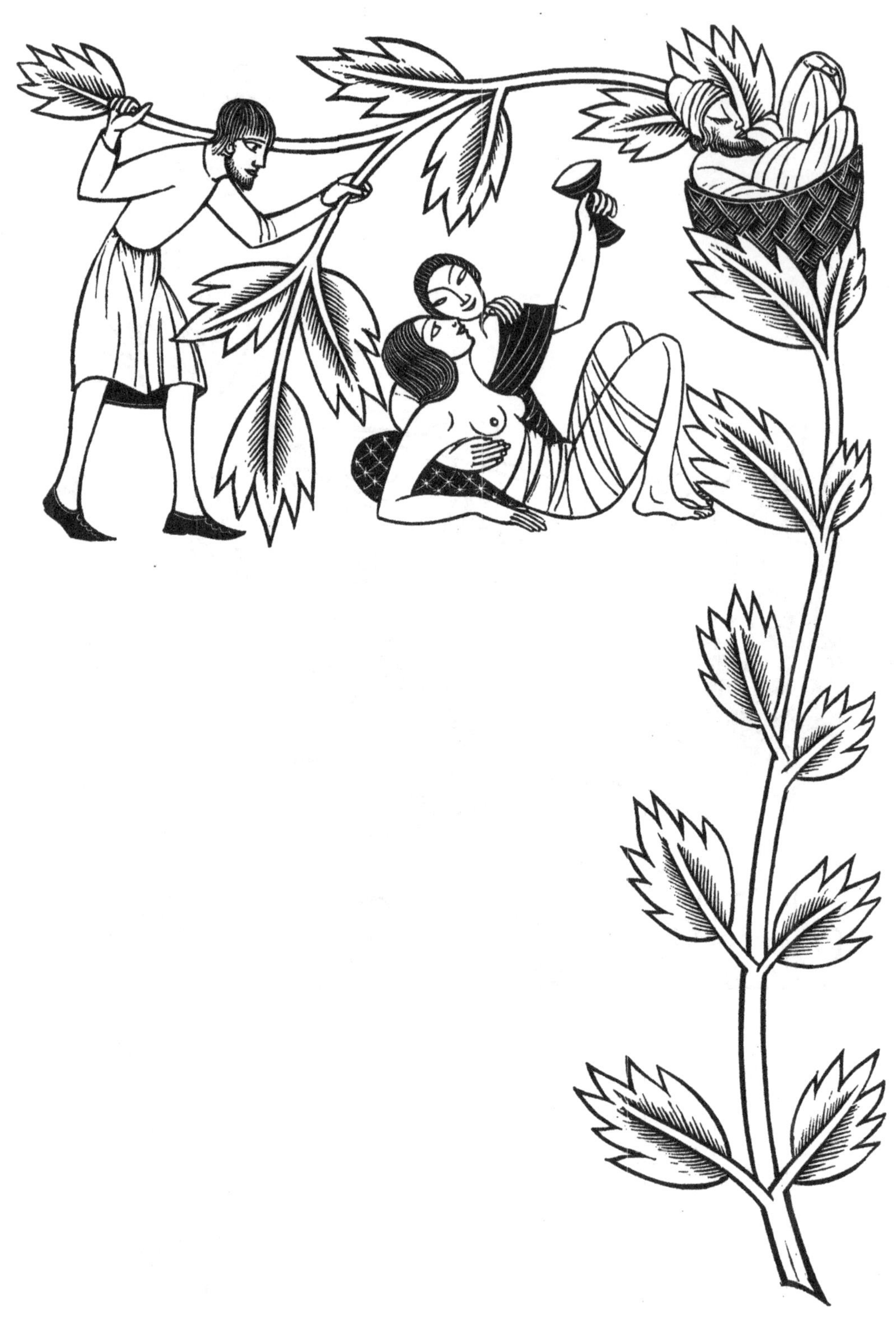

56 The Miller's Tale
1928
The Canterbury Tales

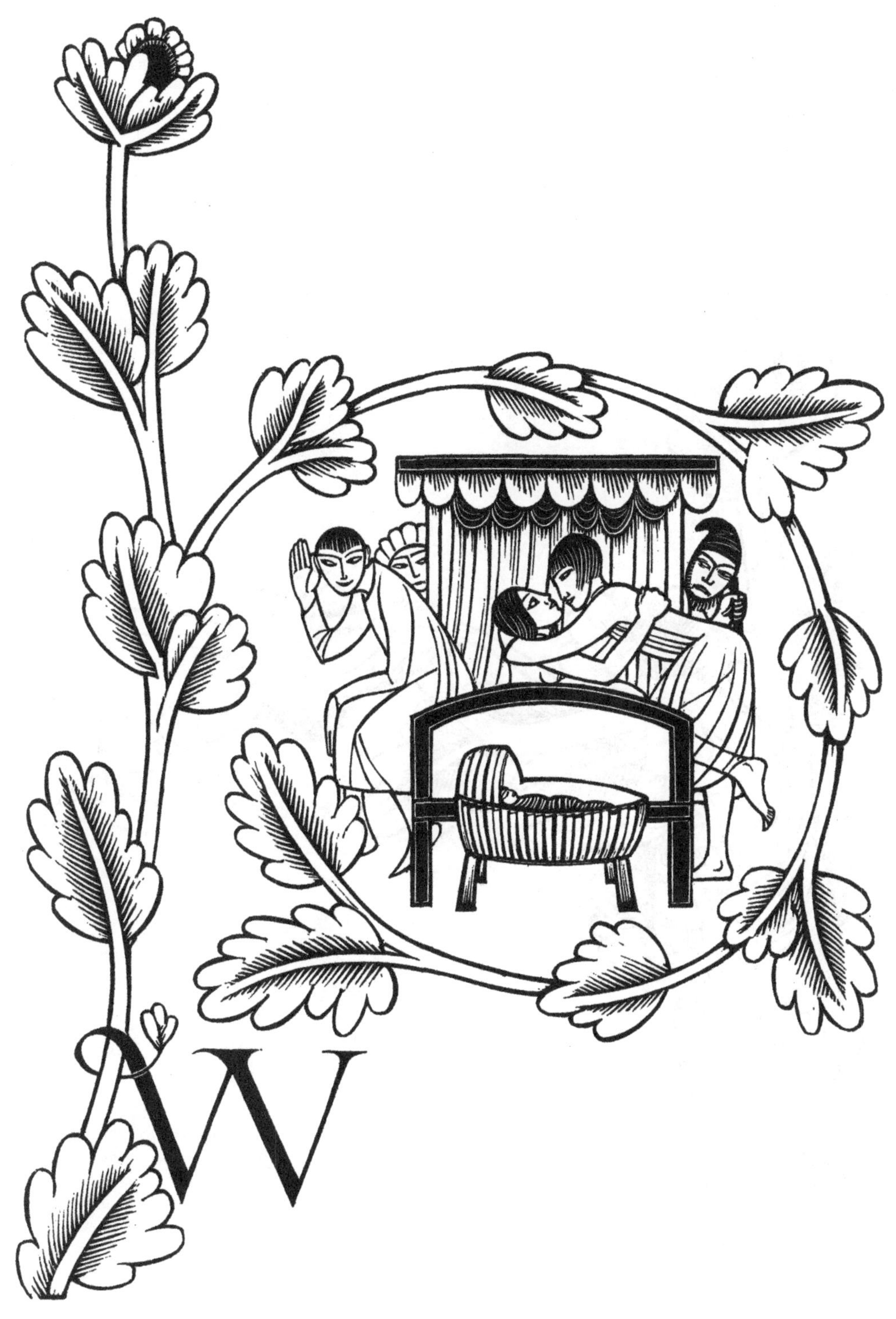

57 The Reeve's Tale
1928
The Canterbury Tales

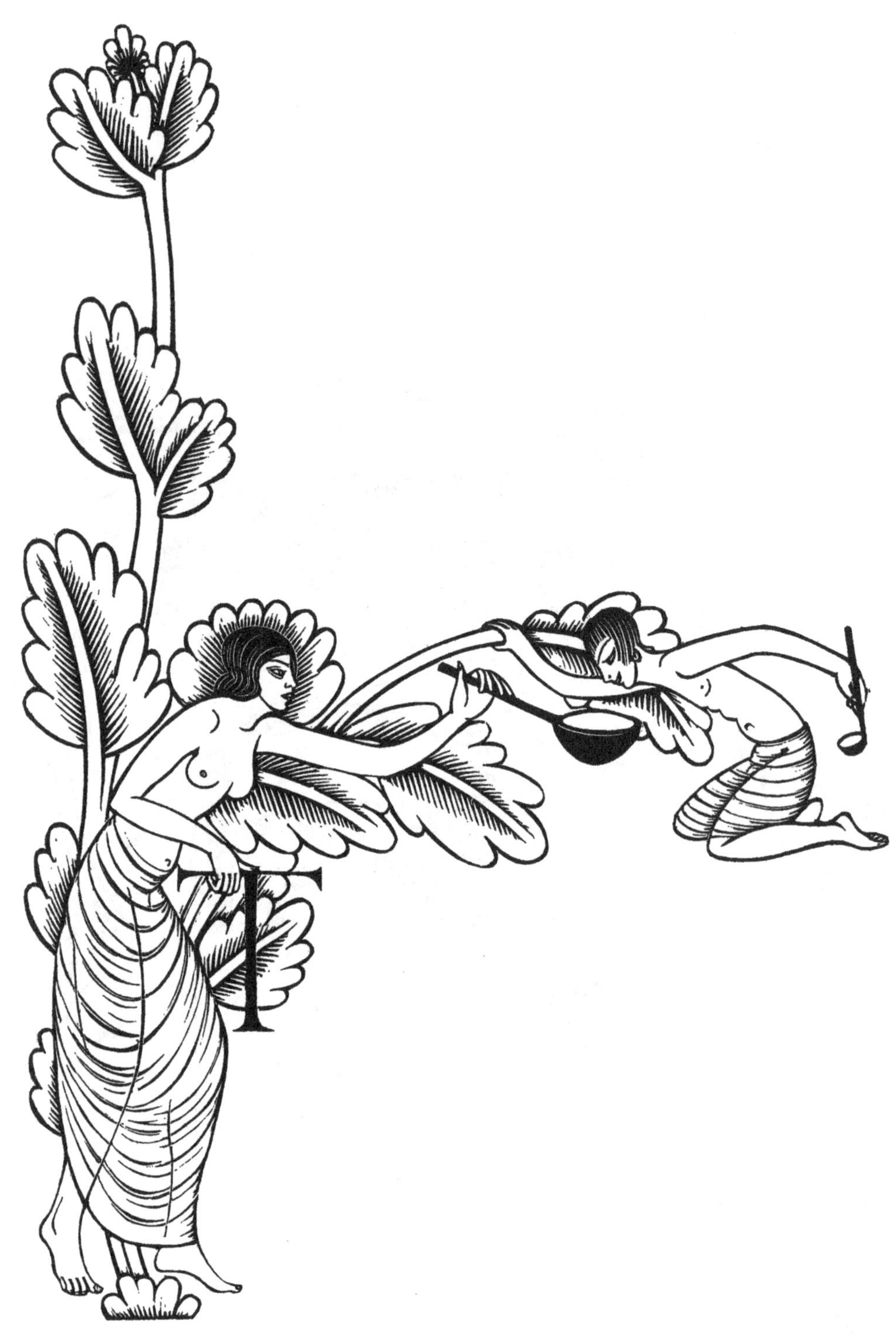

58 The Cook's Tale
1928
The Canterbury Tales

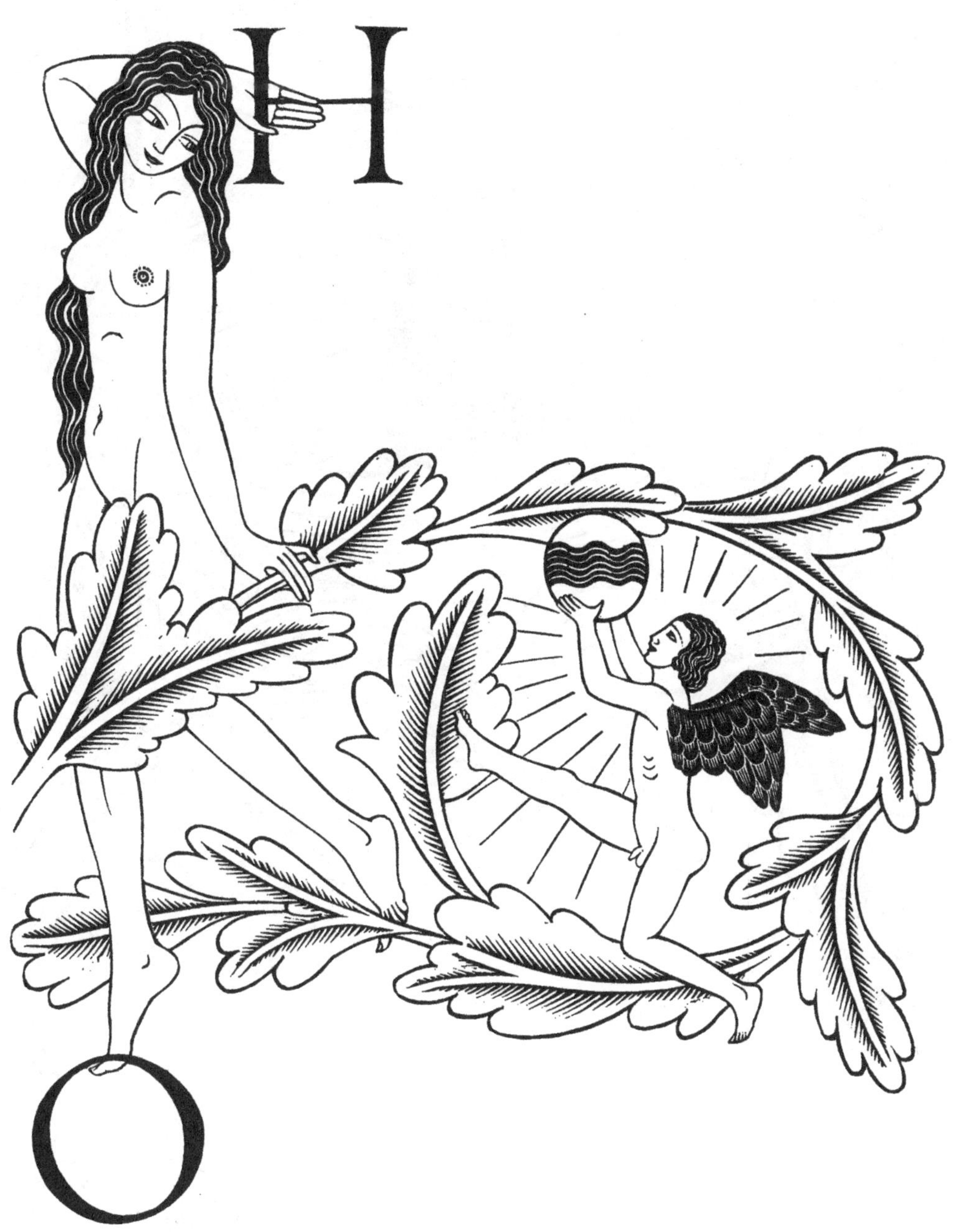

59 Cupid Playing Football with the World,
And Initials H and O with Venus Modestly Holding Spray
1929
The Canterbury Tales

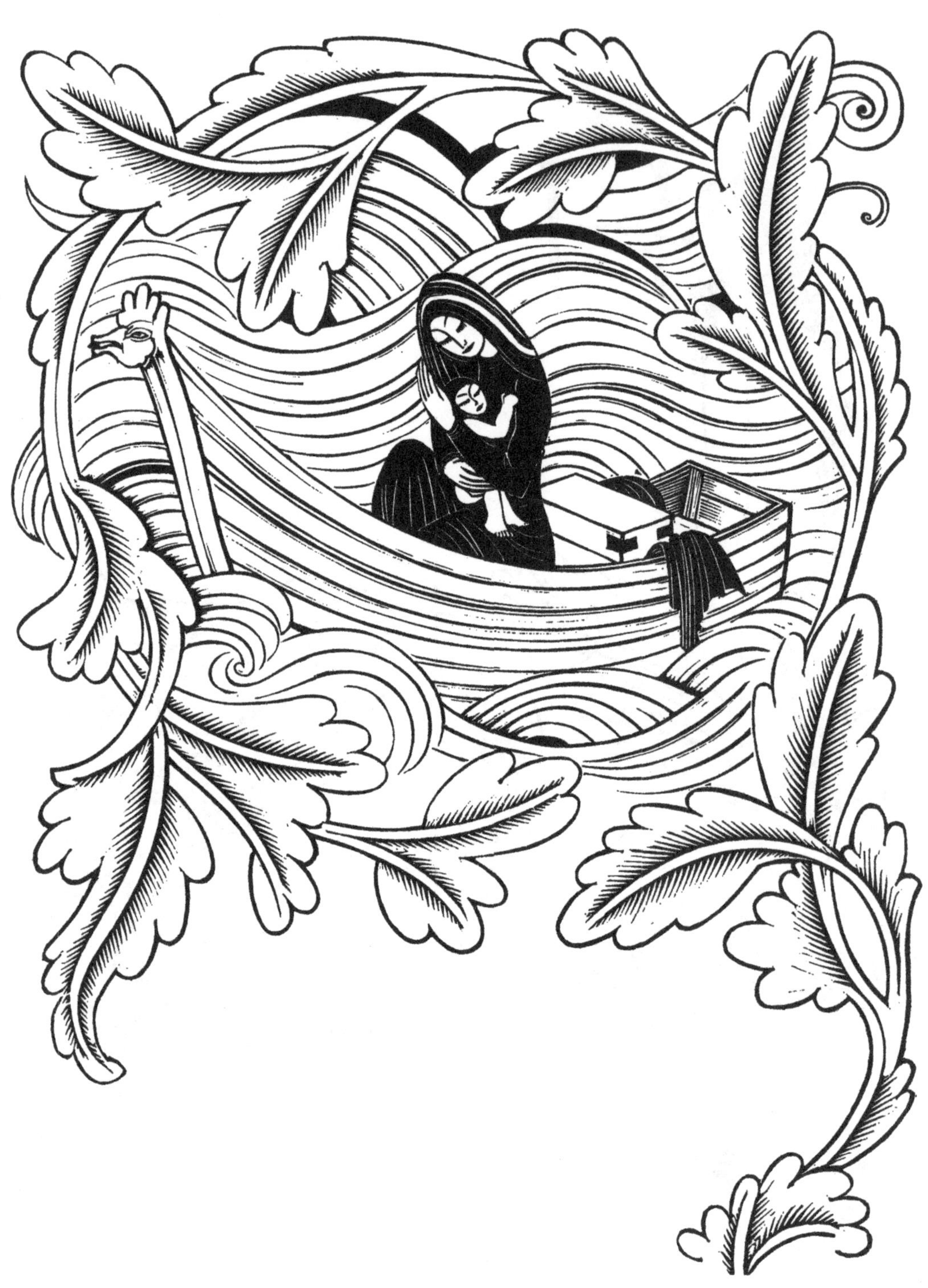

60 The Lawyer's Tale
1929
The Canterbury Tales

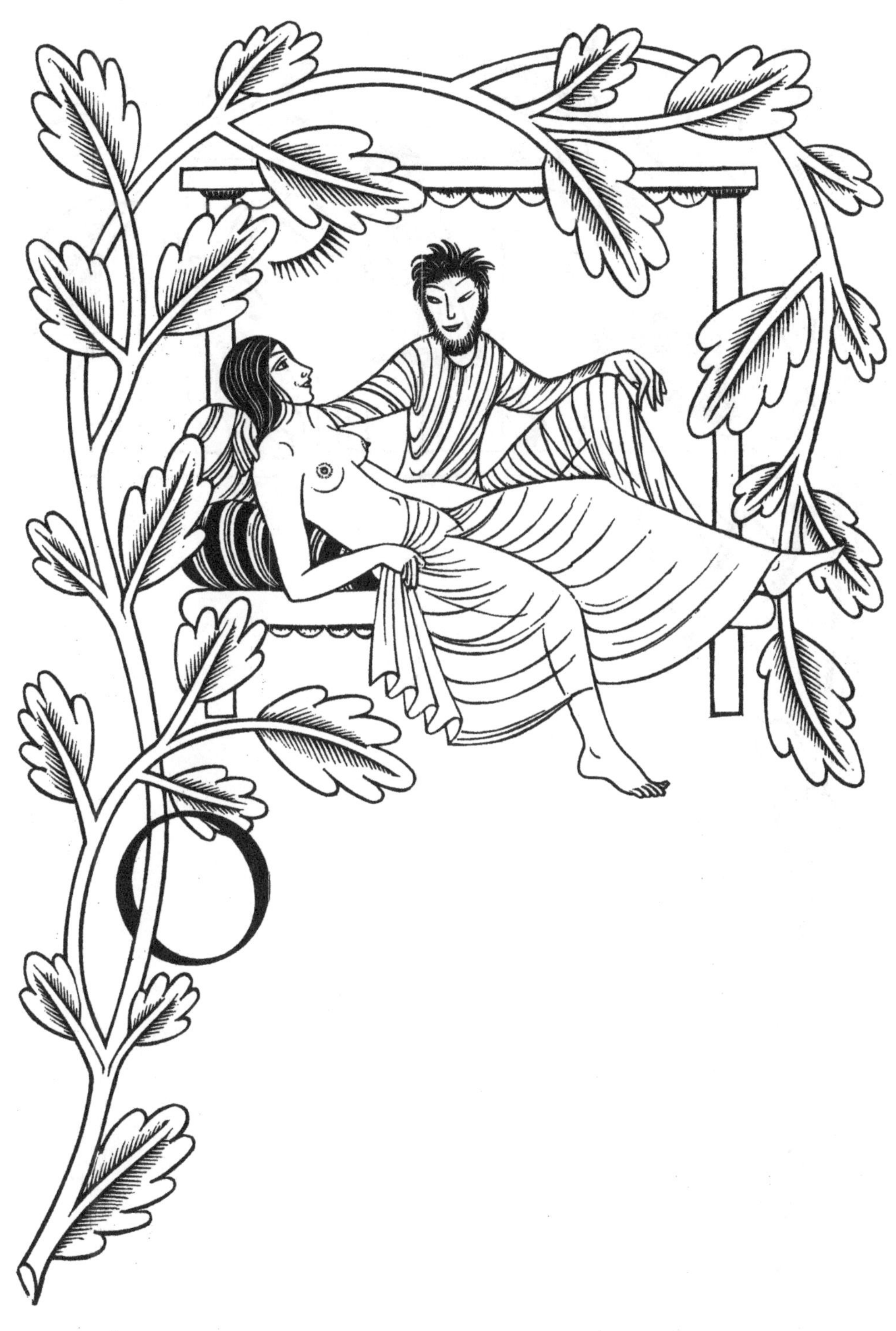

61 The Shipman's Tale
1929
The Canterbury Tales

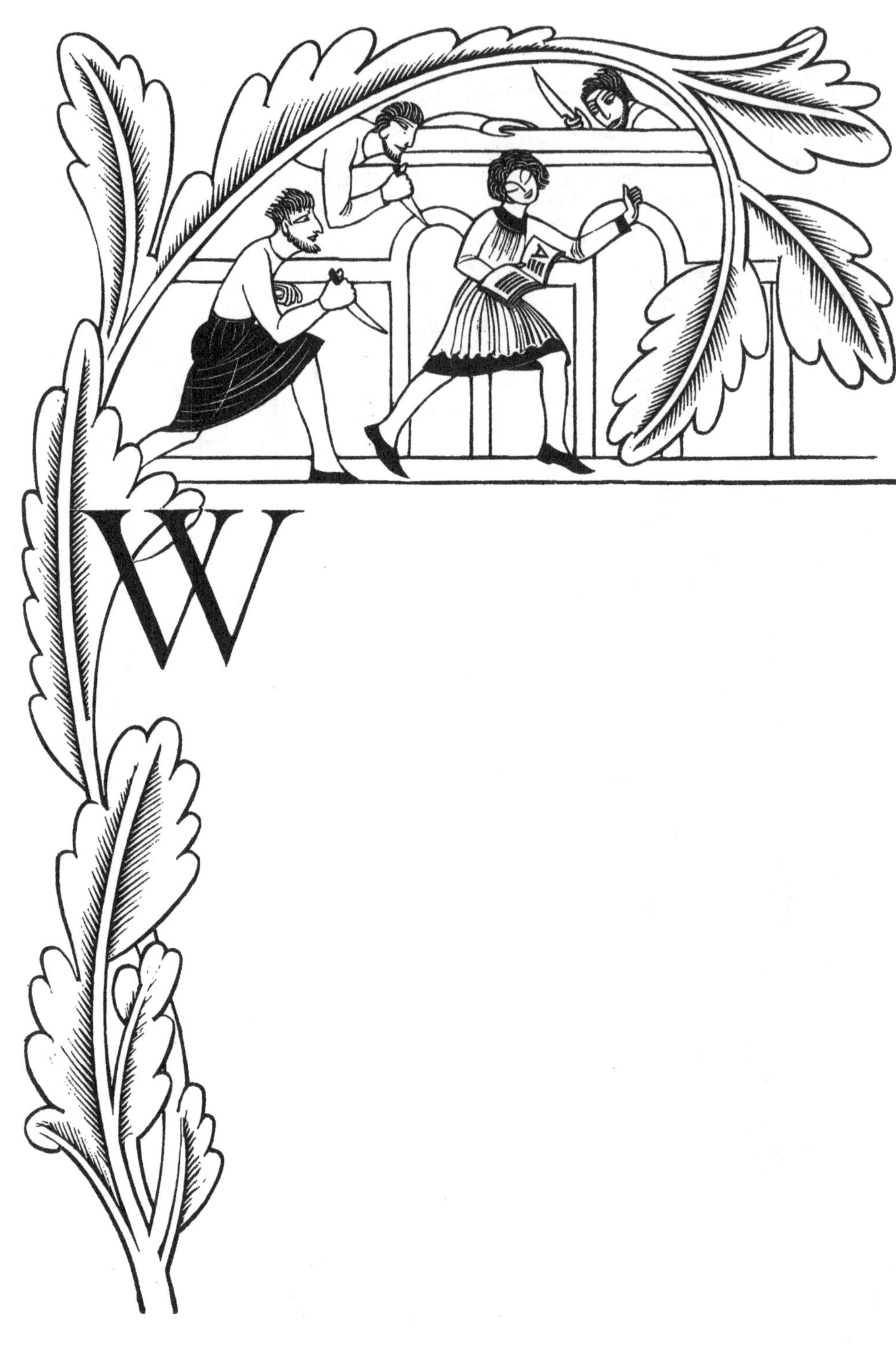

62 The Prioress's Tale
1929
The Canterbury Tales

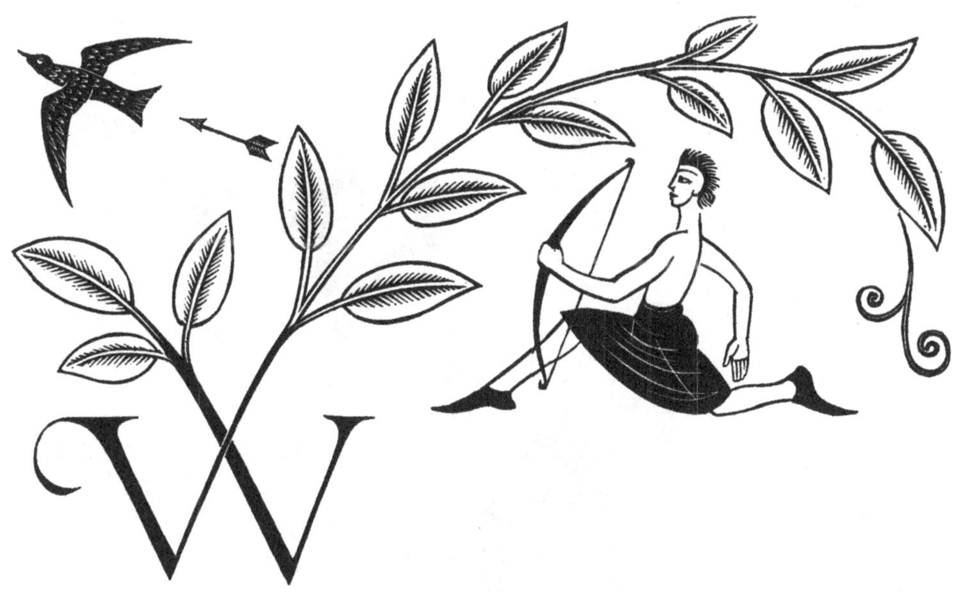

63 The Tale of Sir Topas
1929
The Canterbury Tales

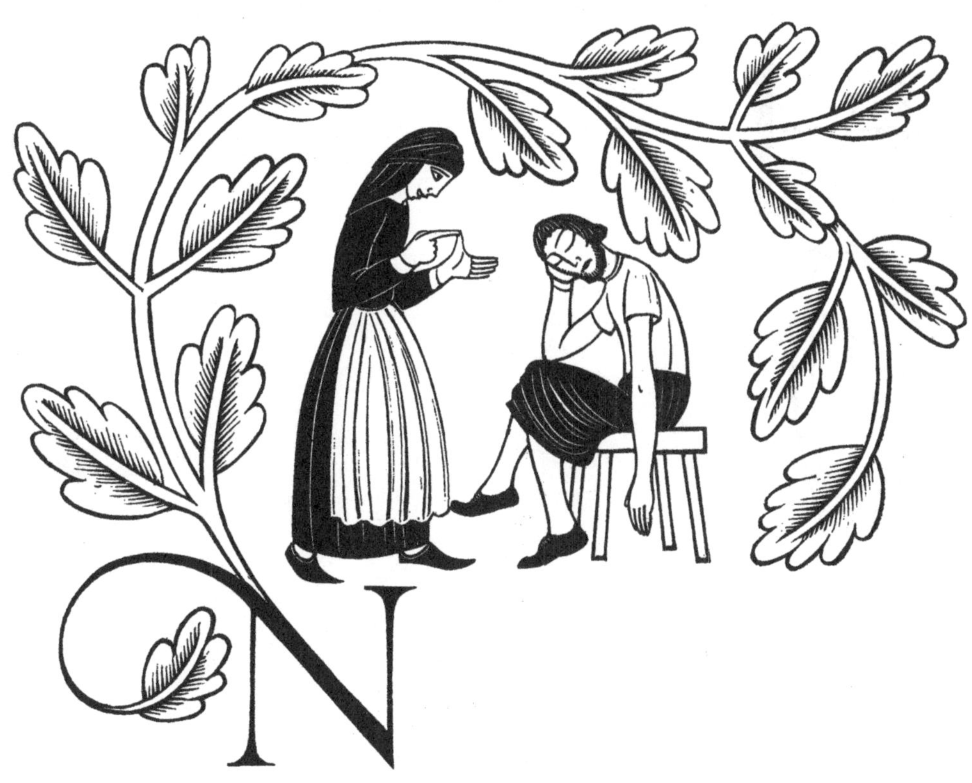

64 The Tale of Melibeus
1929
The Canterbury Tales

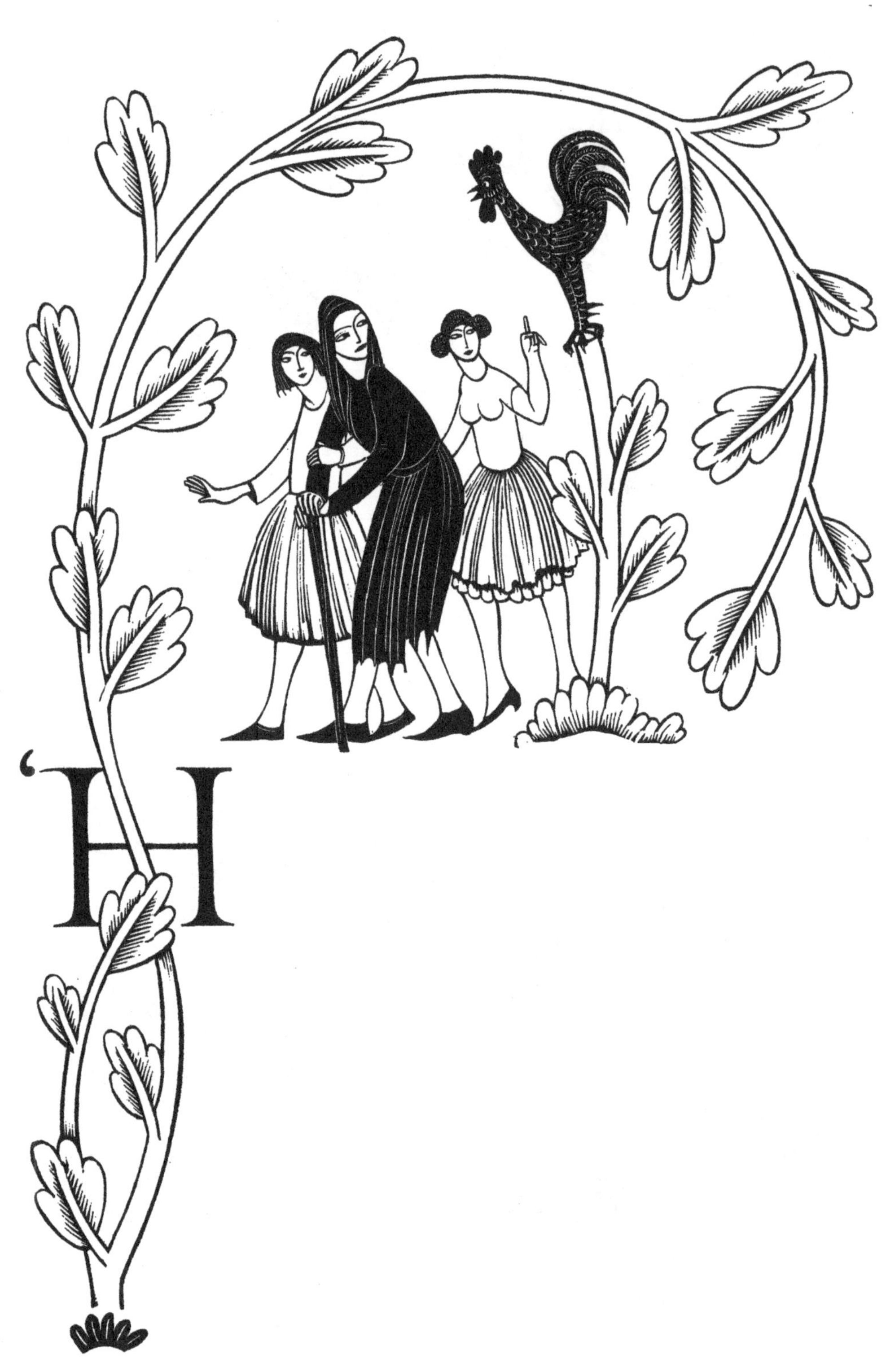

65 The Nun's Priest's Tale
1929
The Canterbury Tales

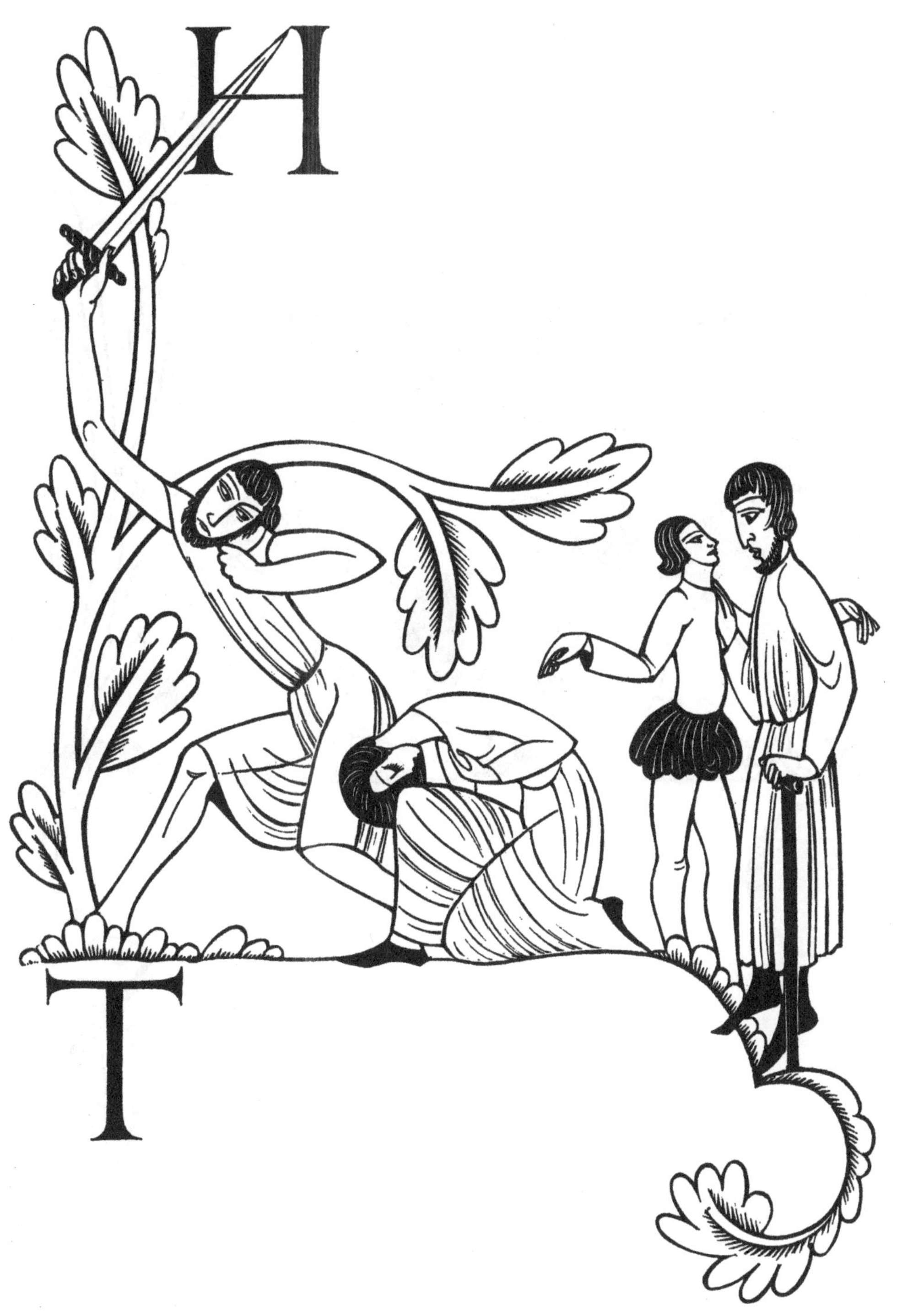

66 The Doctor's Tale
1930
The Canterbury Tales

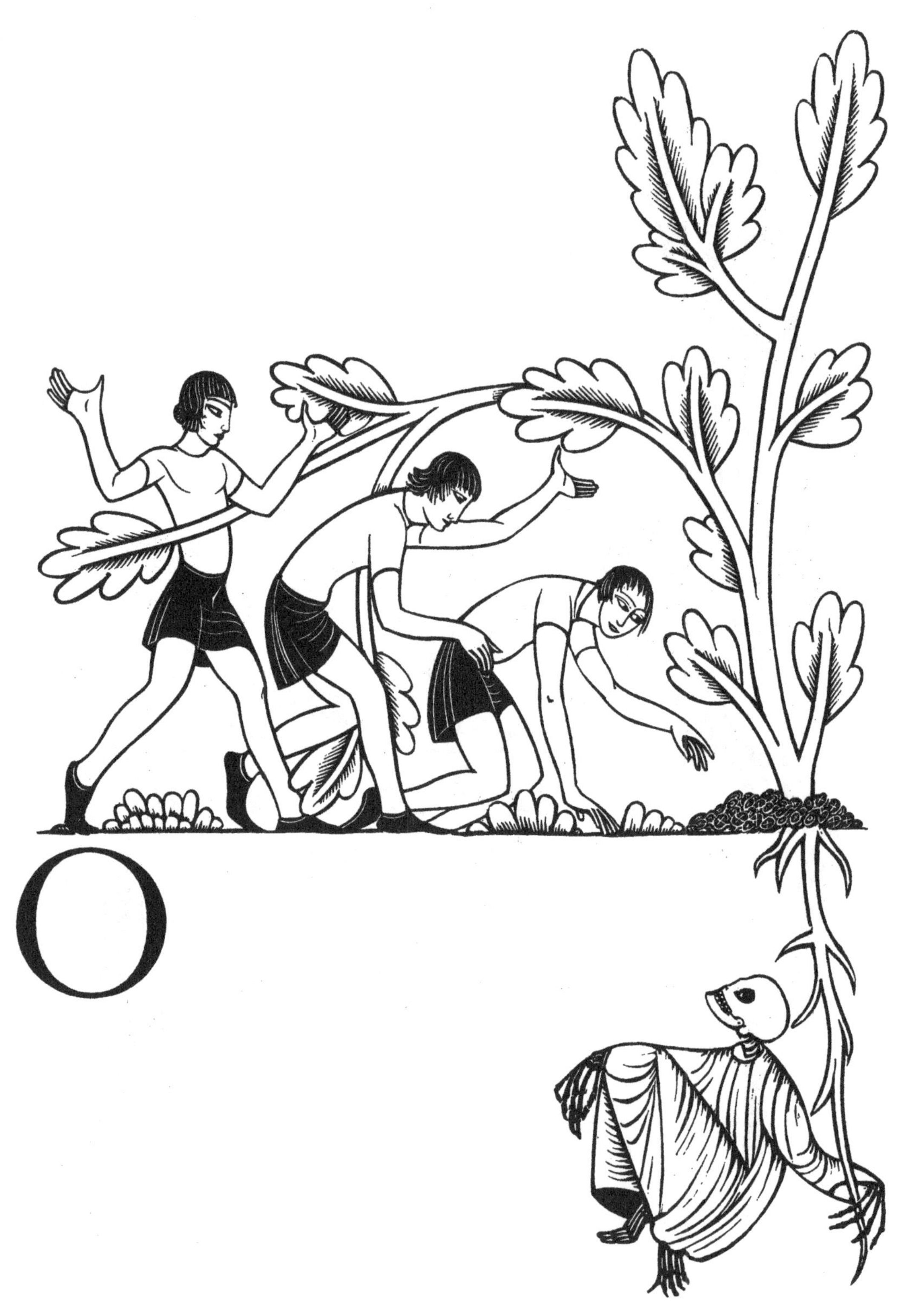

67 The Pardoner's Tale
1930
The Canterbury Tales

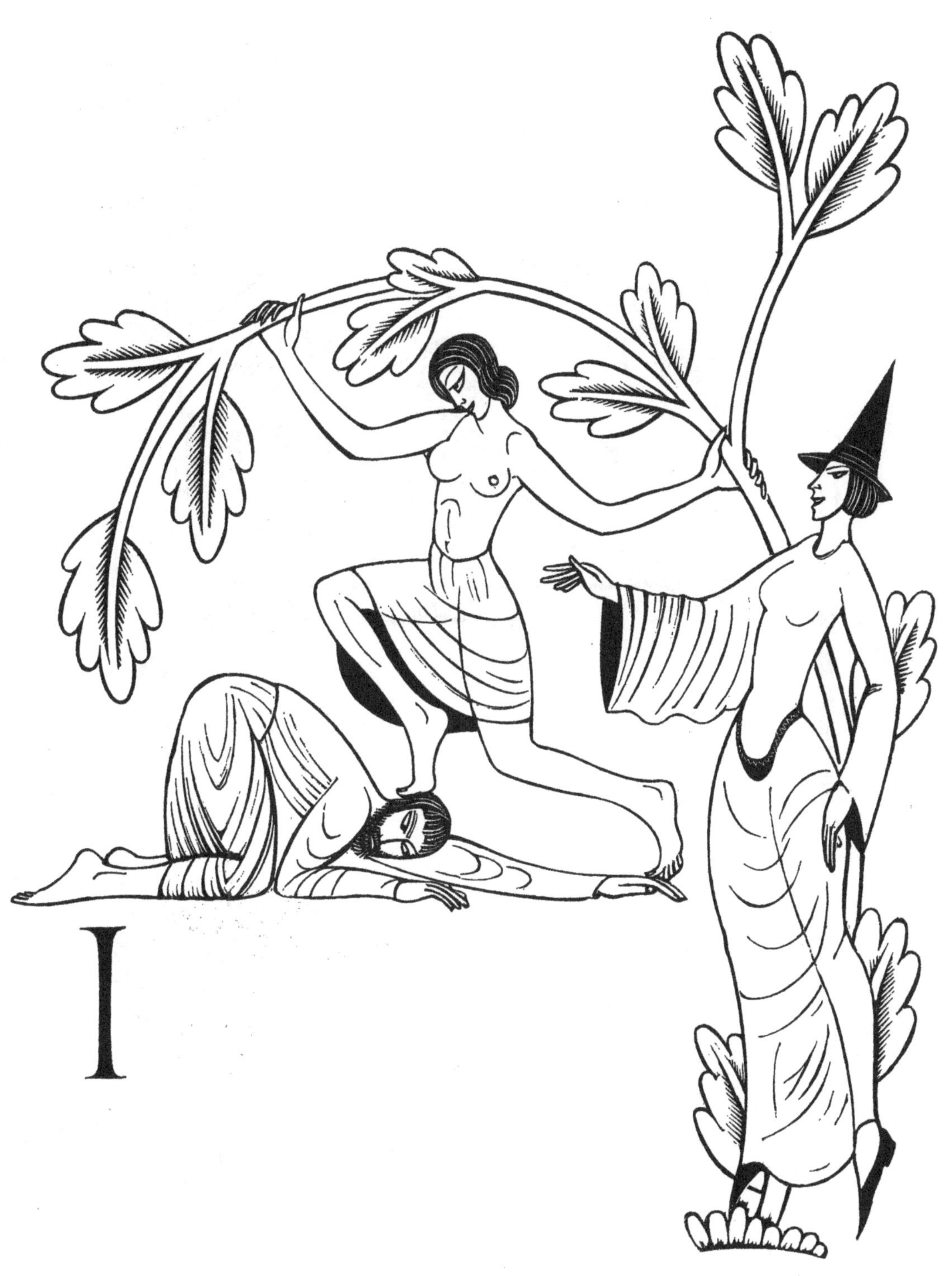

68 The Wife of Bath's Tale
1930
The Canterbury Tales

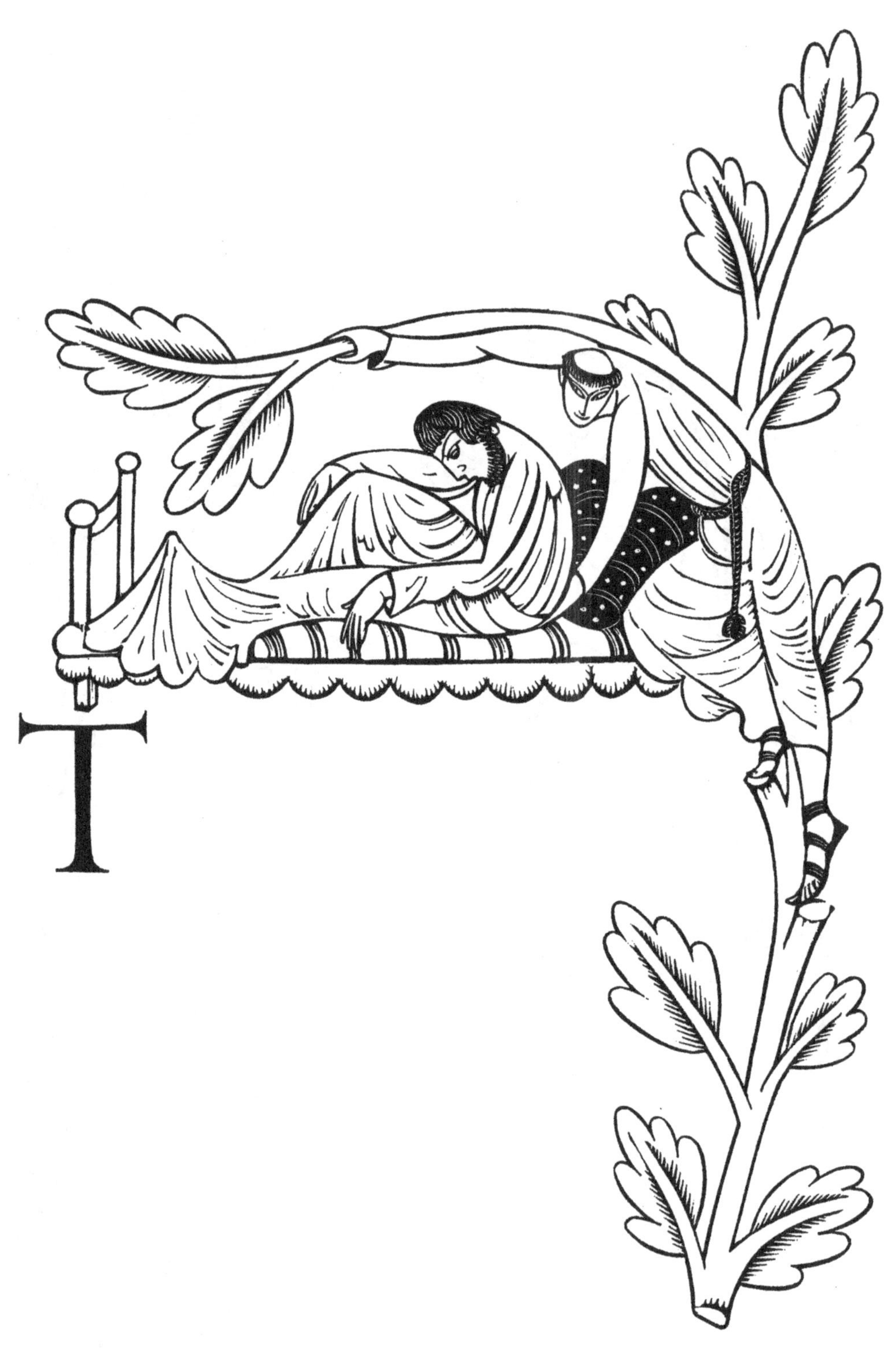

69 The Summoner's Tale
1930
The Canterbury Tales

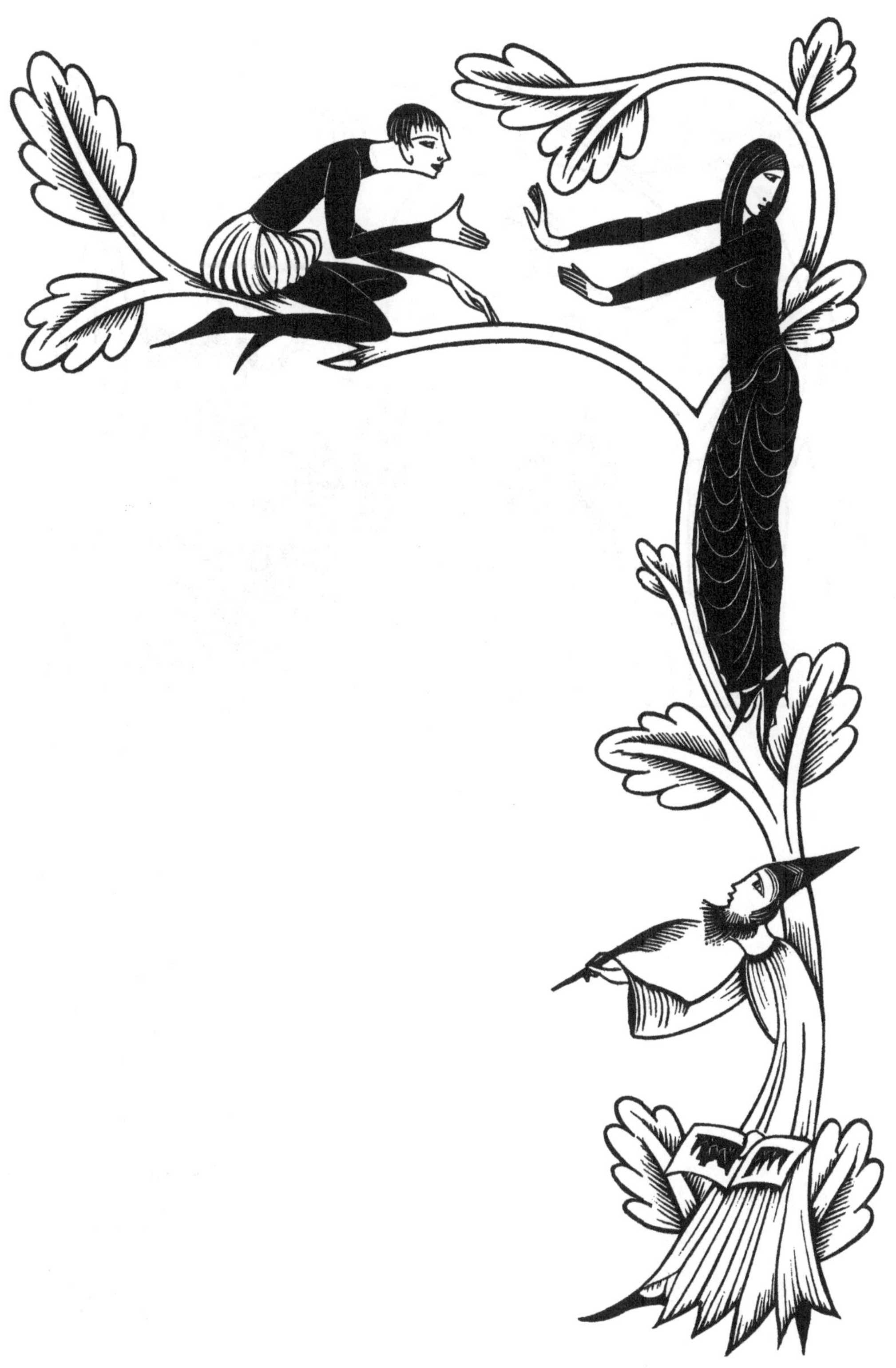

70 The Franklyn's Tale
1930
The Canterbury Tales

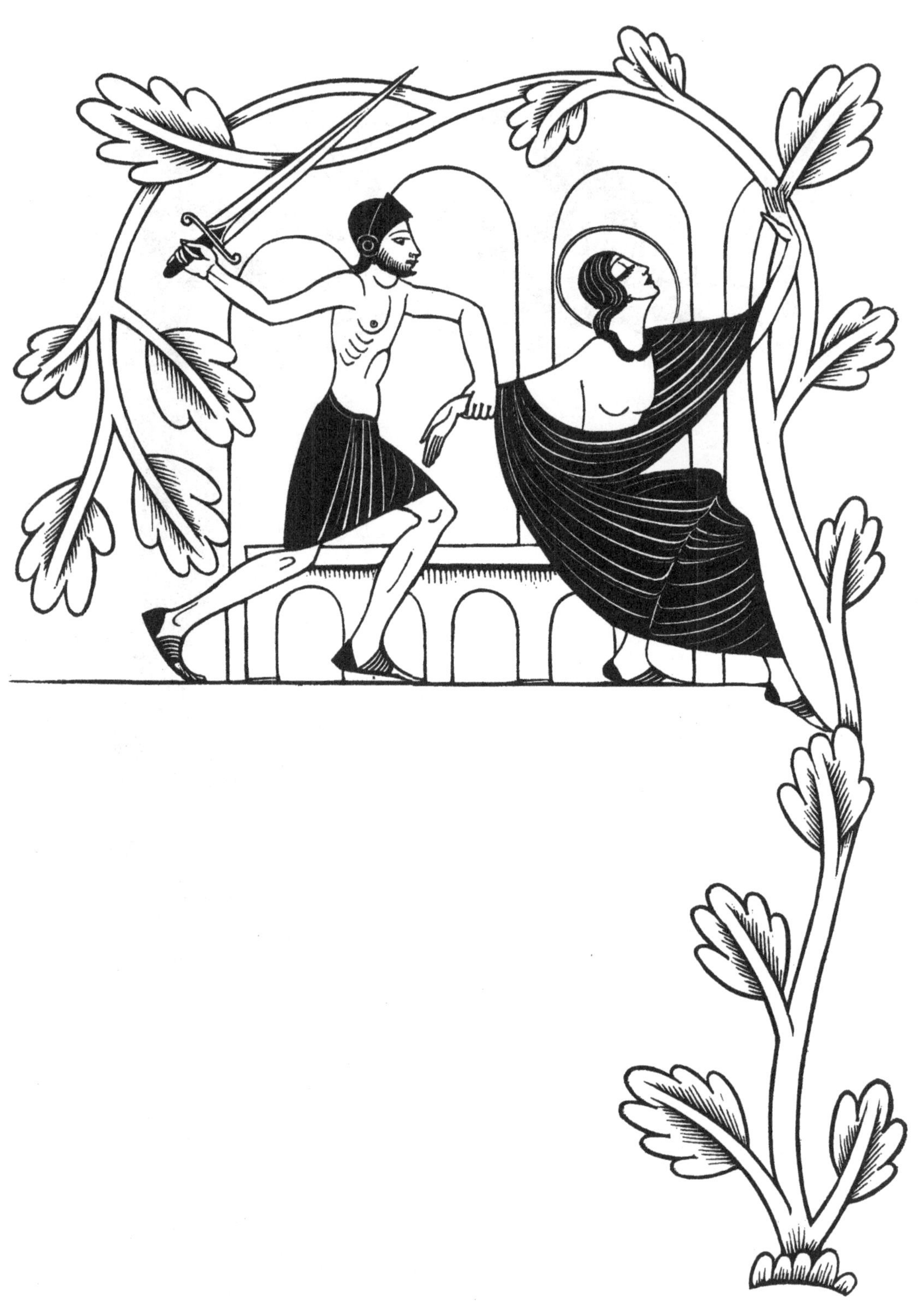

71 The Second Nun's Tale
1930
The Canterbury Tales

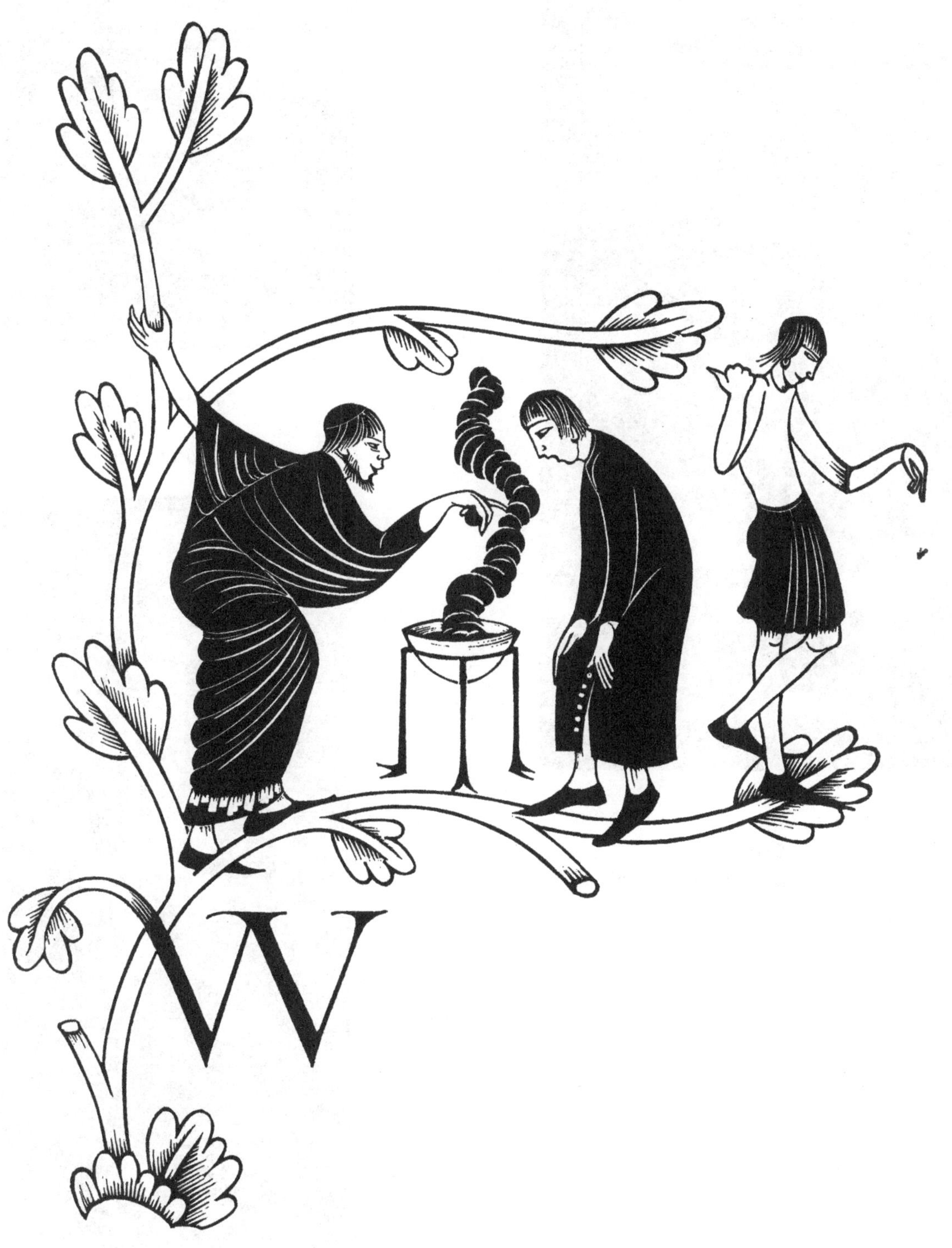

72 The Yeoman's Tale
1930
The Canterbury Tales

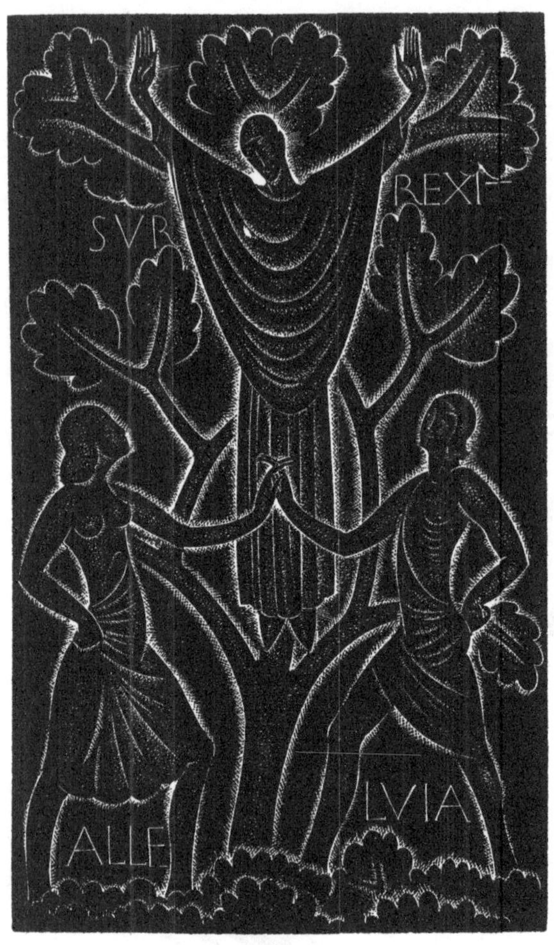

73 Surrexit Alleluia
1930
The Lesson and Gospels for the Seasons of Lent

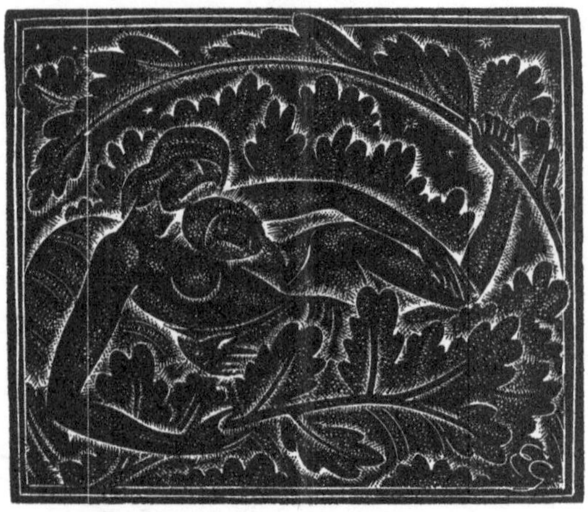

74 Inter Ubera Mea
1930
Canticum Canticorum

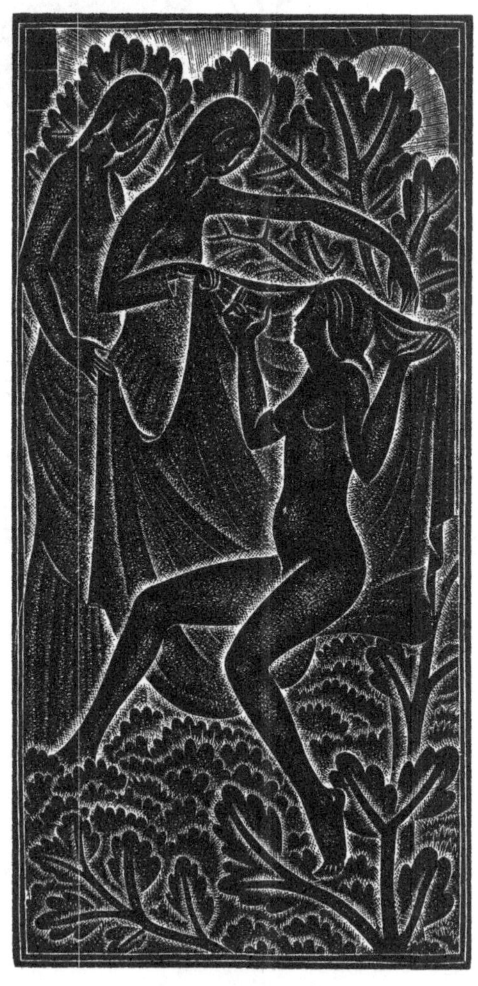

75 Nigra Sum Sed Formosa
1929
Canticum Canticorum

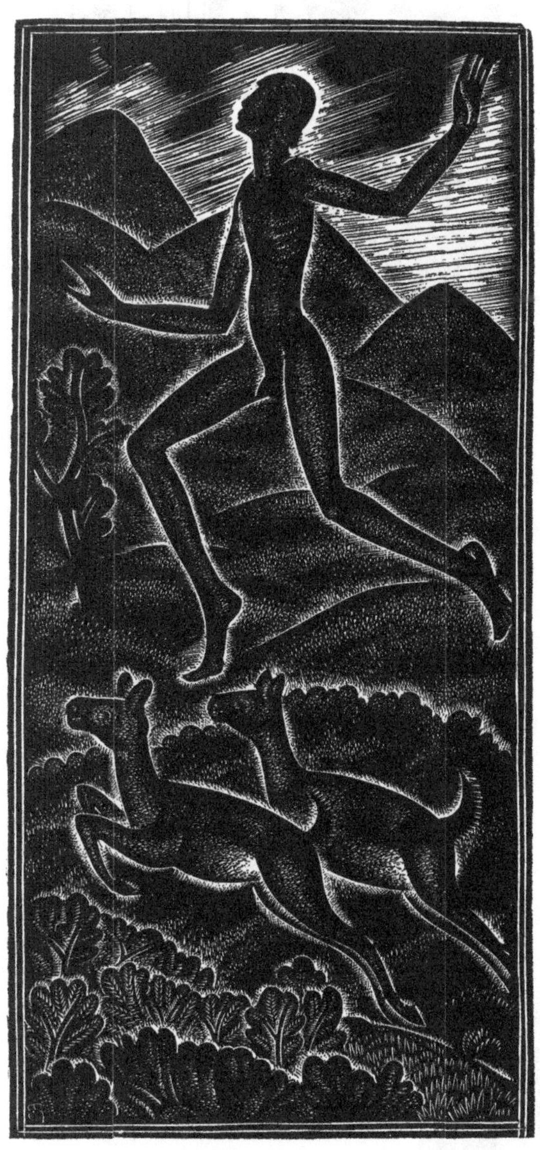

76 Transiliens Colles
1930
Canticum Canticorum

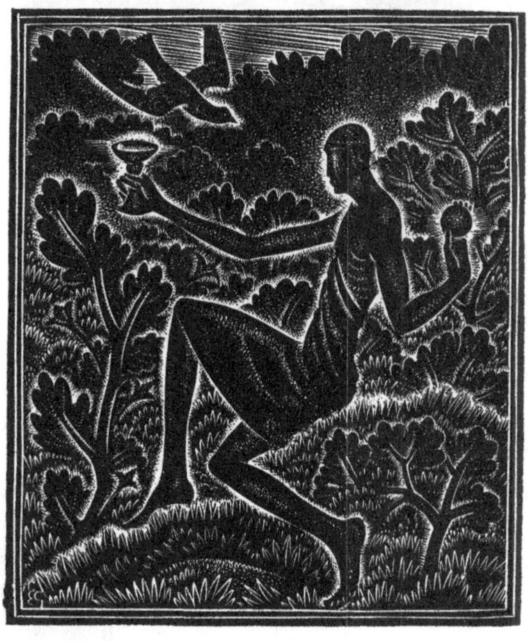

77 Qui Pascitur Inter Lilia
1930
Canticum Canticorum

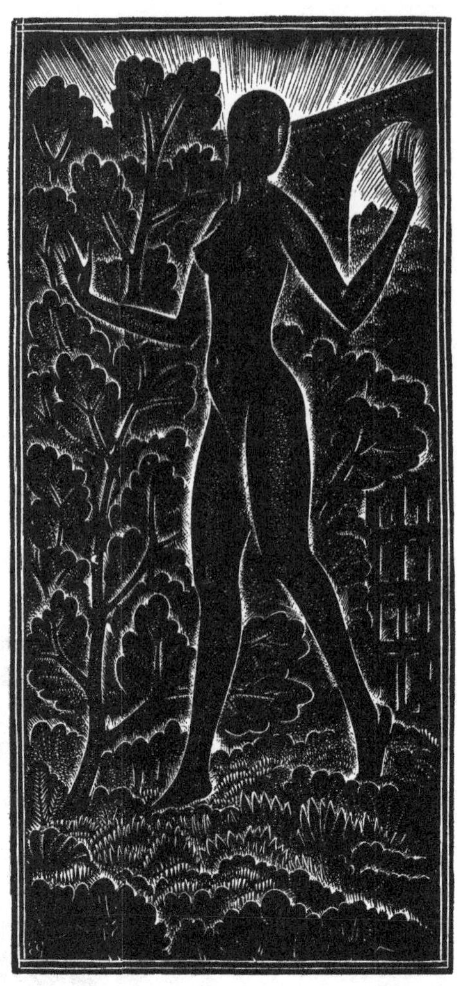

78 Hortus Conclusus
1930
Canticum Canticorum

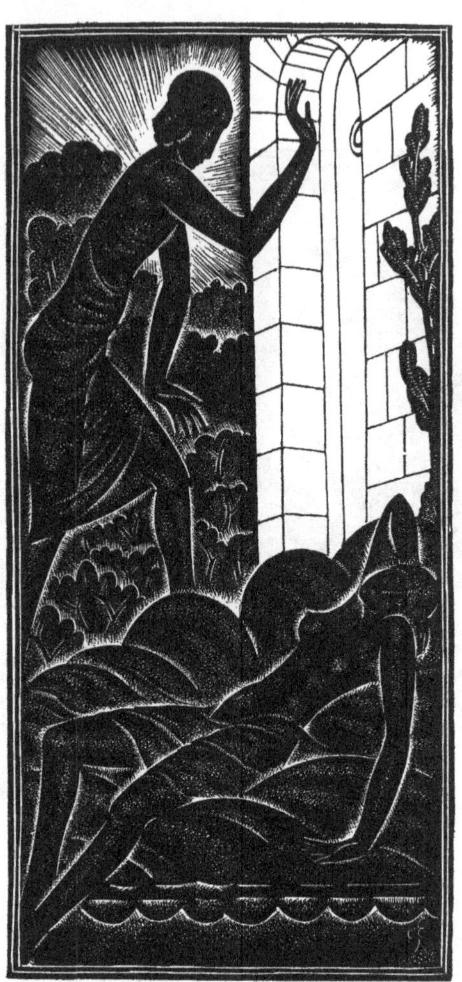

79 Dilecti Mei Pulsantis
1930
Canticum Canticorum

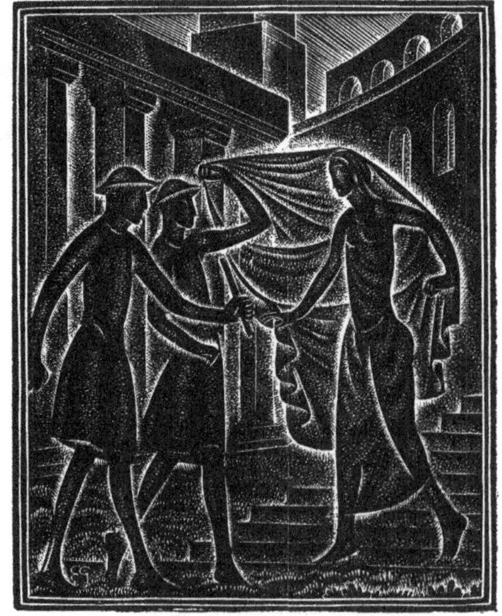

80 Invenerunt Me Custodes
1930
Canticum Canticorum

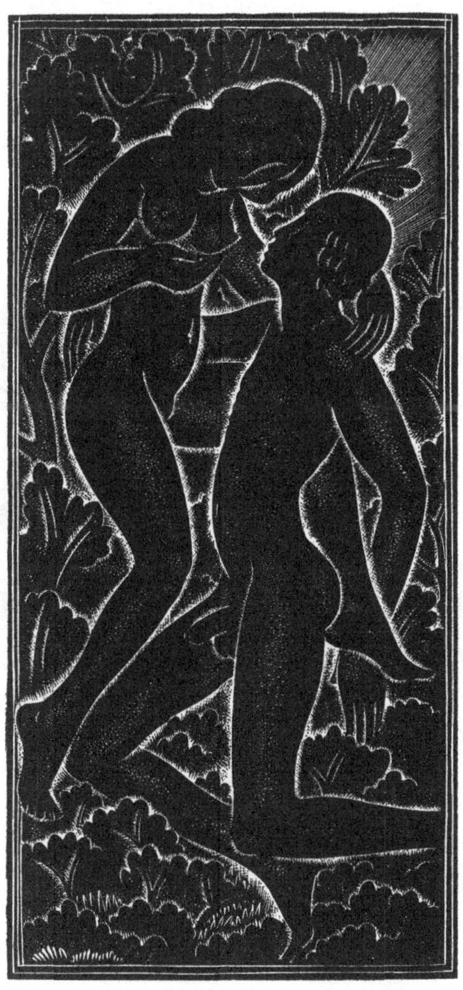

81 Ibi Dabo Tibi
1930
Canticum Canticorum

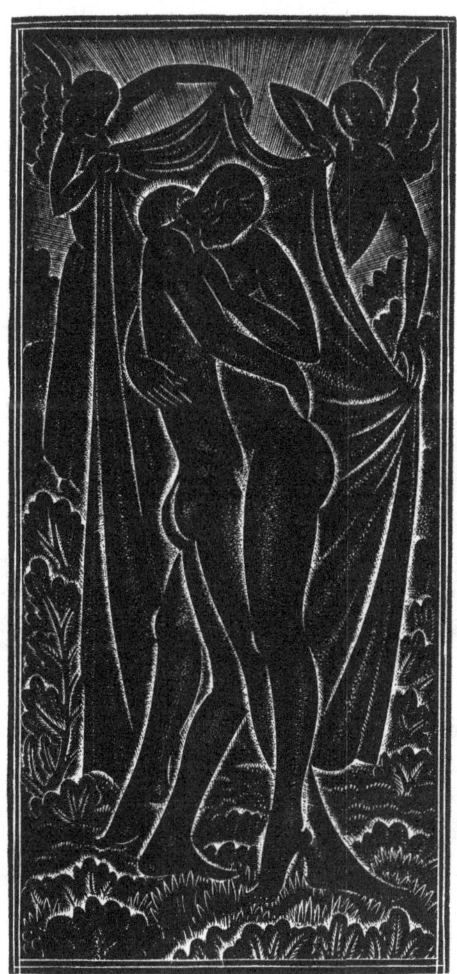

82 In Domum Matris Meae
1930
Canticum Canticorum

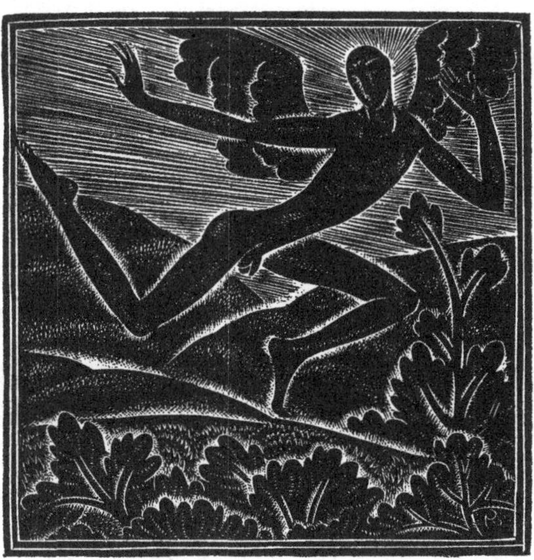

83 Fuge, Dilecti Me
1930
Canticum Canticorum

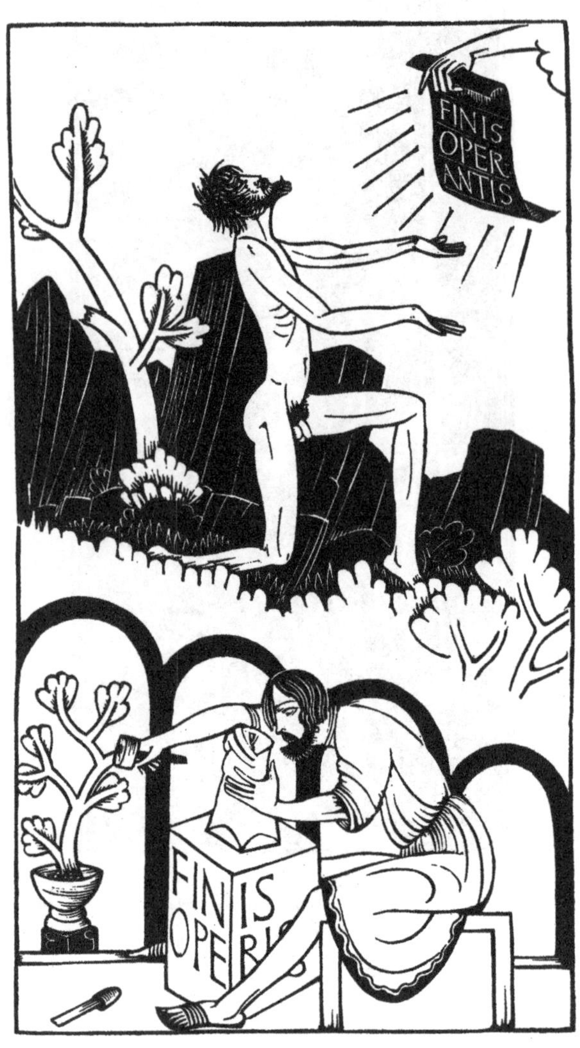

84 Art and Prudence
1930
Clothes

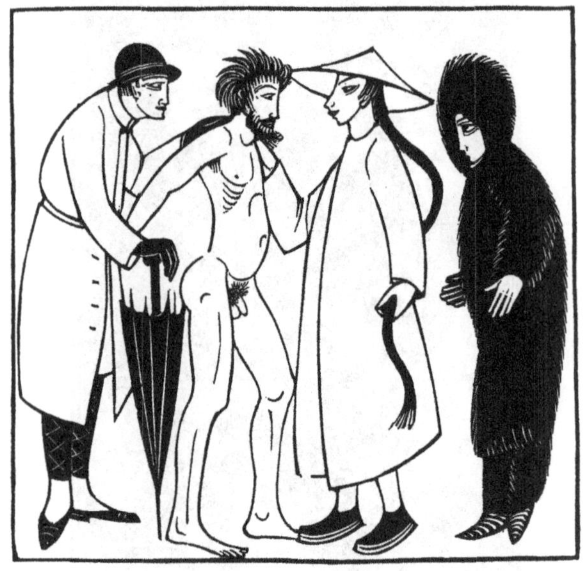

85 Clothes as Houses
1930
Clothes

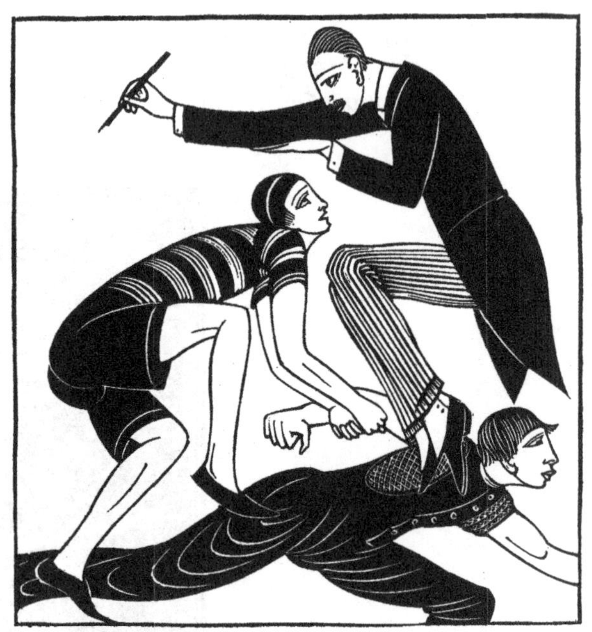

86 Clothes as Workshops
1930
Clothes

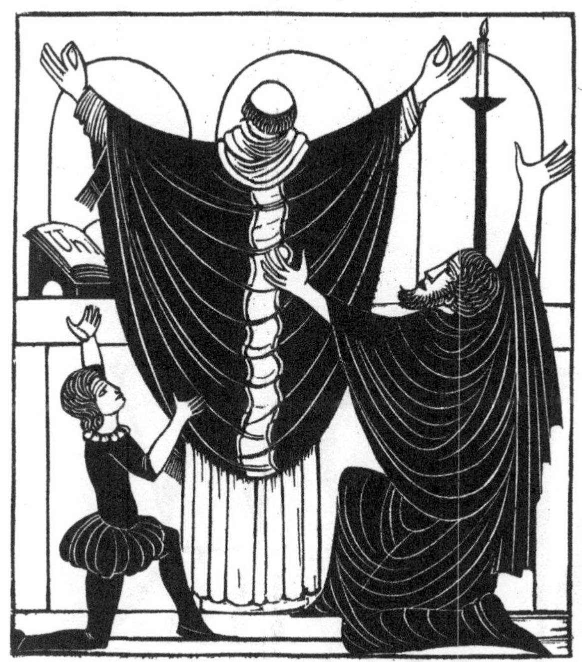

87 Clothes as Churches and Town Halls
1930
Clothes

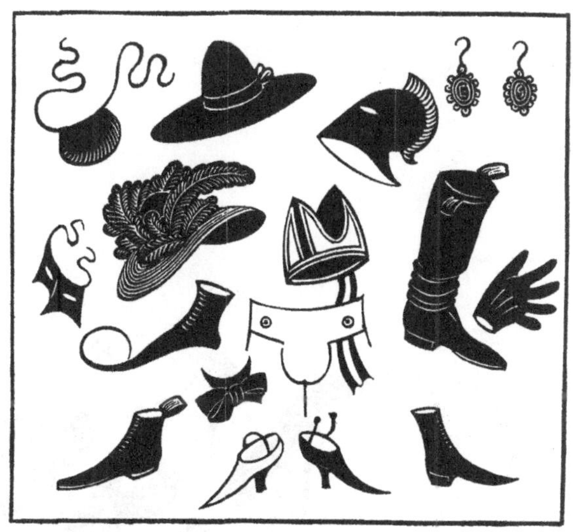

88 Clothes for Special Parts
1930
Clothes

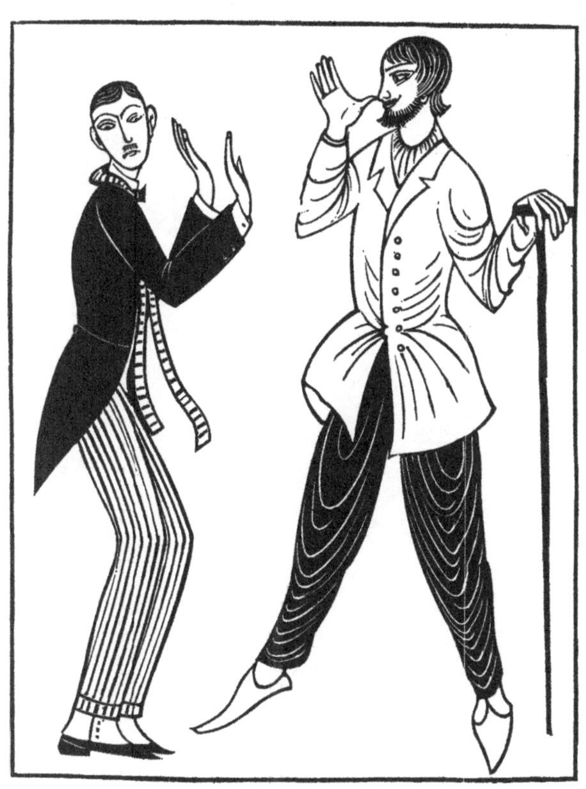

89 The Tyranny of Tailors
1930
Clothes

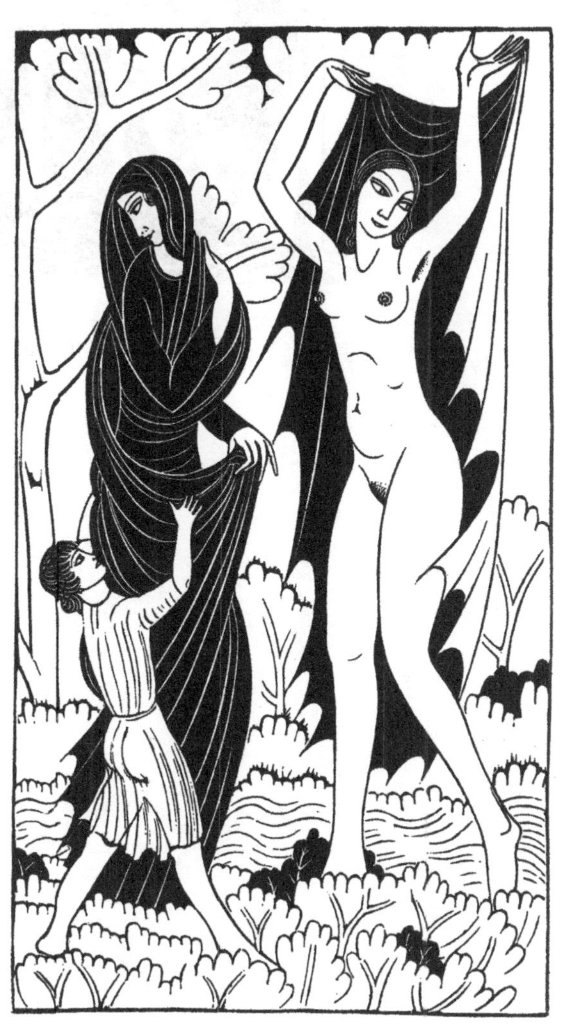

90 Nature and Nakedness
1930
Clothes

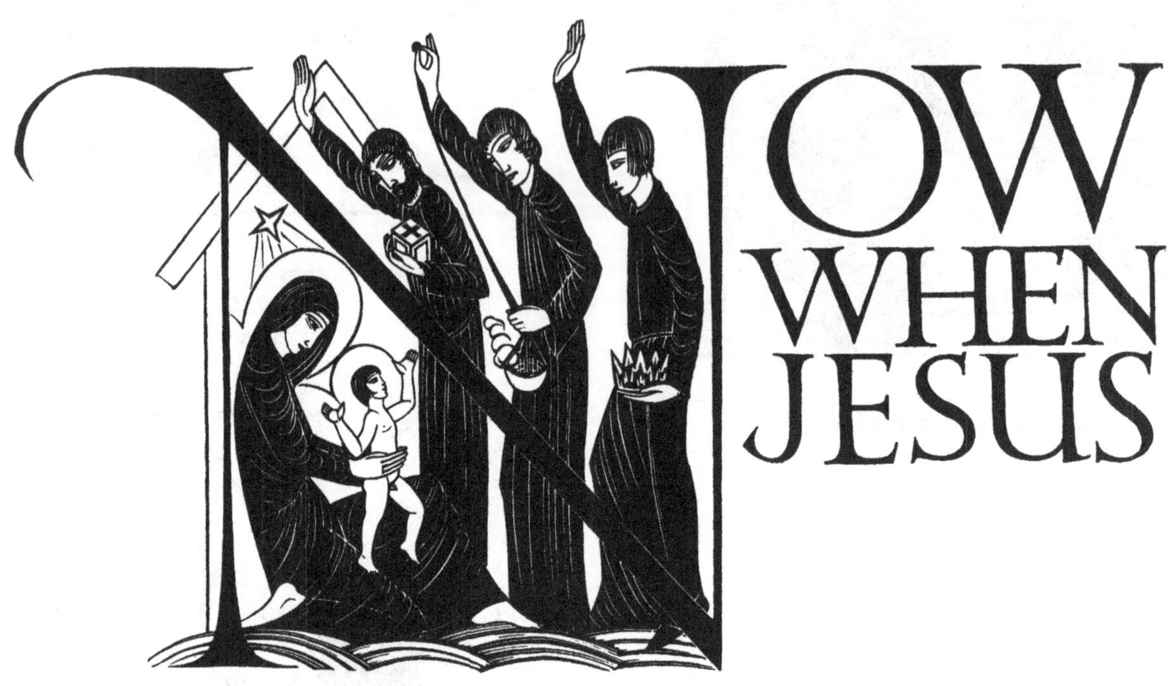

91 Initial Letter N and The Epiphany
1930
The Four Gospels

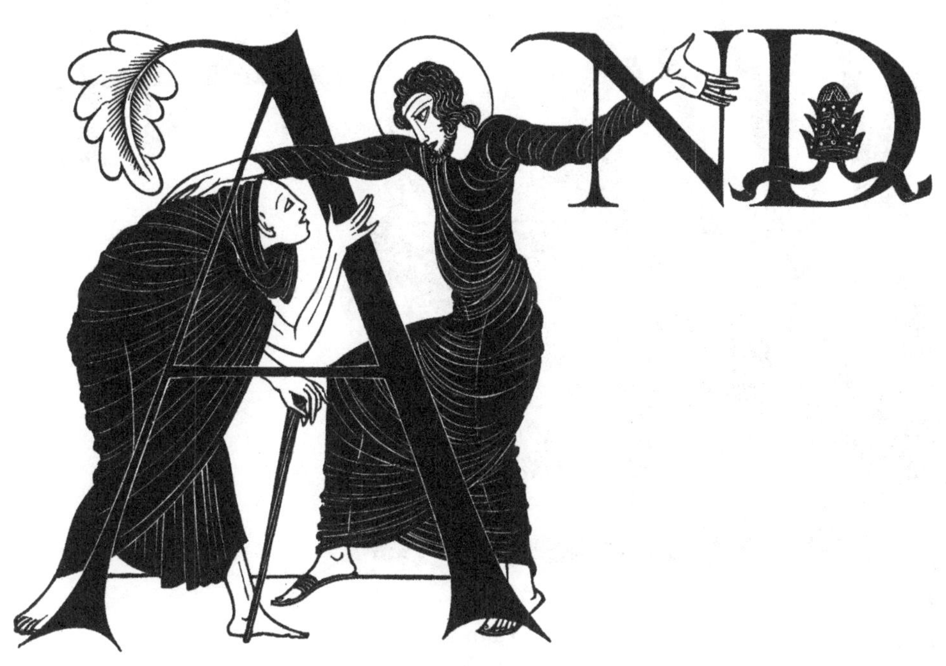

92 Christ and the Leper
1931
The Four Gospels

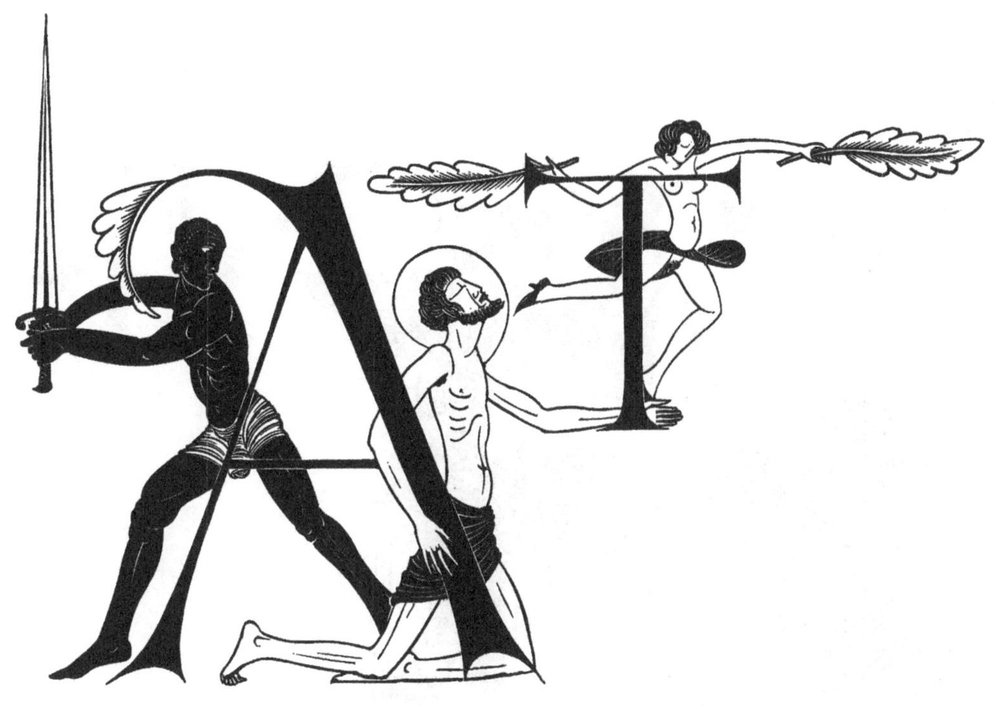

93 John the Baptist's Beheading
1931
The Four Gospels

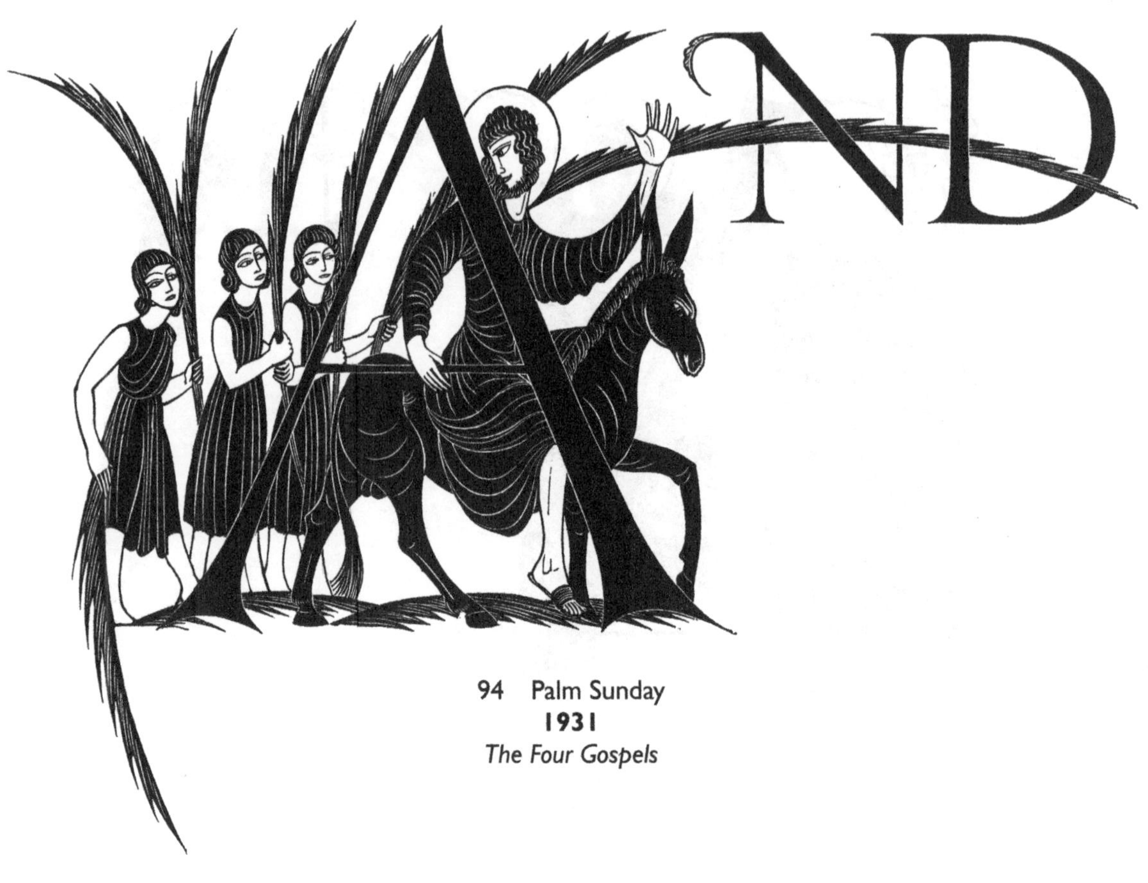

94 Palm Sunday
1931
The Four Gospels

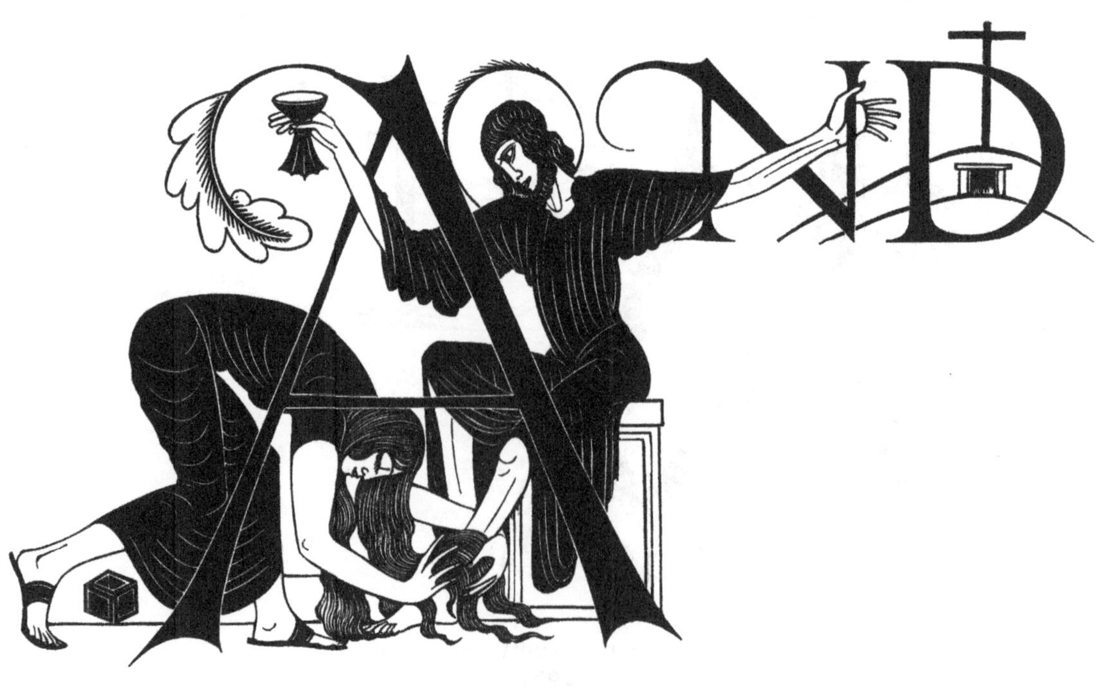

95 Mary Magdalen
1931
The Four Gospels

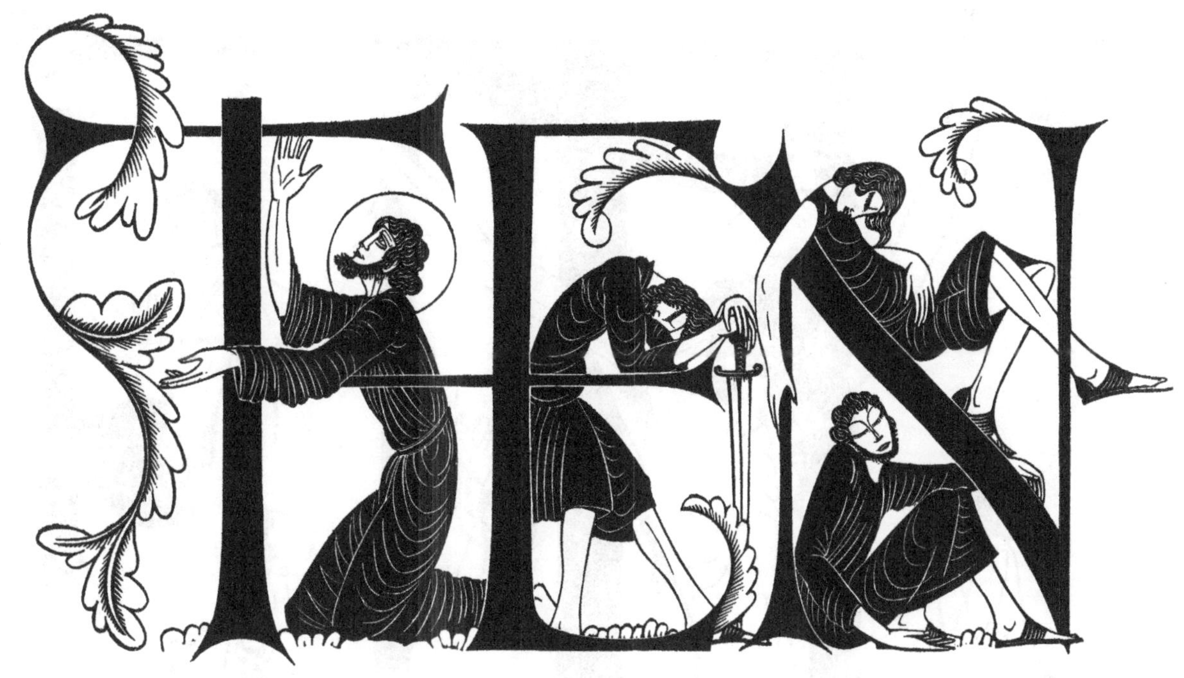

96 Gethsemane
1931
The Four Gospels

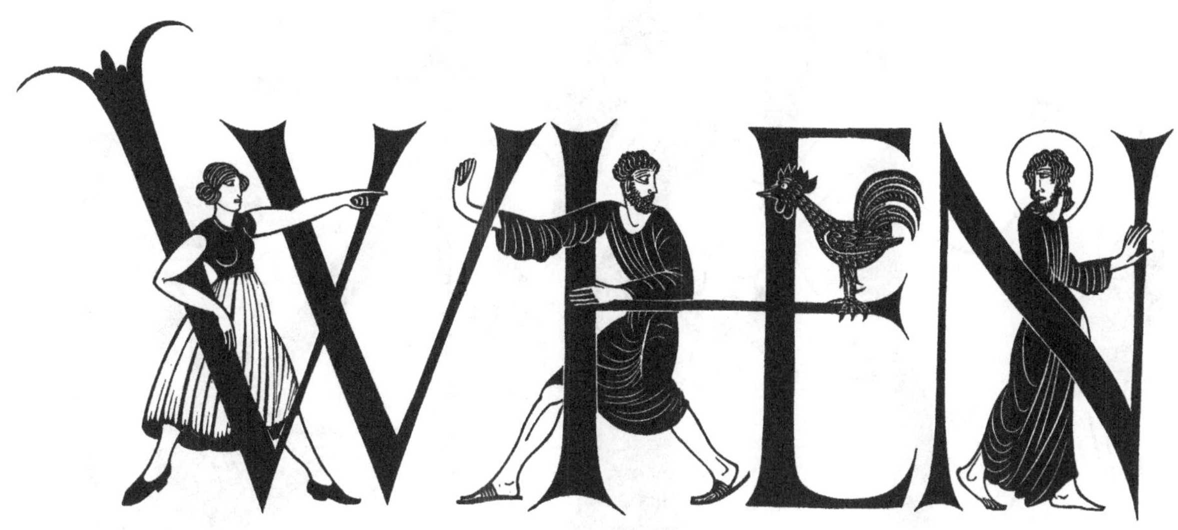

97 Peter and the Cock
1931
The Four Gospels

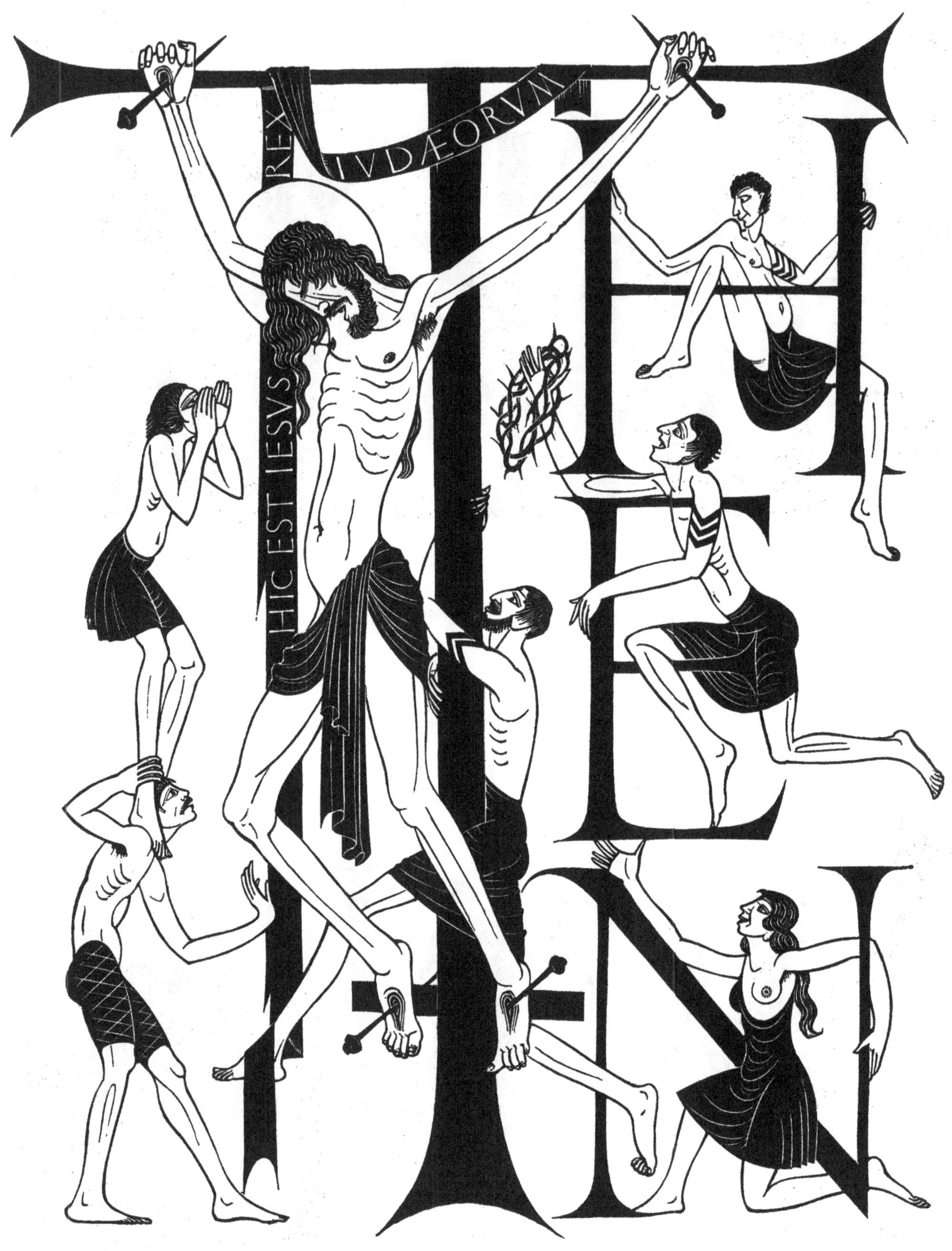

98 The Crucifixion
1931
The Four Gospels

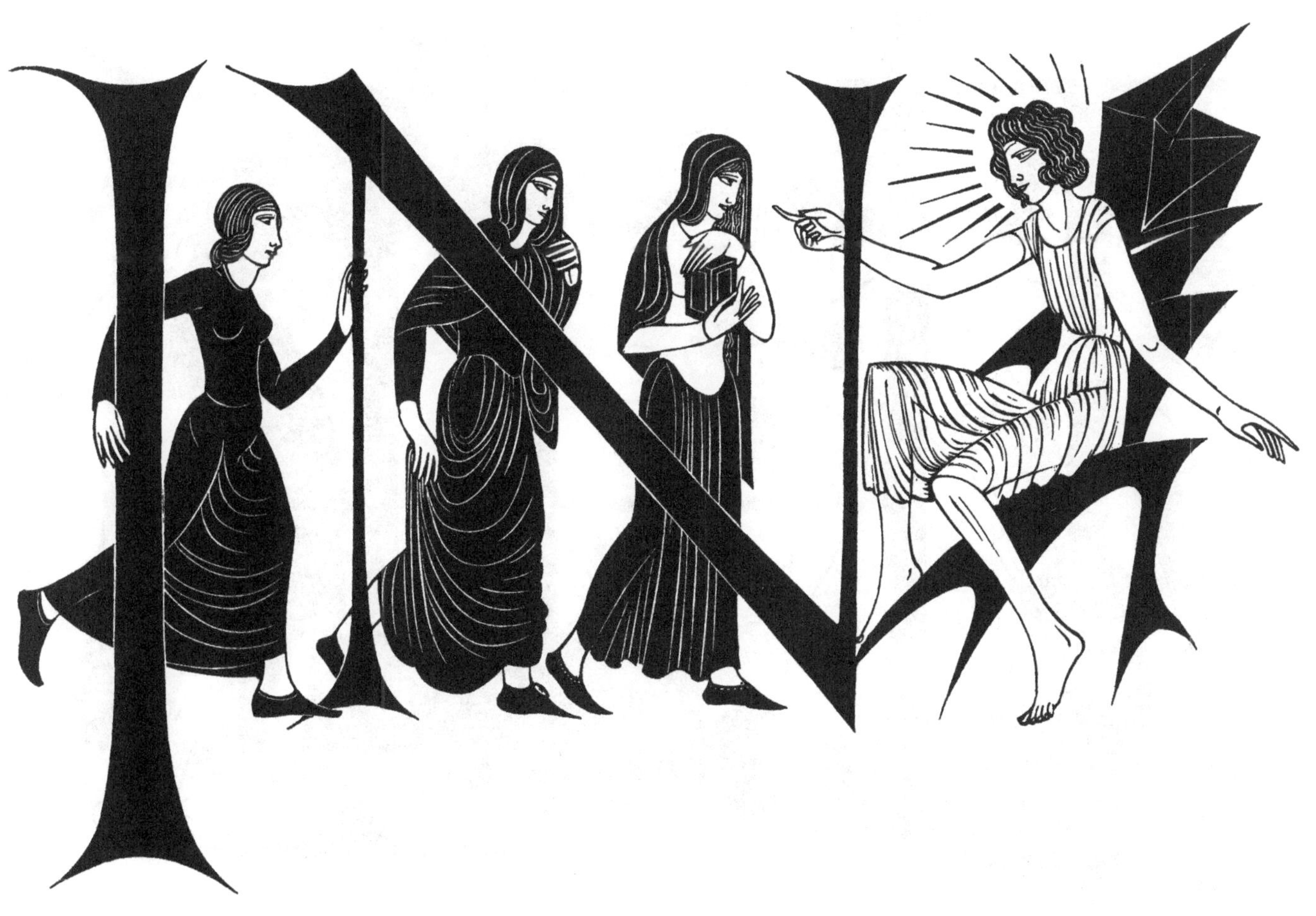

99 Mary at the Tomb
1931
The Four Gospels

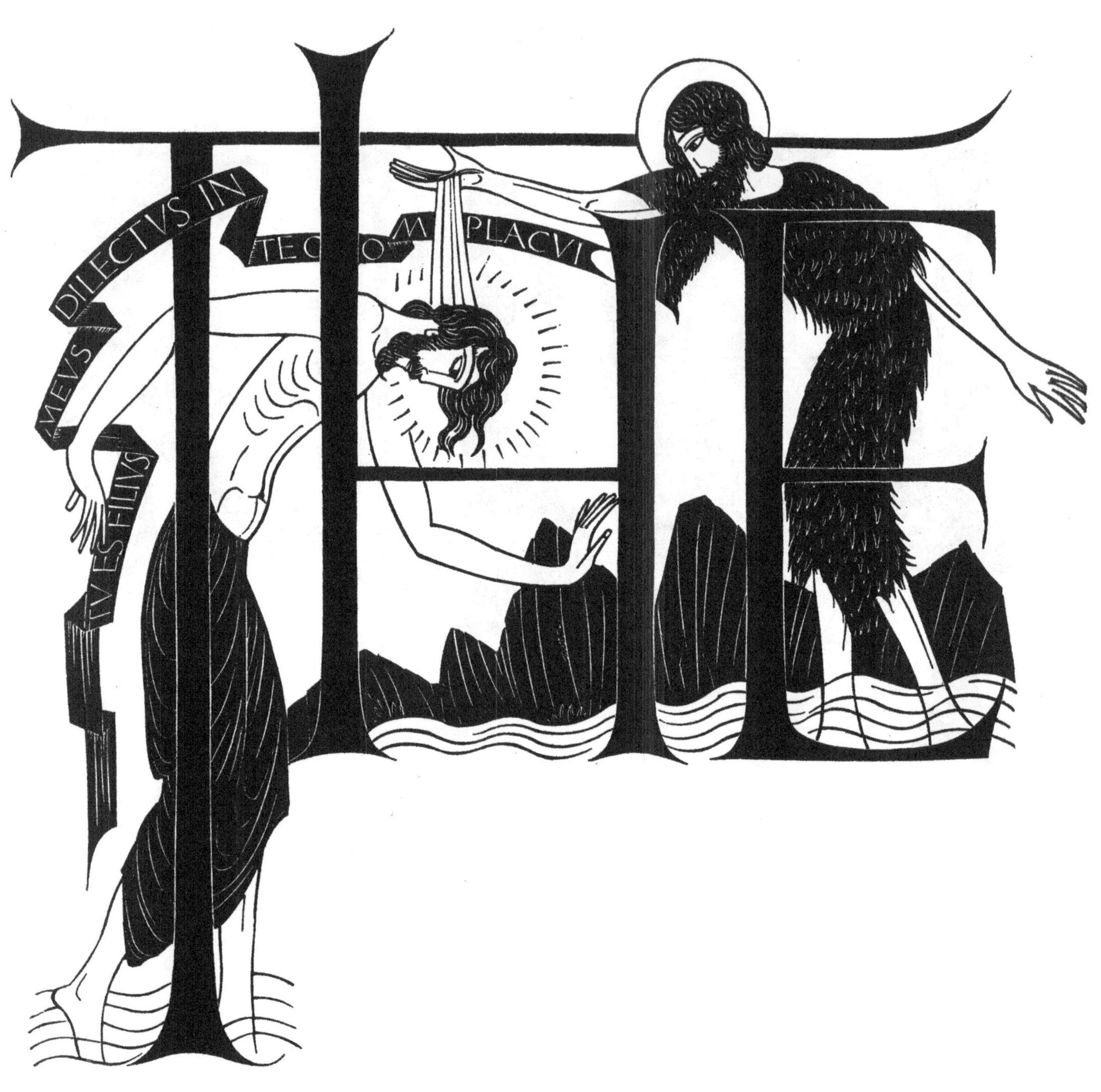

100 The Baptism of Jesus
1931
The Four Gospels

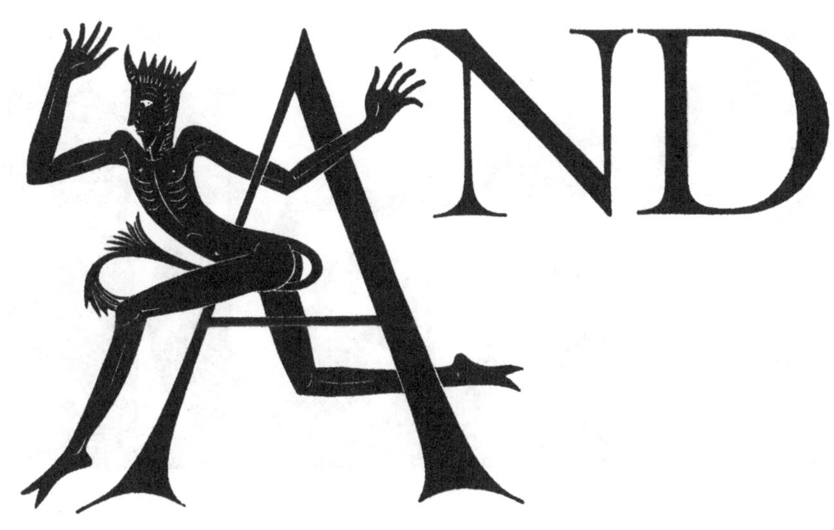

101 The Devil
1931
The Four Gospels

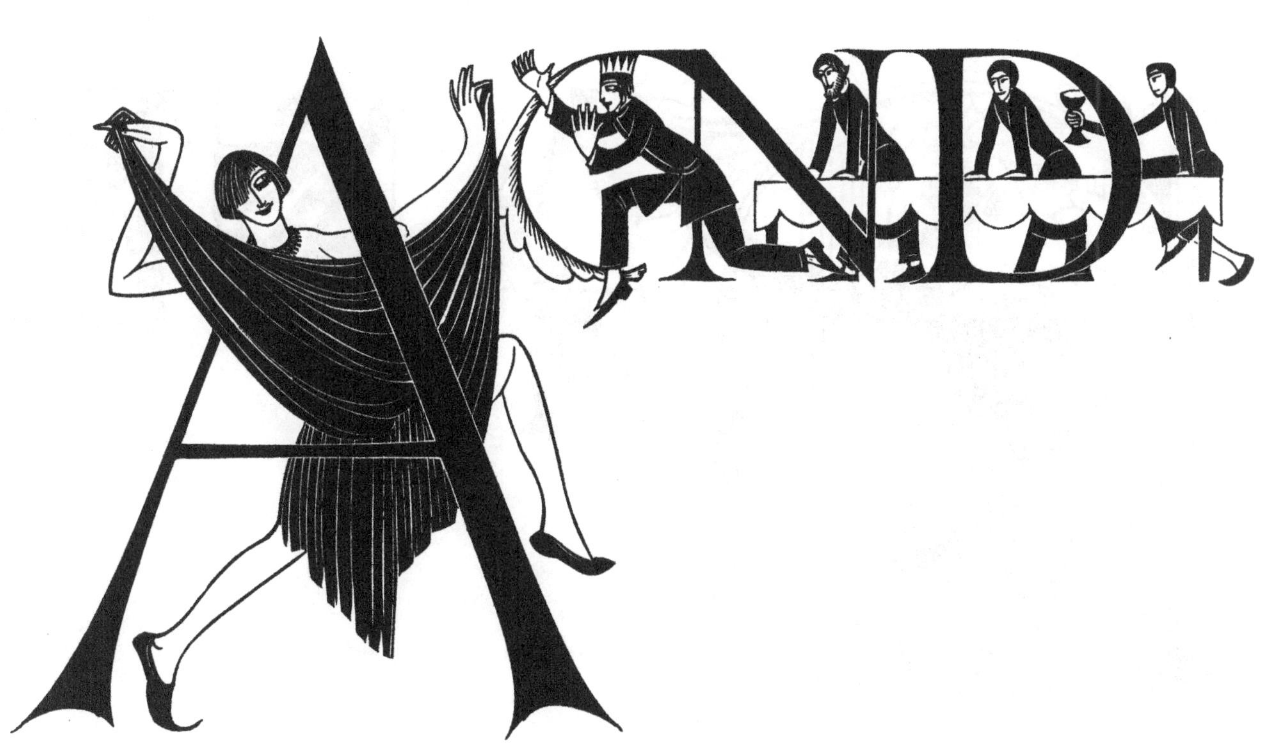

102 Herod's Feast
1931
The Four Gospels

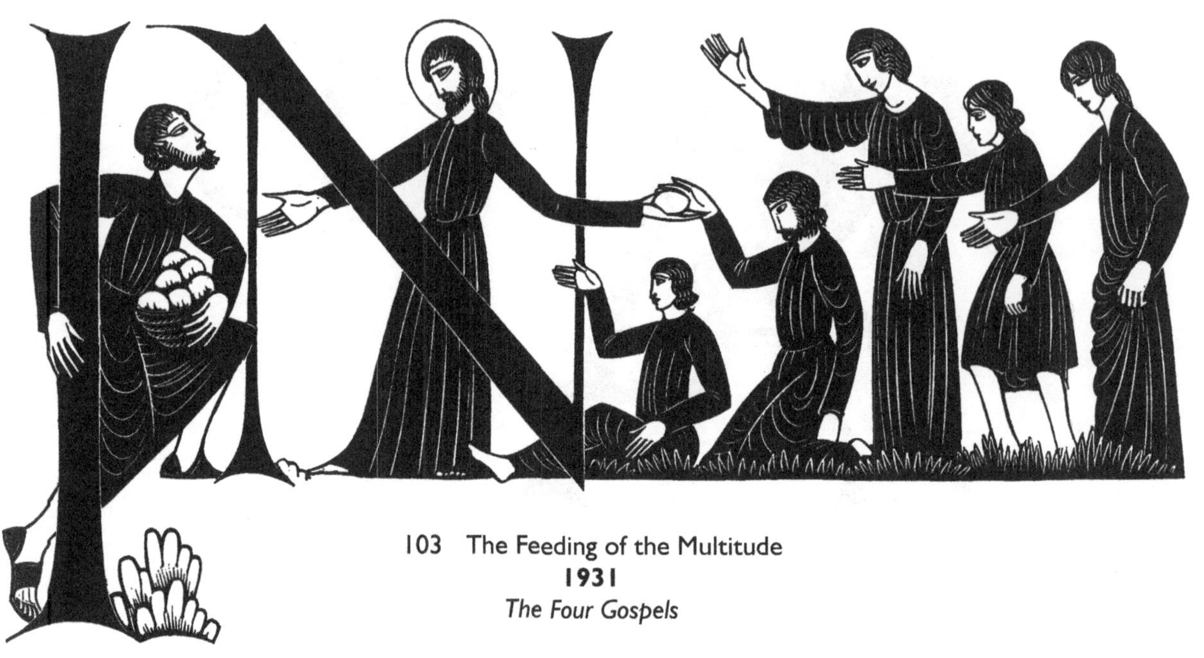

103 The Feeding of the Multitude
1931
The Four Gospels

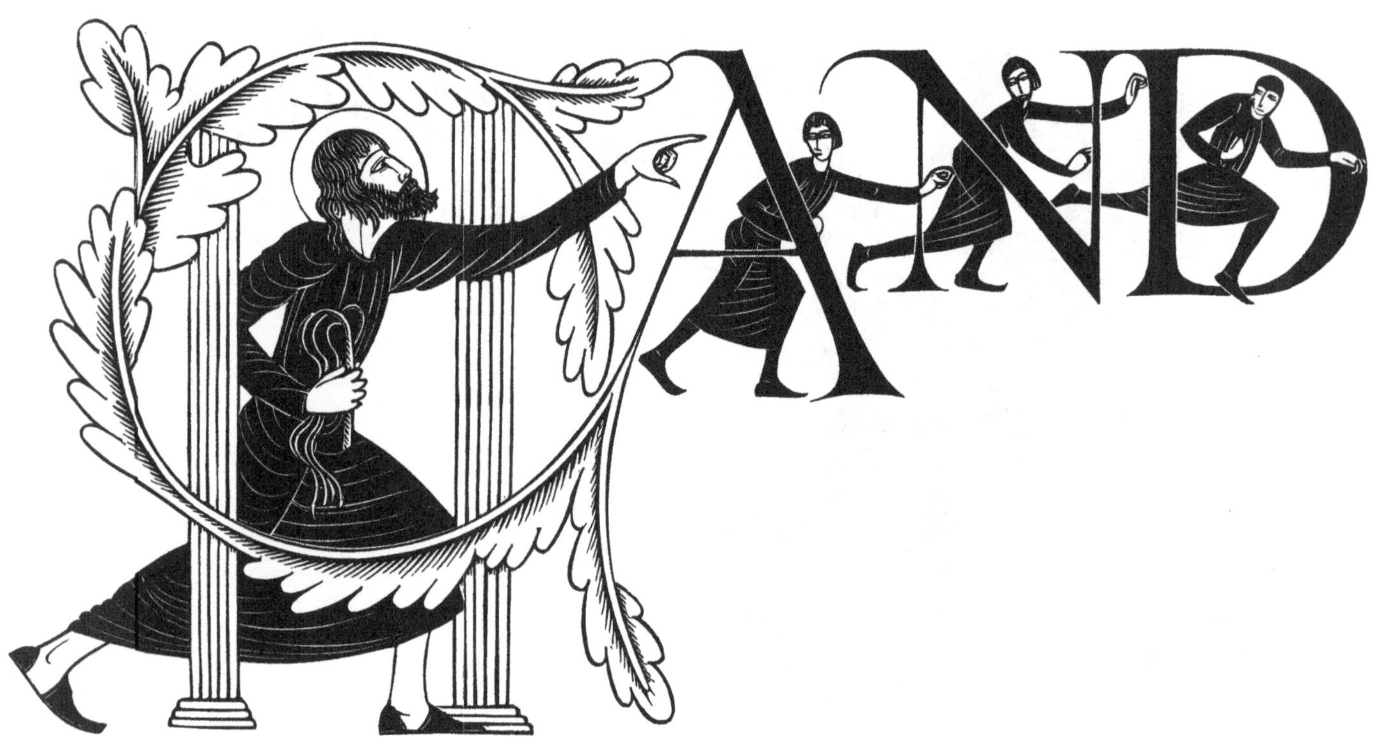

104 The Money Changers
1931
The Four Gospels

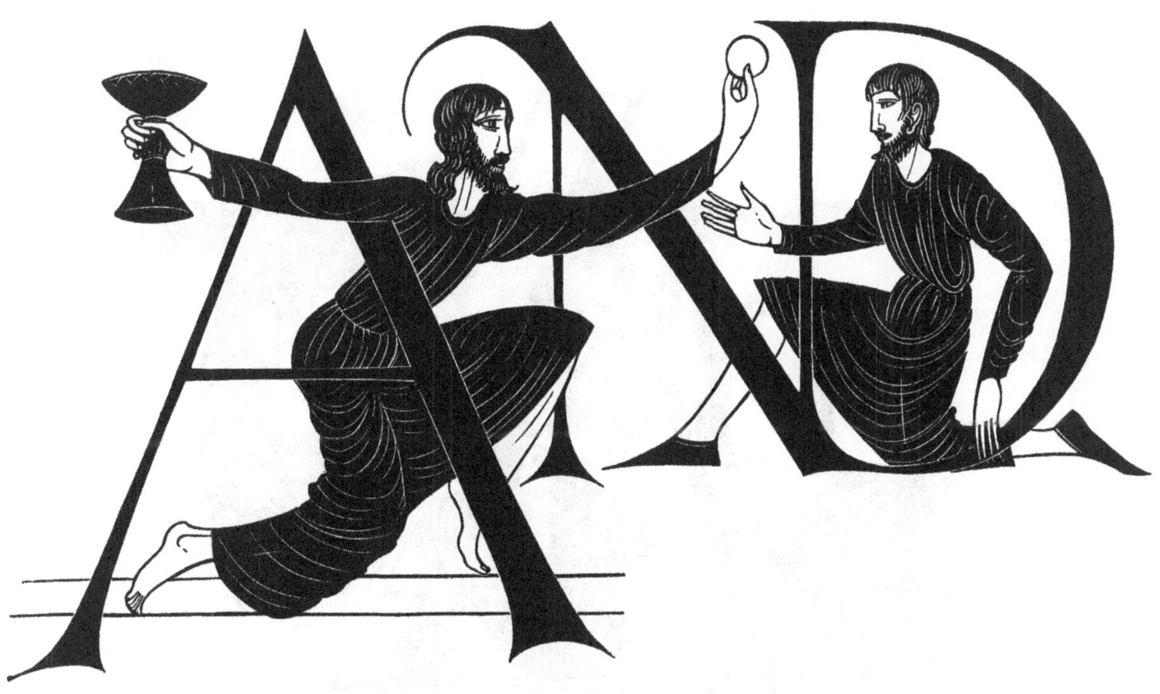

105 The Last Supper
1931
The Four Gospels

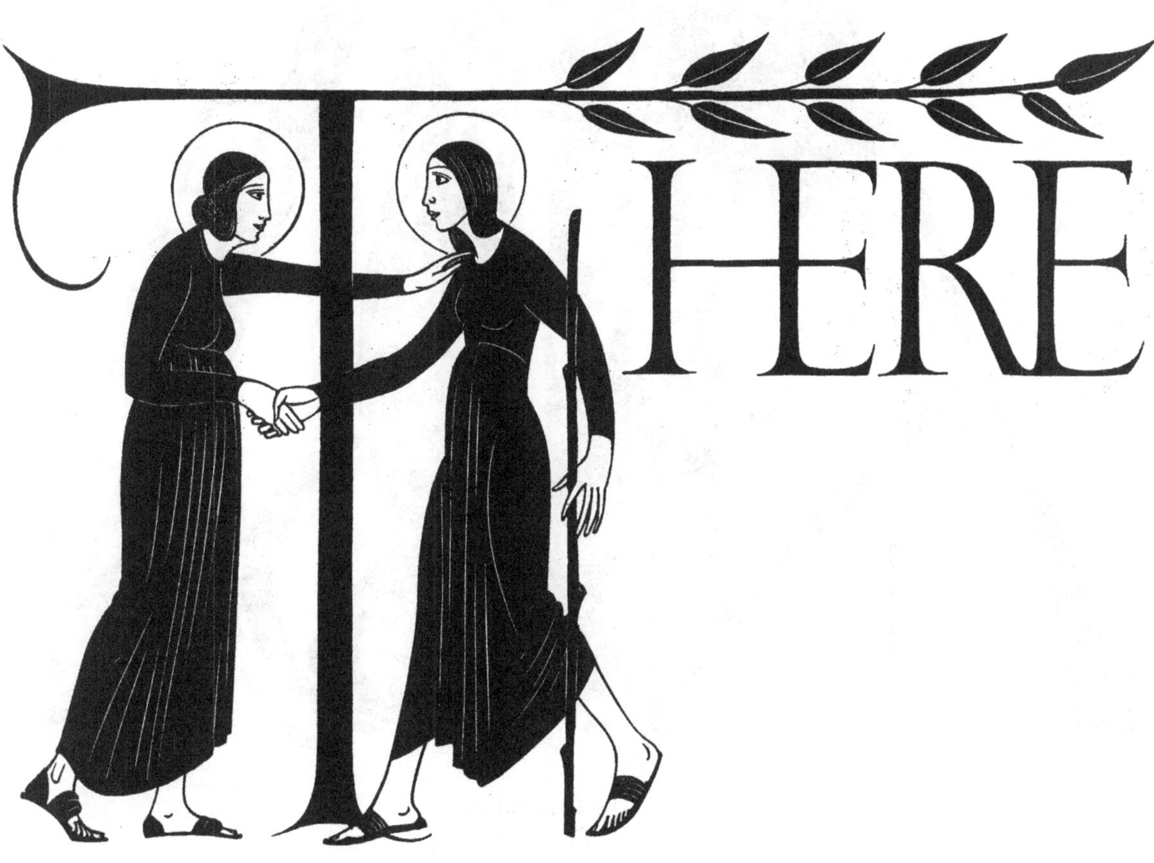

106 The Visitation
1931
The Four Gospels

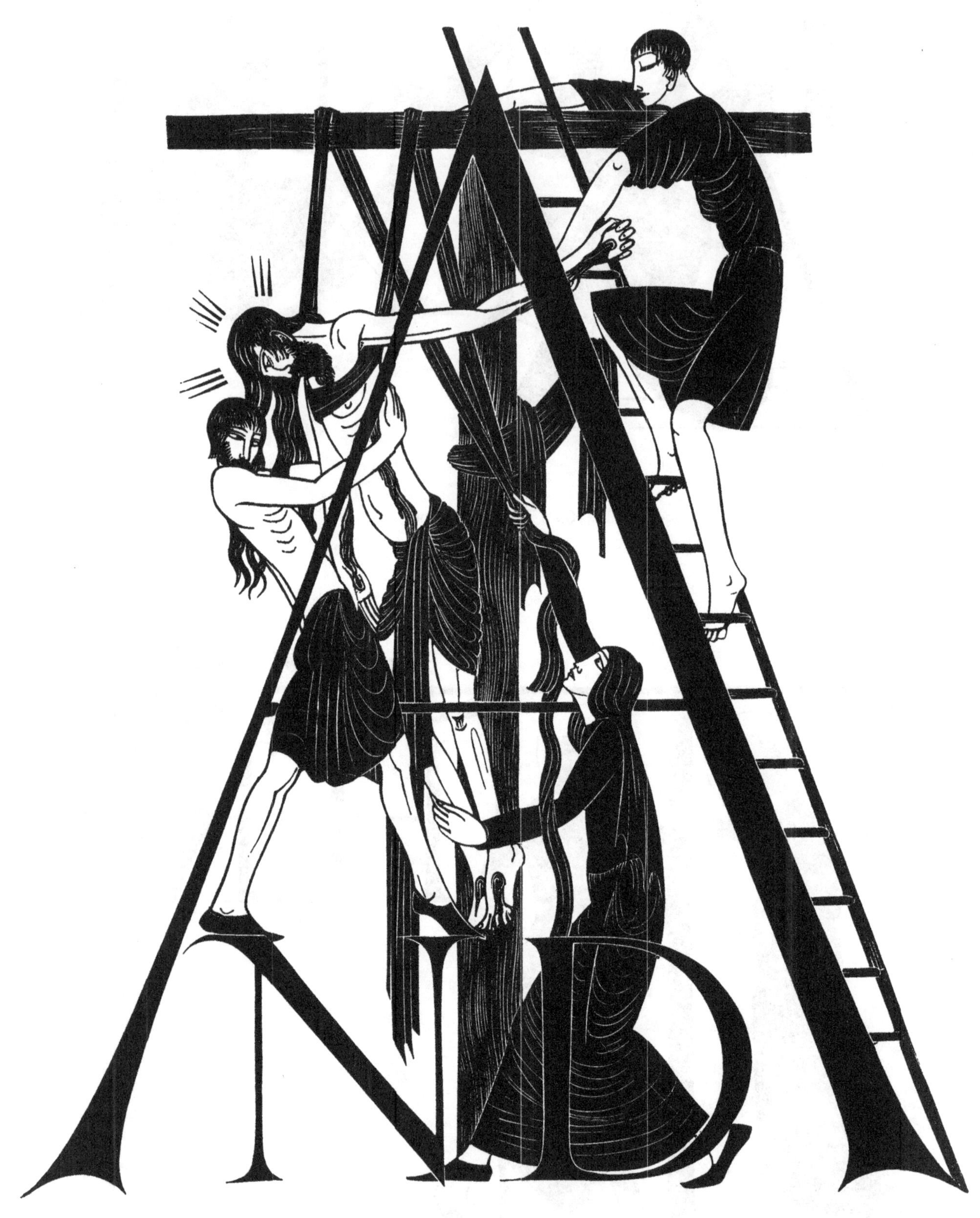

107 The Deposition
1931
The Four Gospels

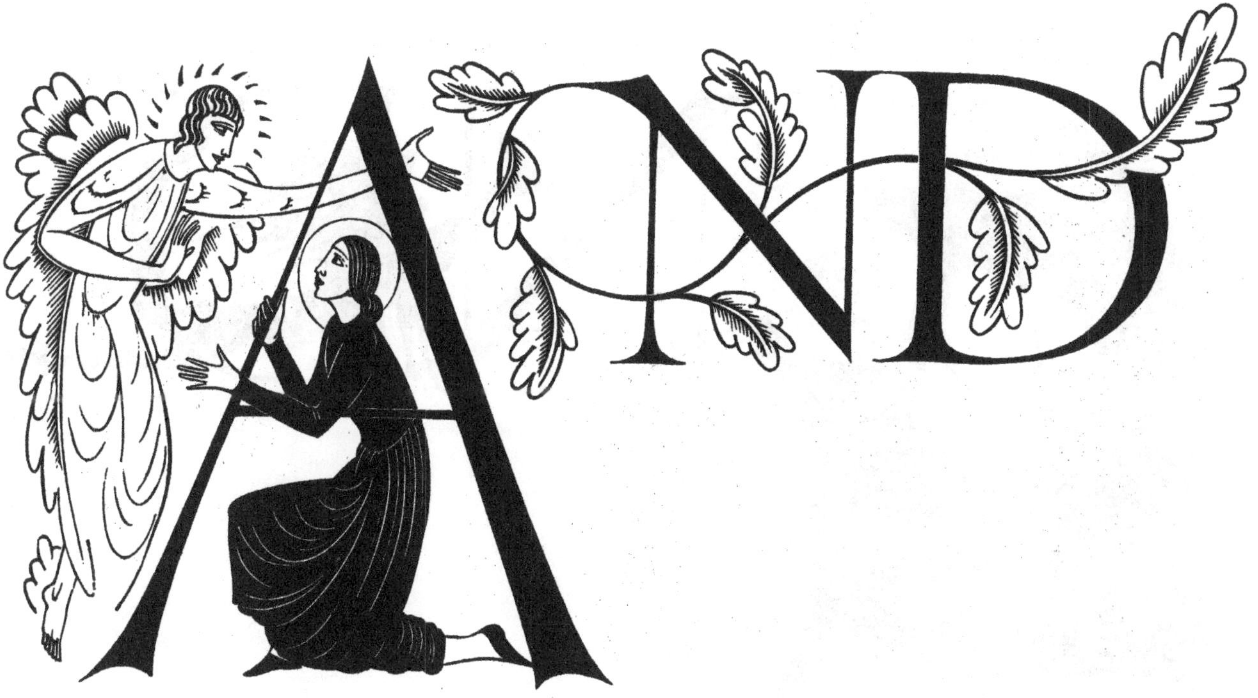

108 The Annunciation
1931
The Four Gospels

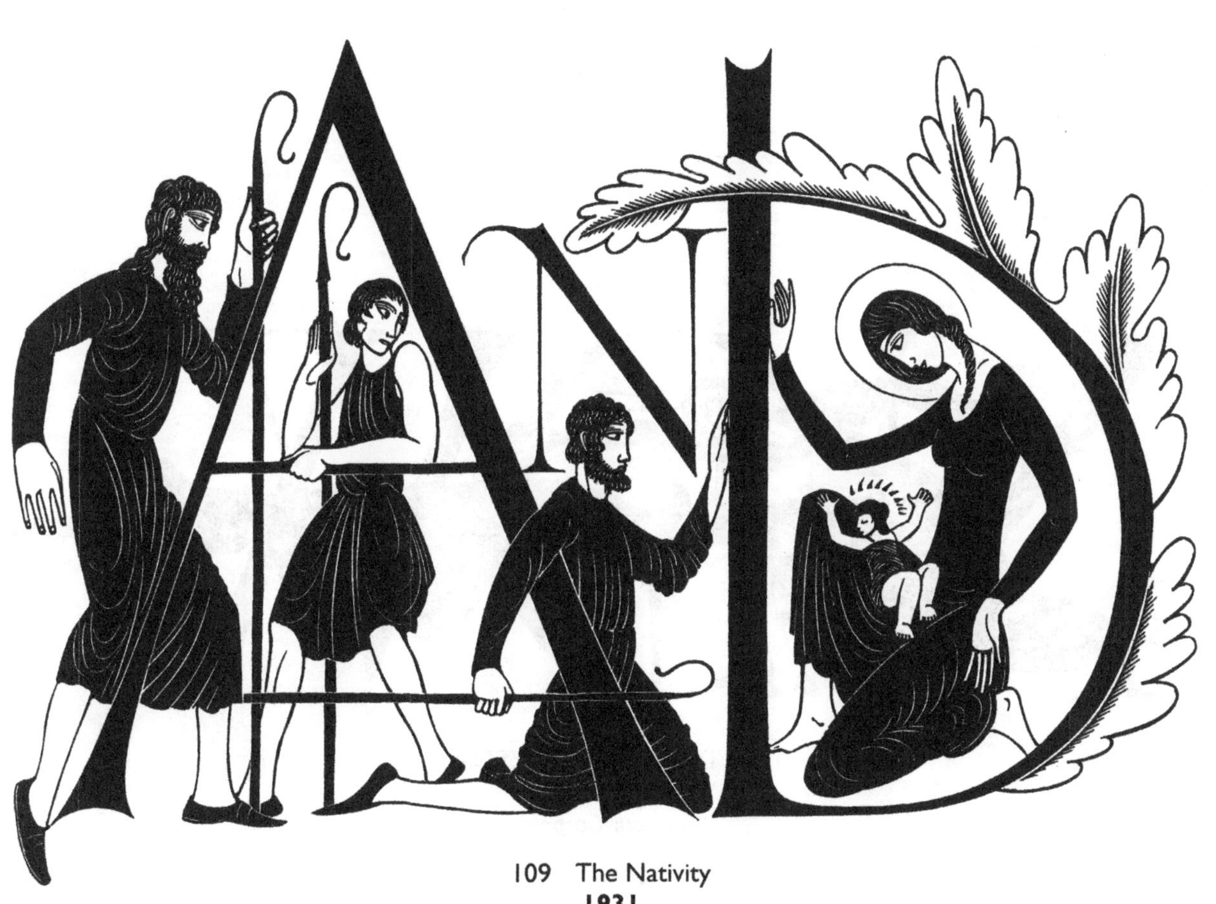

109 The Nativity
1931
The Four Gospels

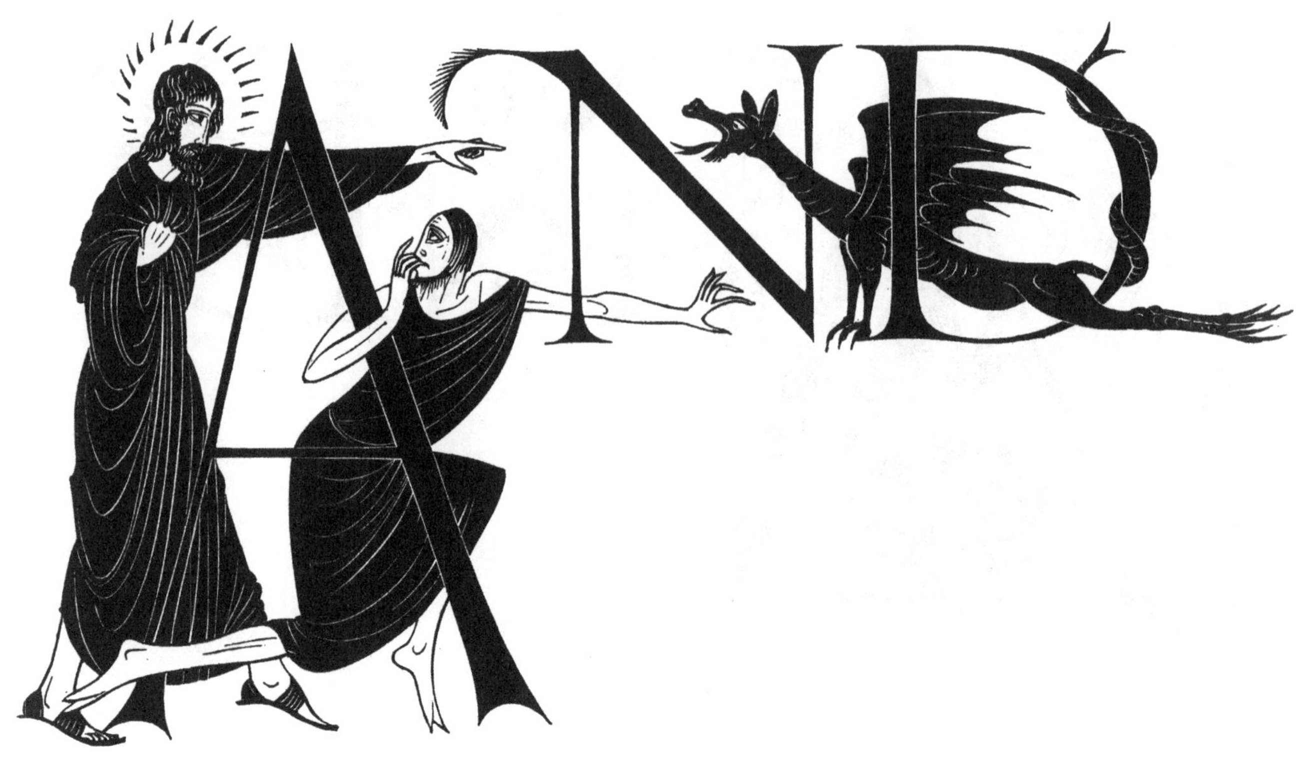

110 The Temptation
1931
The Four Gospels

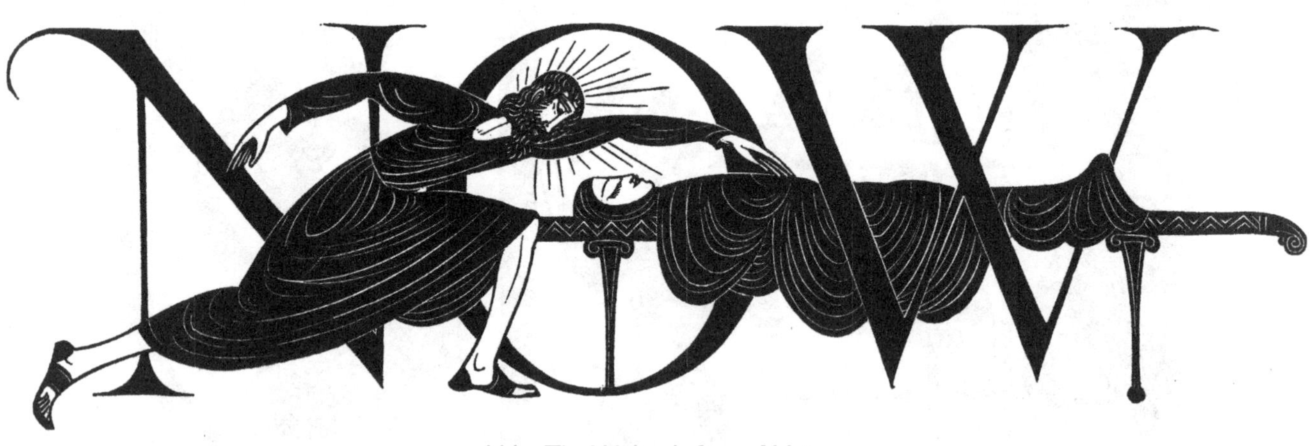

111 The Widow's Son of Nain
1931
The Four Gospels

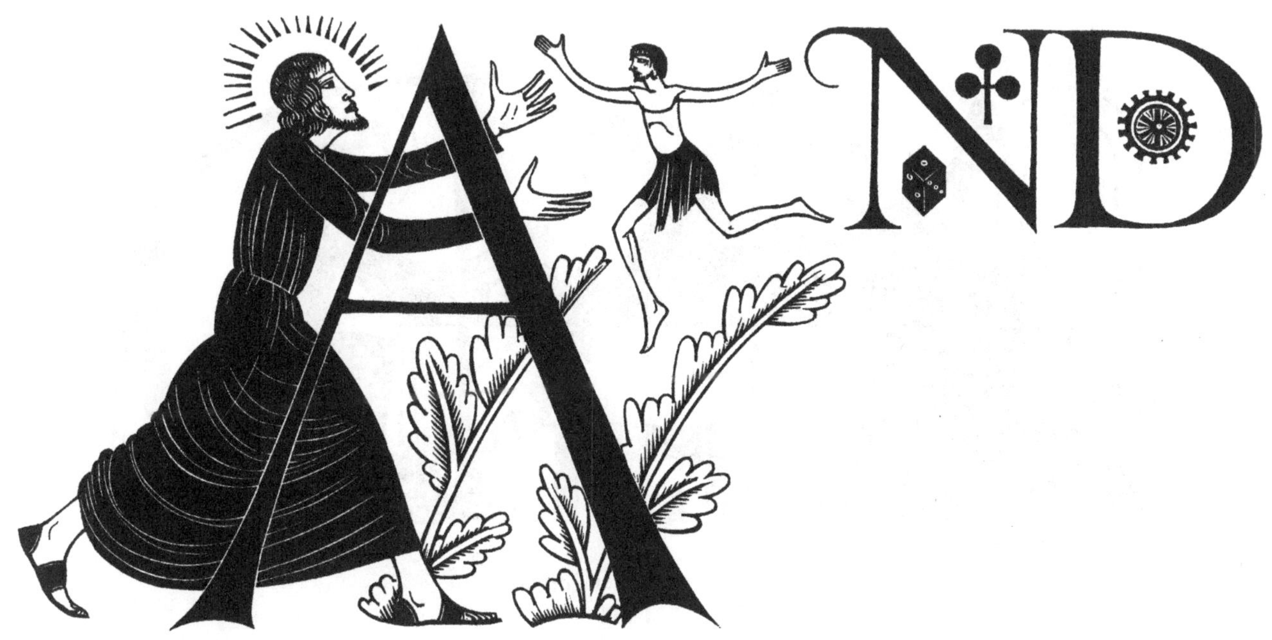

112 The Prodigal Son
1931
The Four Gospels

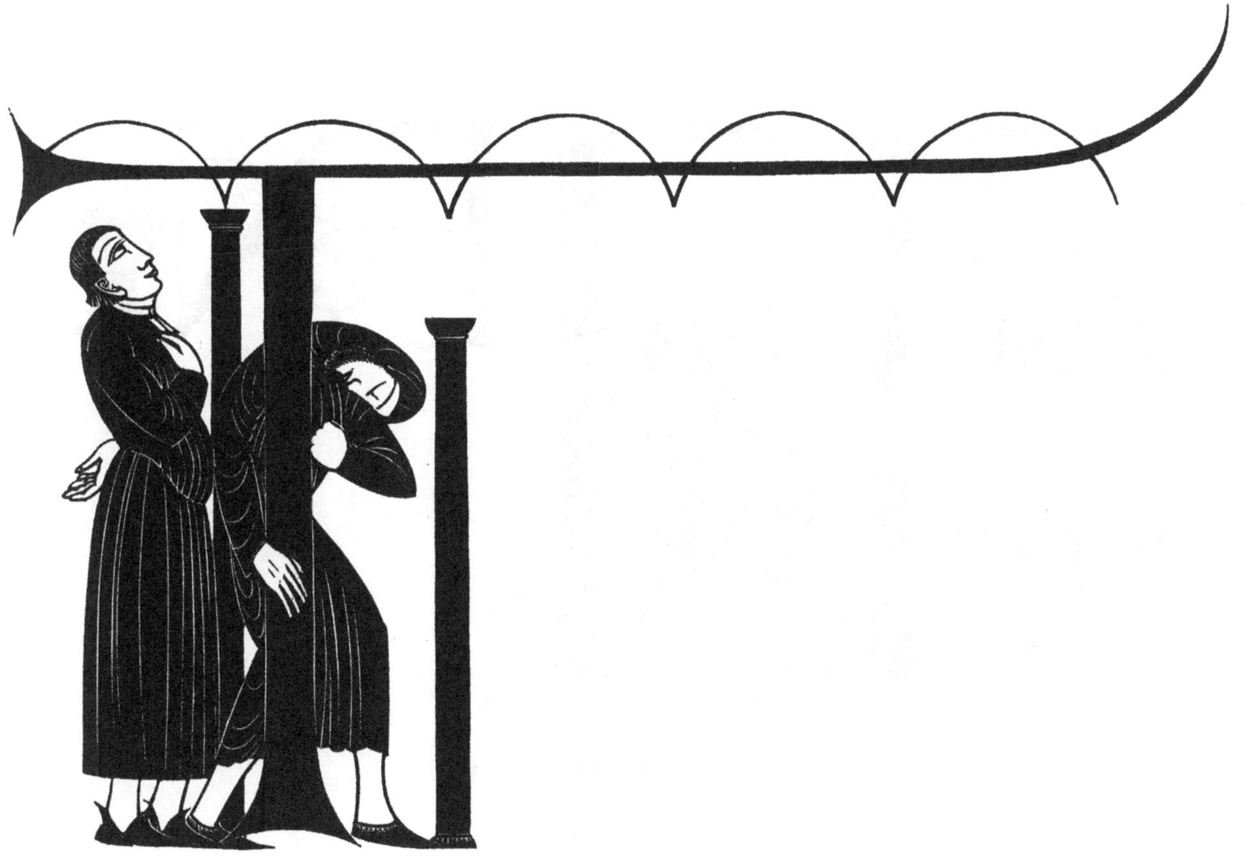

113 The Pharisee and the Publican
1931
The Four Gospels

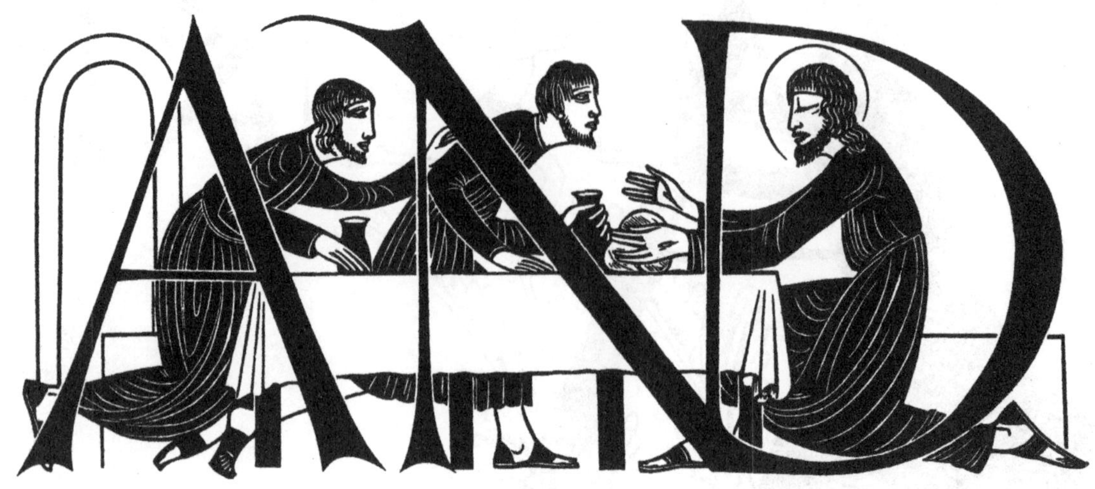

114 Christ at Emmaus
1931
The Four Gospels

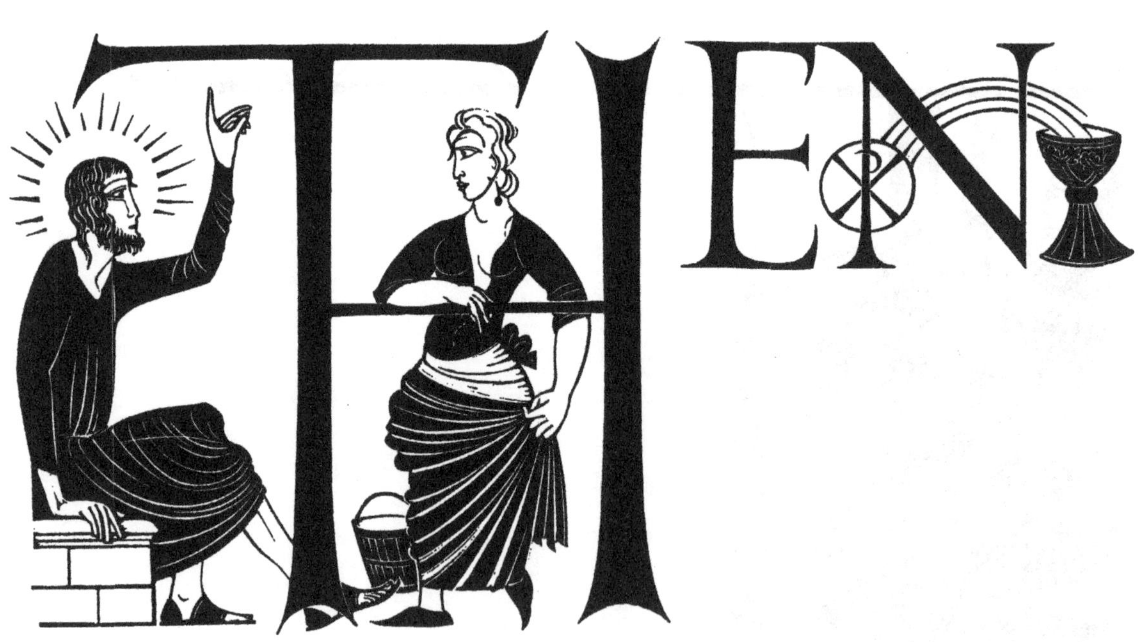

115 The Woman of Samaria
1931
The Four Gospels

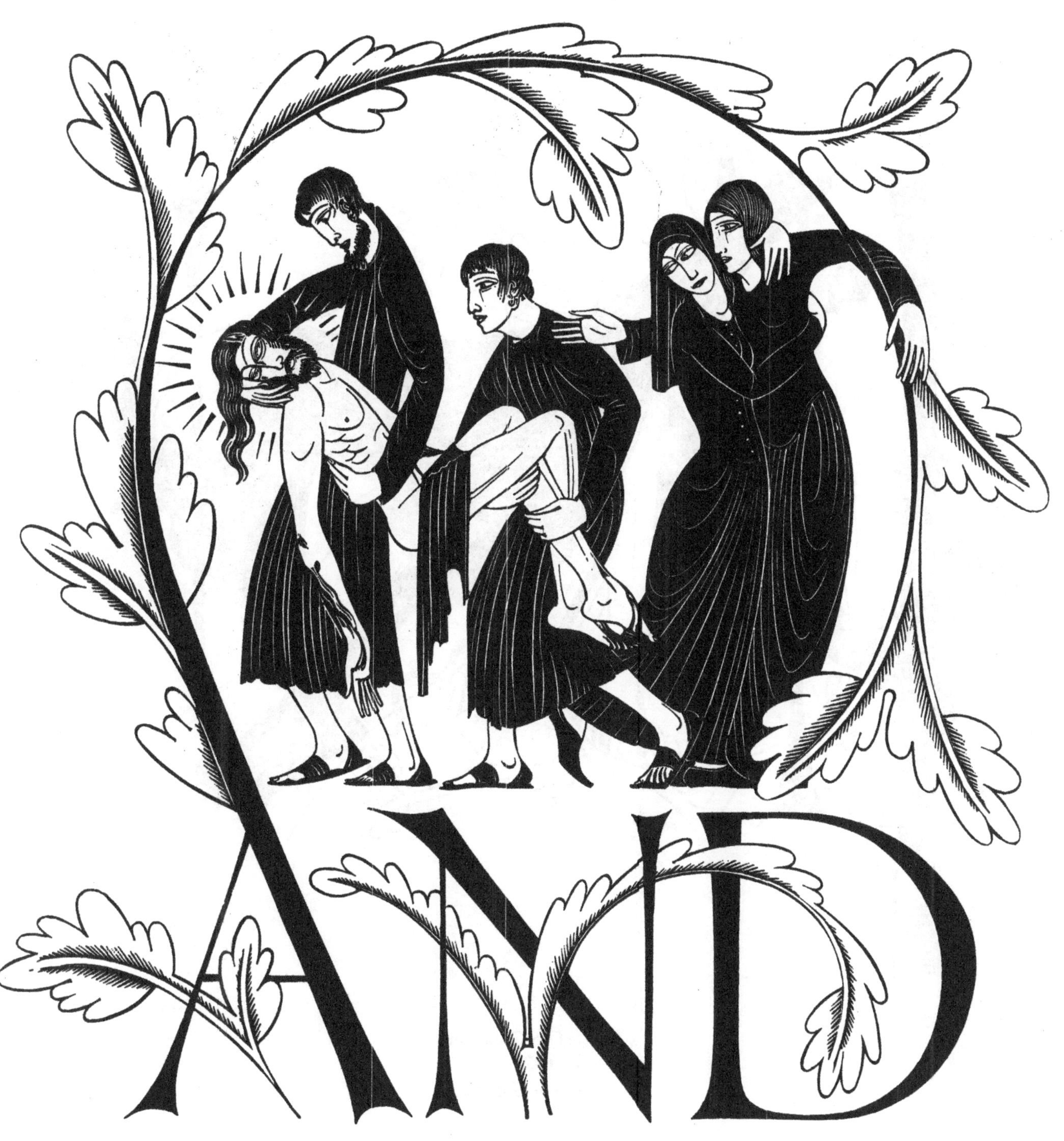

116 The Burial of Christ
1931
The Four Gospels

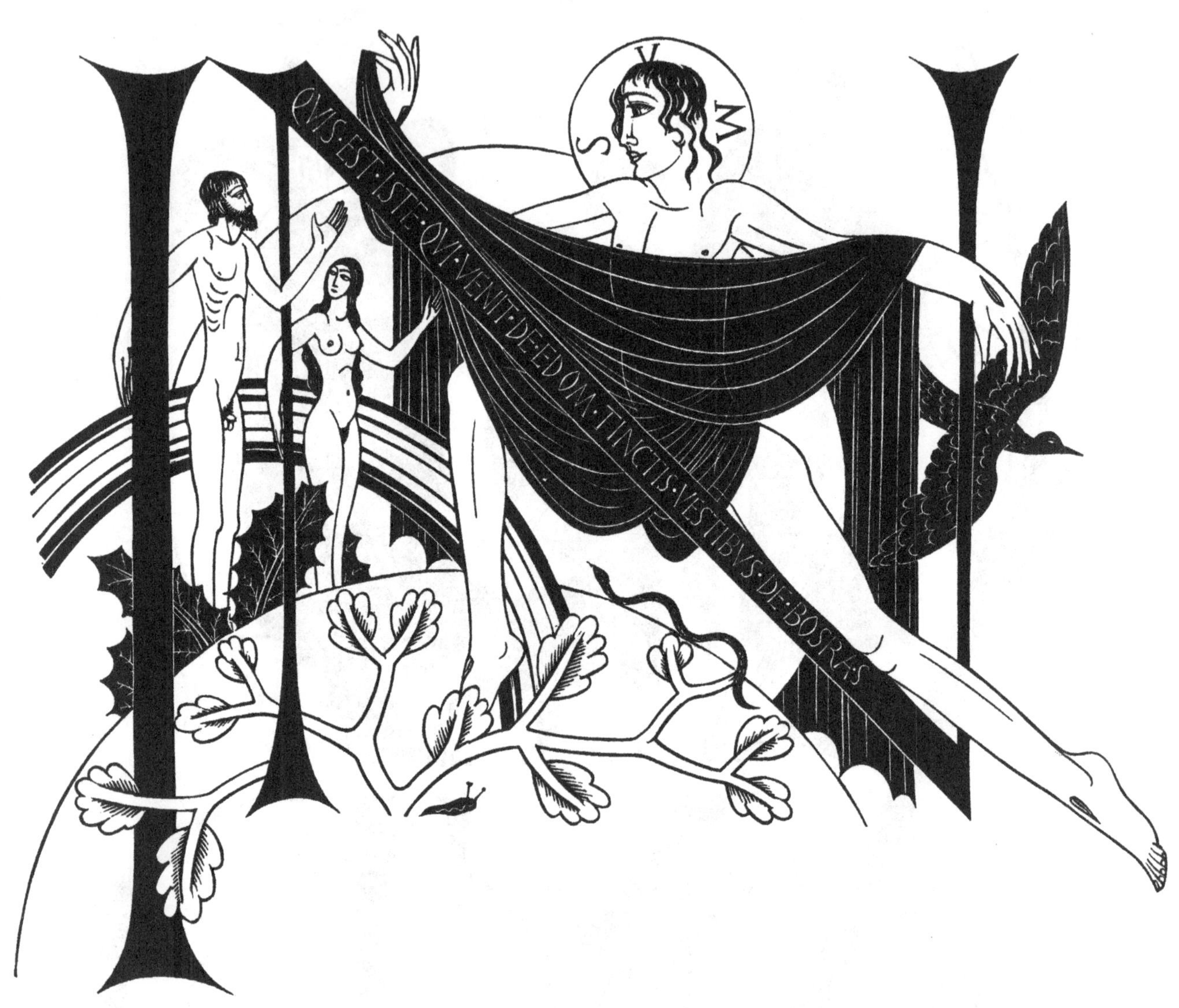

117 The Creation
1931
The Four Gospels

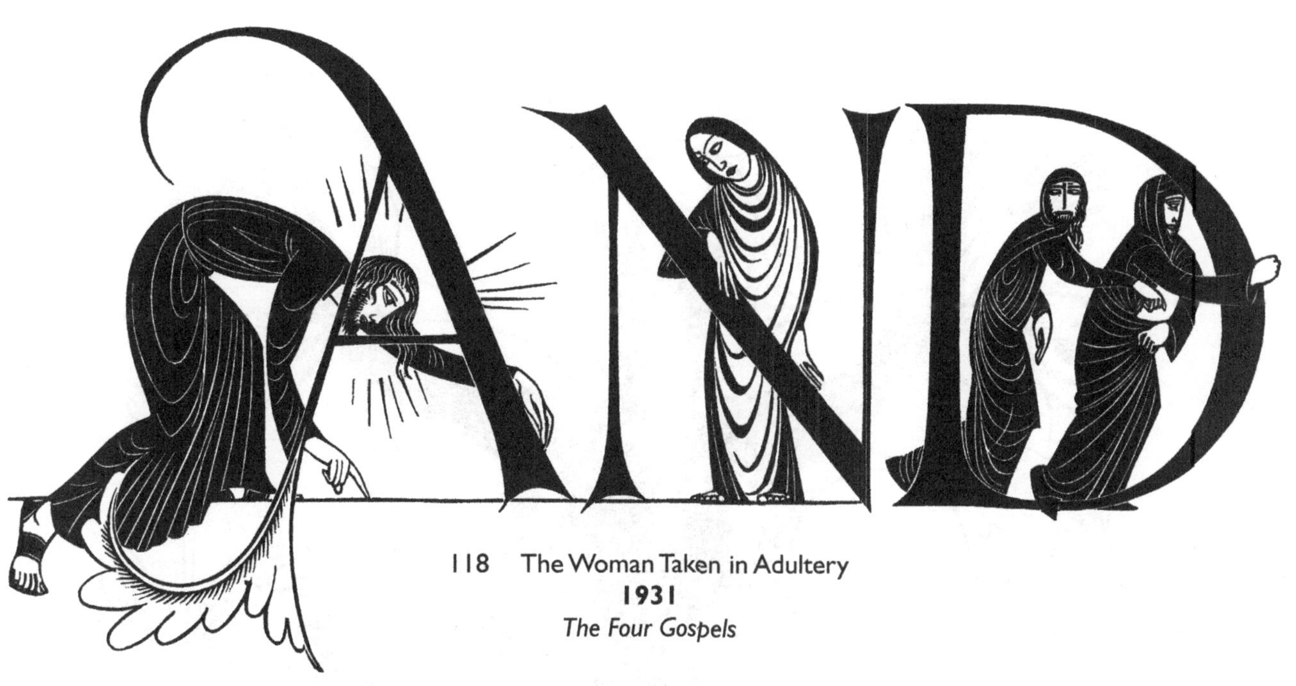

118 The Woman Taken in Adultery
1931
The Four Gospels

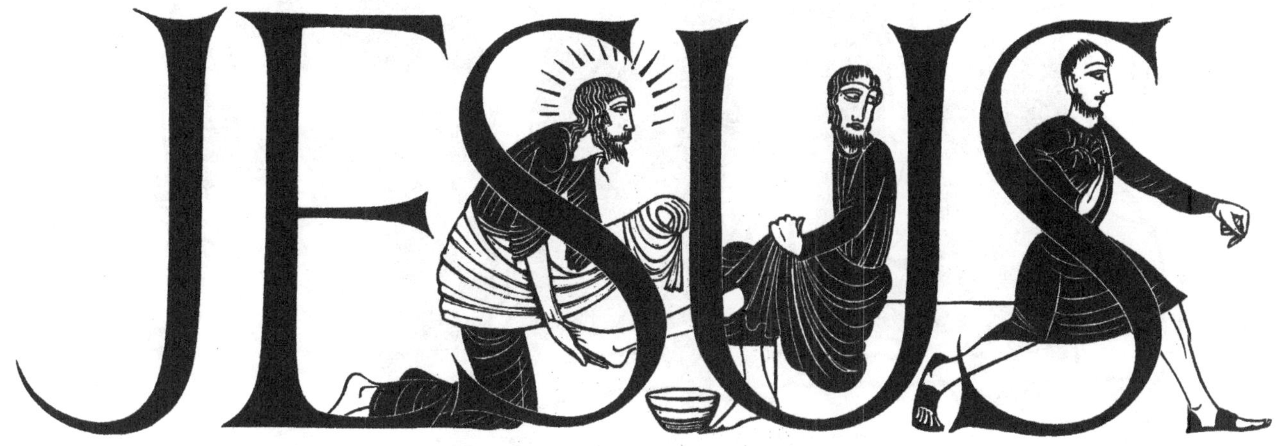

119 Christ Washing Peter's Feet
1931
The Four Gospels

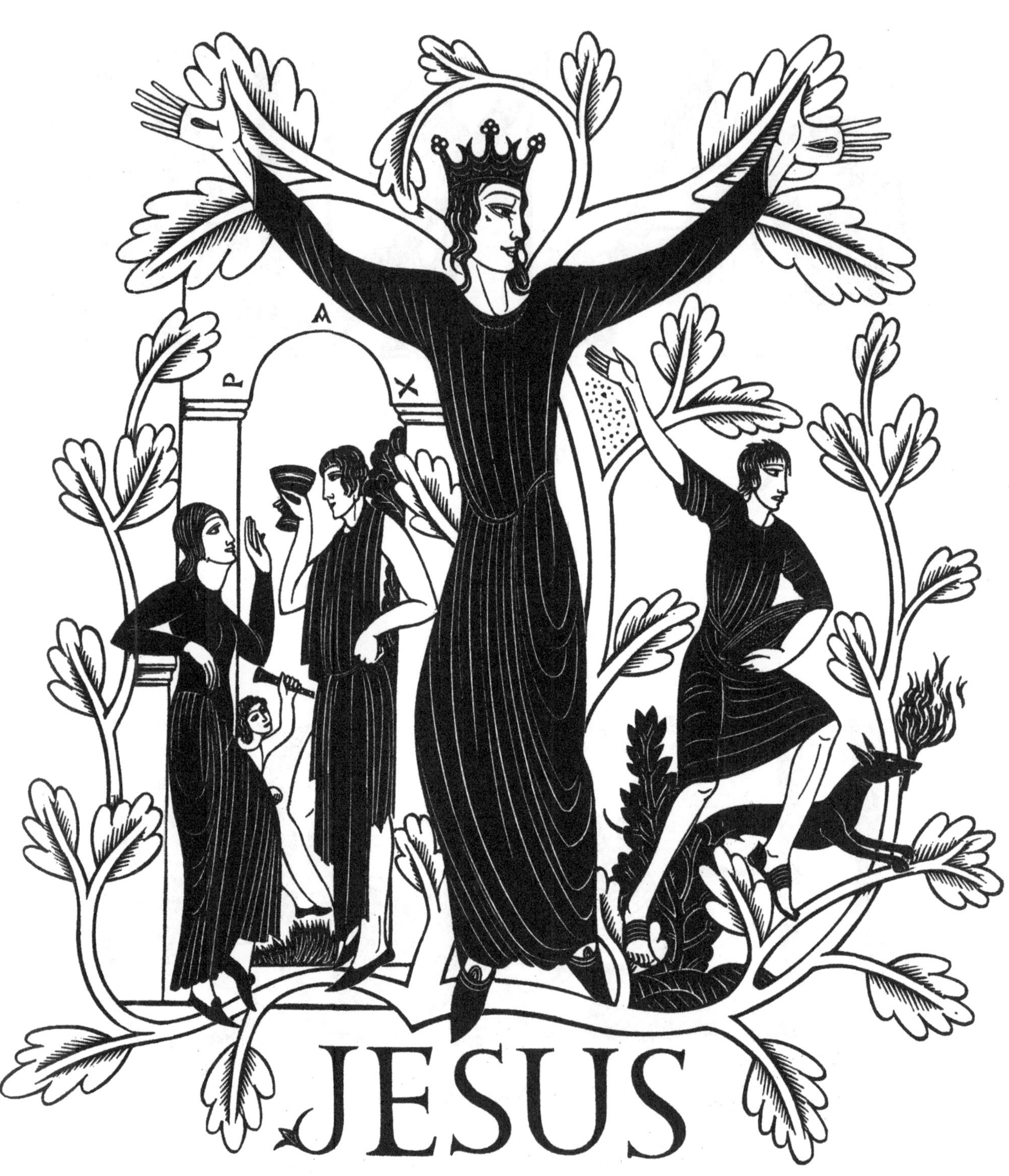

120 Christ Crowned
1931
The Four Gospels

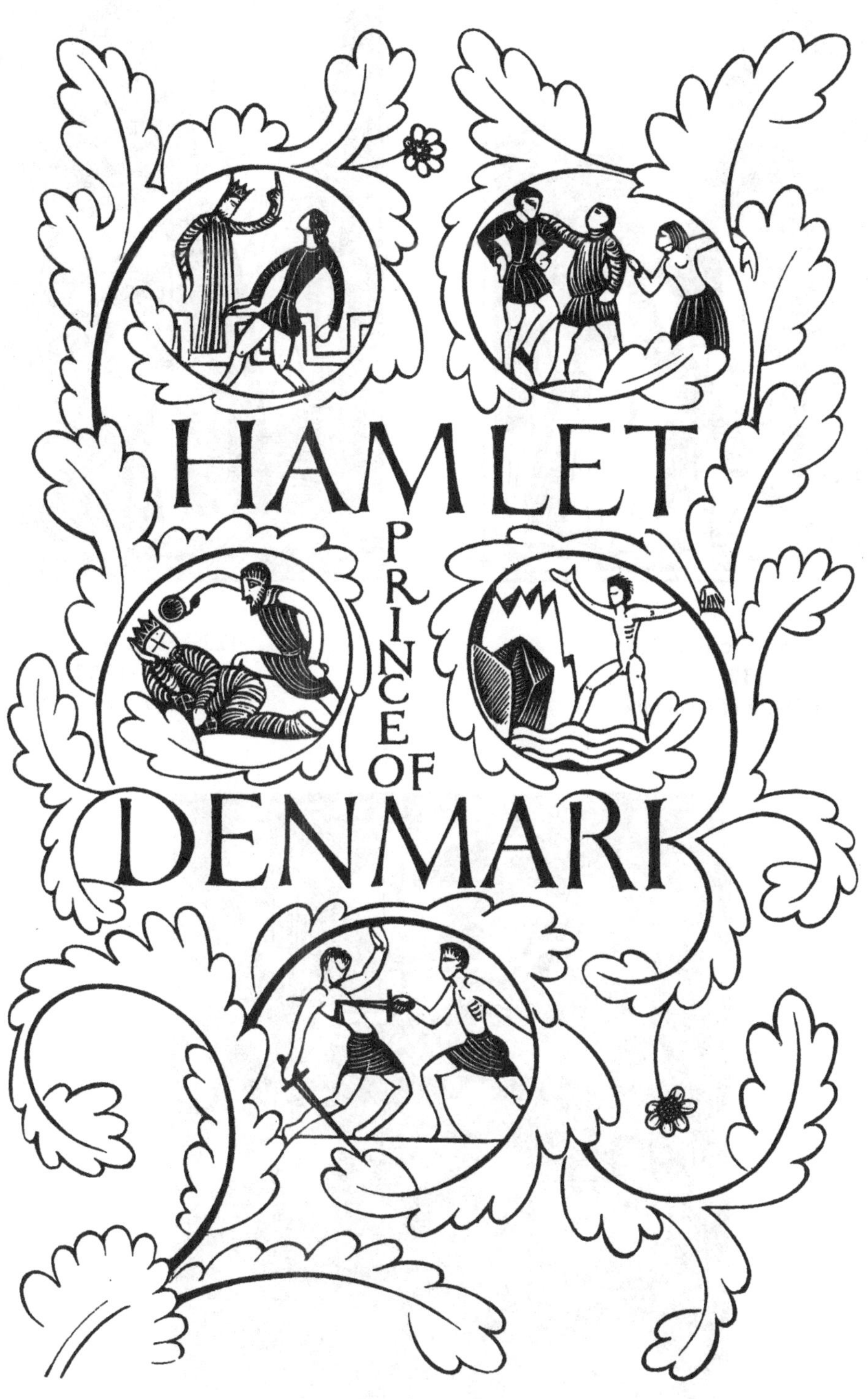

121 Hamlet
1932
Hamlet, Prince of Denmark

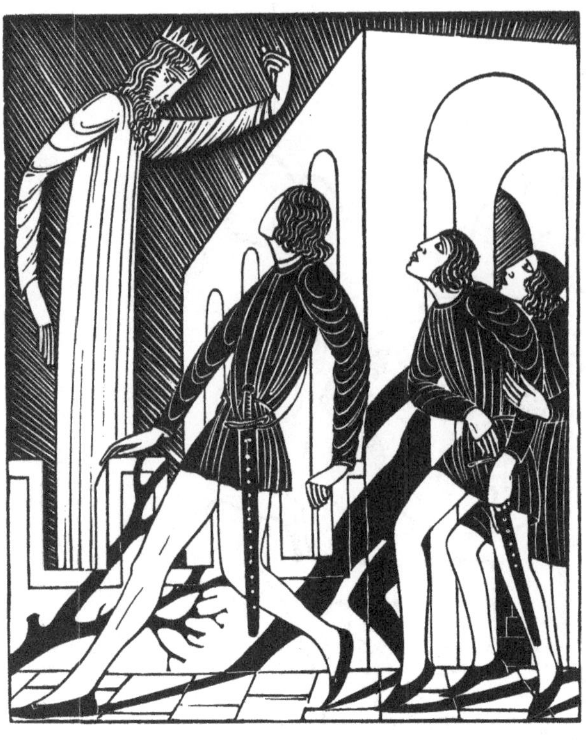

122 Hamlet and the Ghost
1932
Hamlet, Prince of Denmark

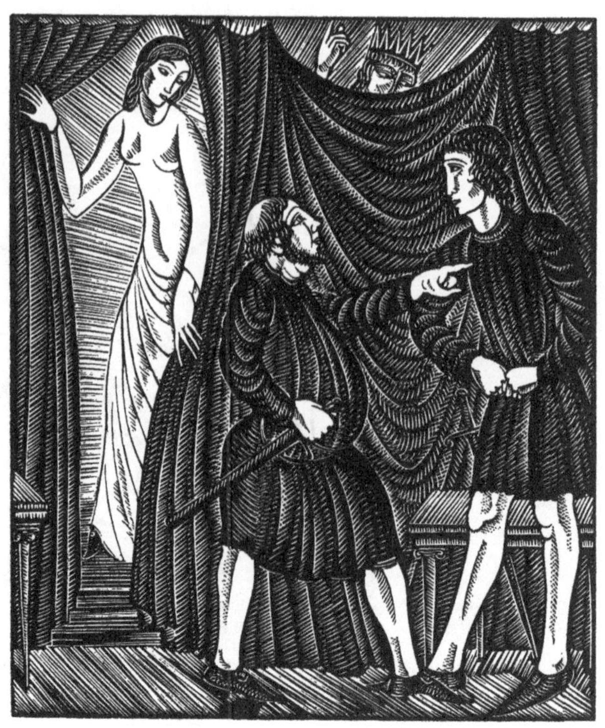

123 Hamlet and Polonius
1932
Hamlet, Prince of Denmark

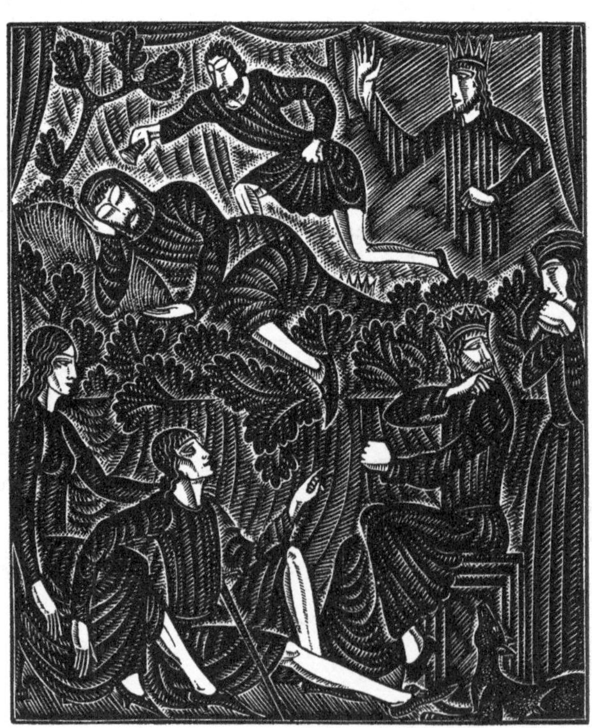

124 The Play Scene
1932
Hamlet, Prince of Denmark

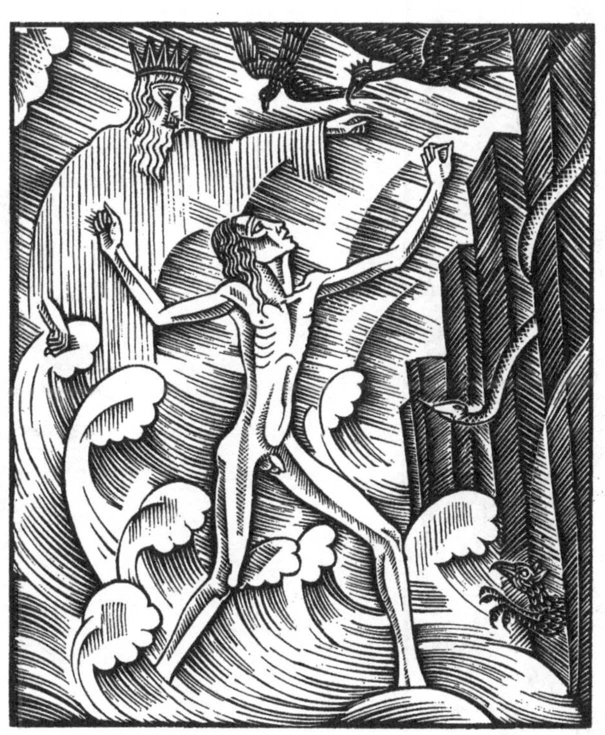

125 'I Am Set Naked on Your Kingdom'
1932
Hamlet, Prince of Denmark

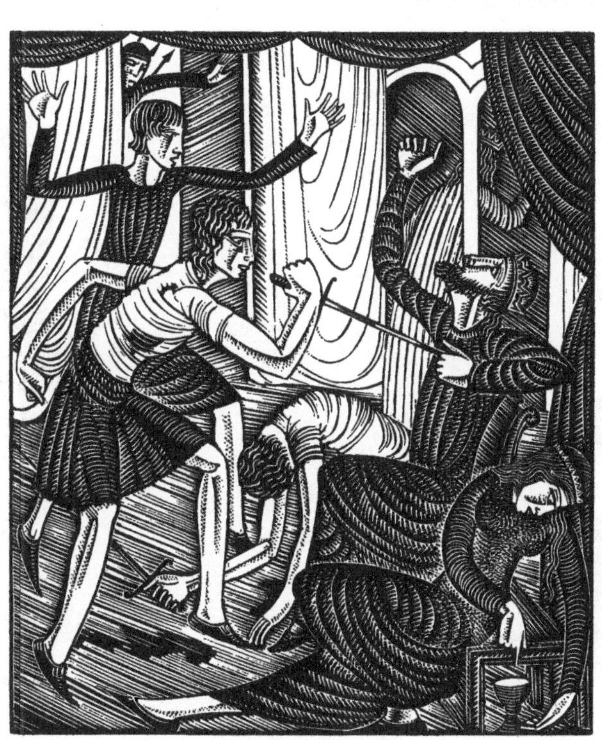

126 The Death of the King
1932
Hamlet, Prince of Denmark

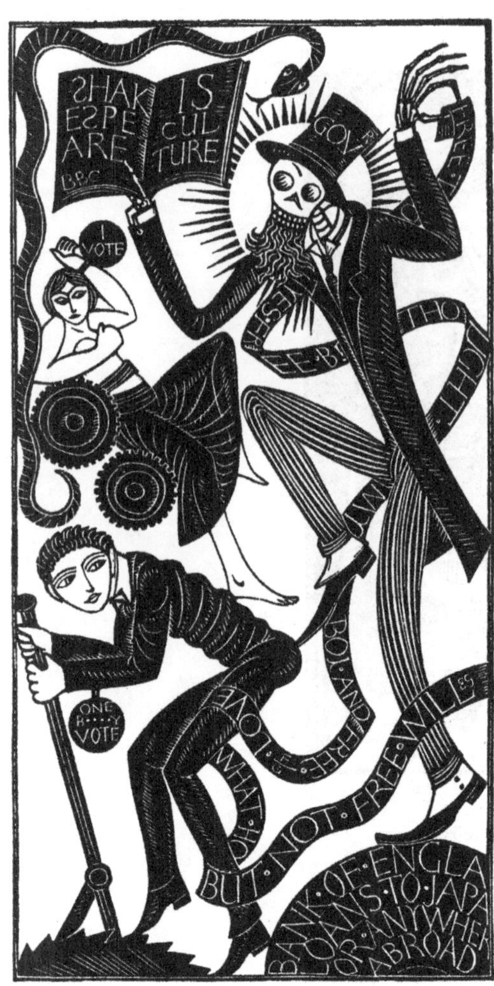

127 The Lord's Song
1934
The Lord's Song

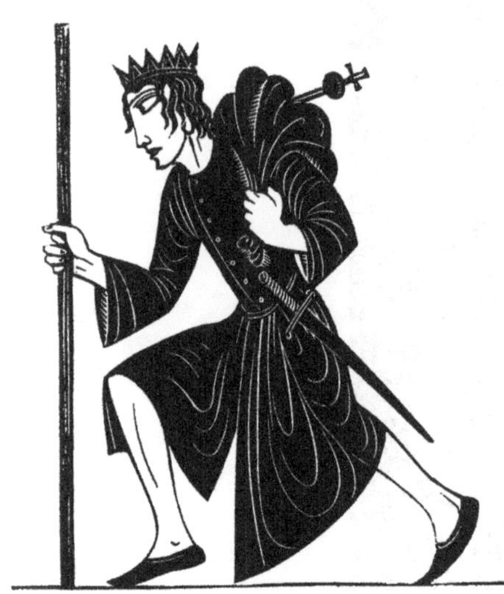

130 History: Man Just Going on Walking
1934
The New Temple Shakespeare

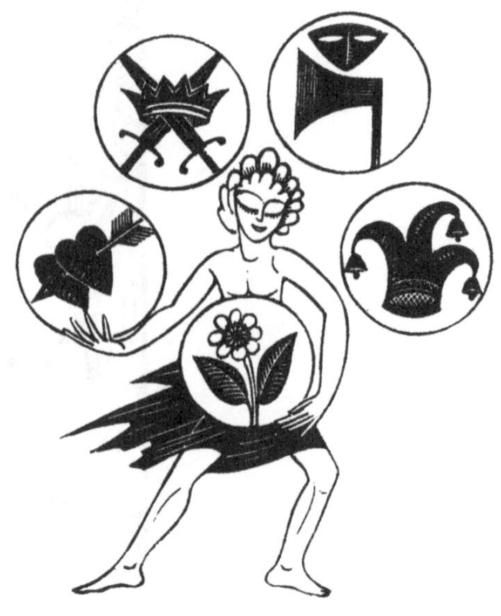

128 Puck Juggling
1934
The New Temple Shakespeare

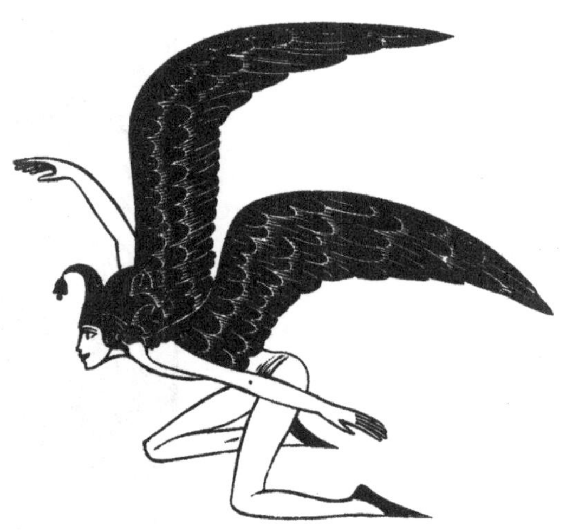

129 Comedy: Man Trying to Fly
1934
The New Temple Shakespeare

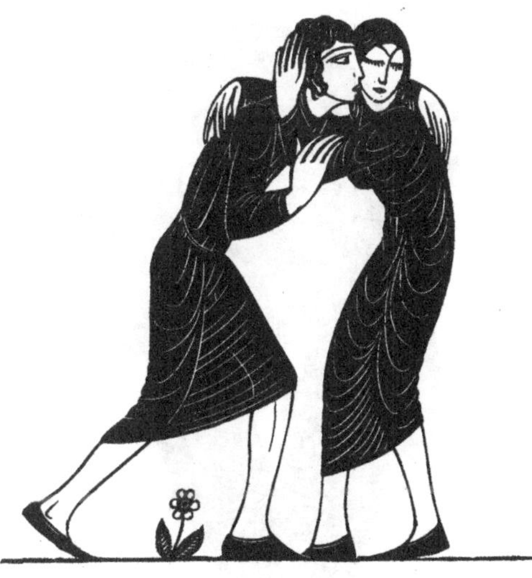

131 Romance: Man Seizing Unreality
1934
The New Temple Shakespeare

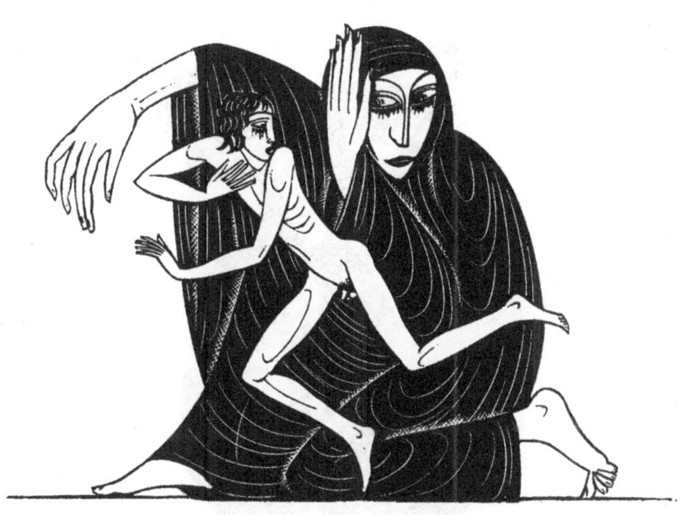

132 Tragedy: Man Trying to Escape
1934
The New Temple Shakespeare

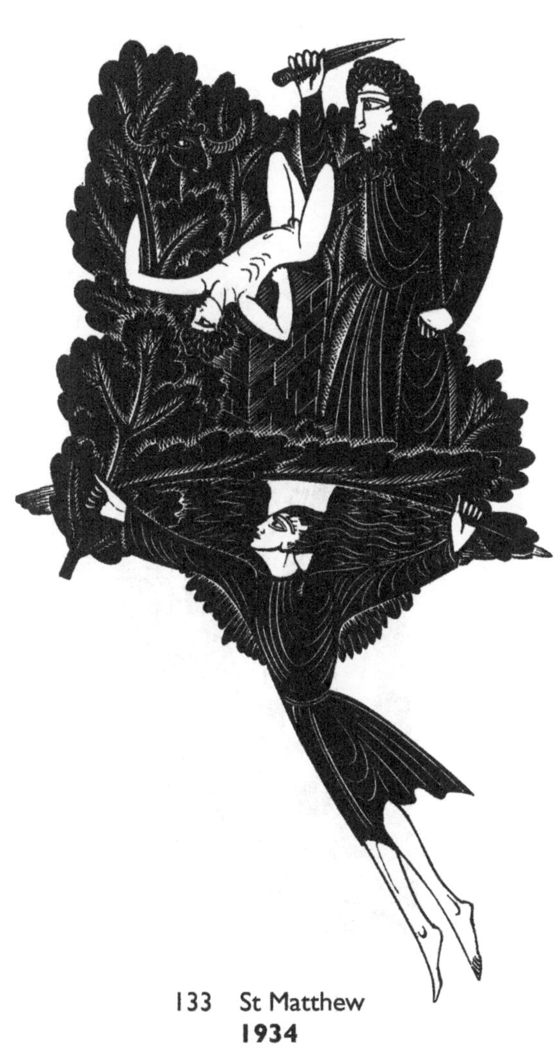

133 St Matthew
1934
The Passion of Our Lord

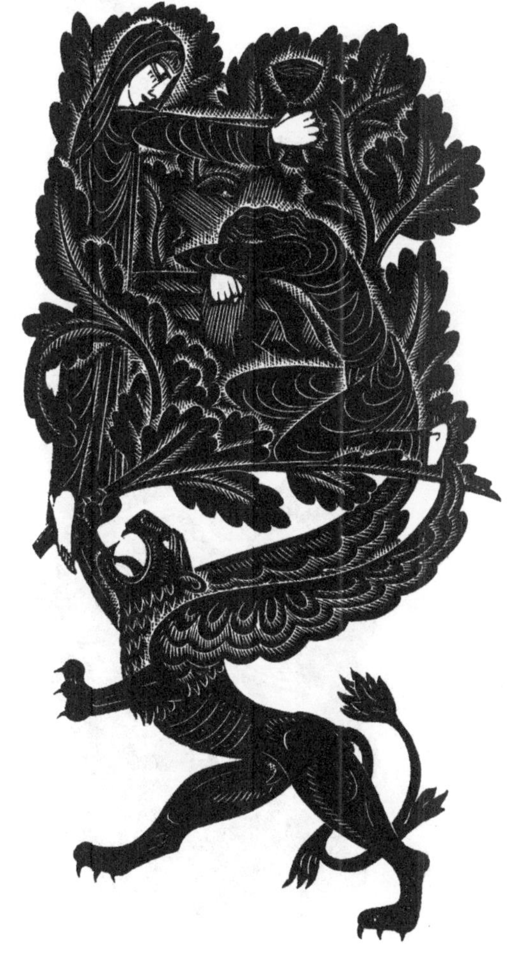

134 St Mark
1934
The Passion of Our Lord

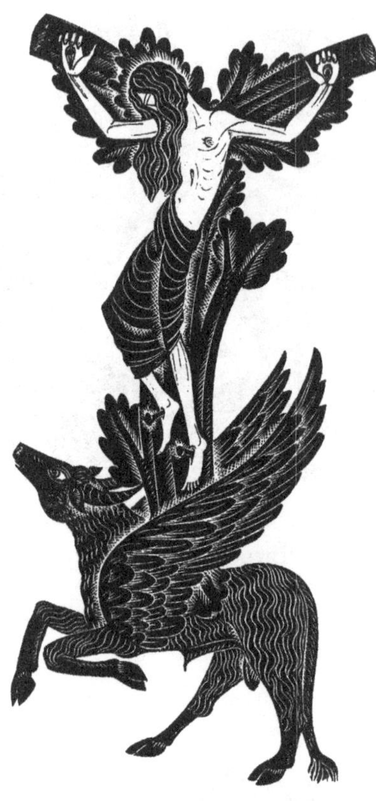

135 St Luke
1934
The Passion of Our Lord

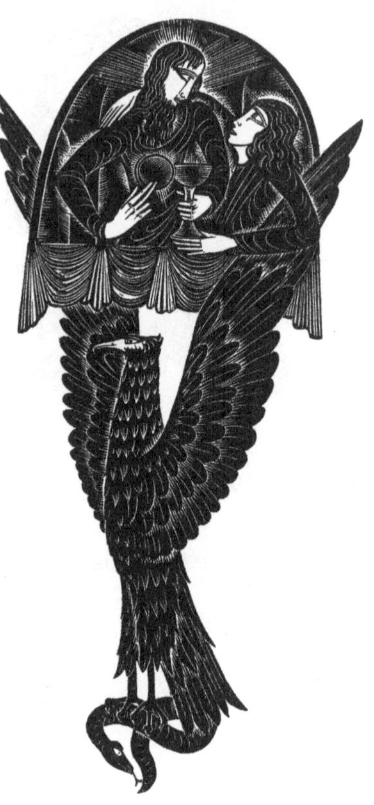

136 St John
1934
The Passion of Our Lord

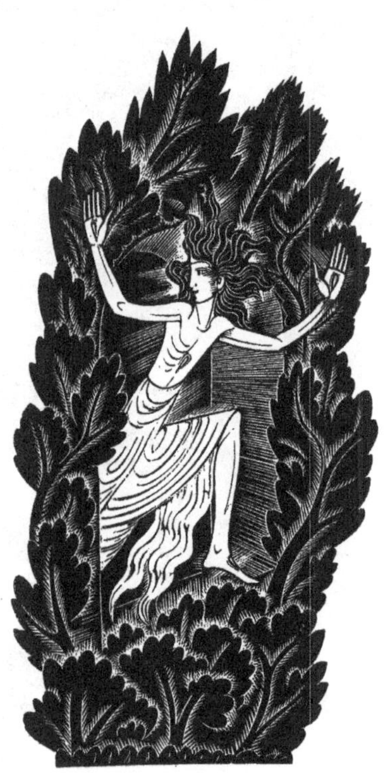

137 Resurrection
1934
The Passion of Our Lord

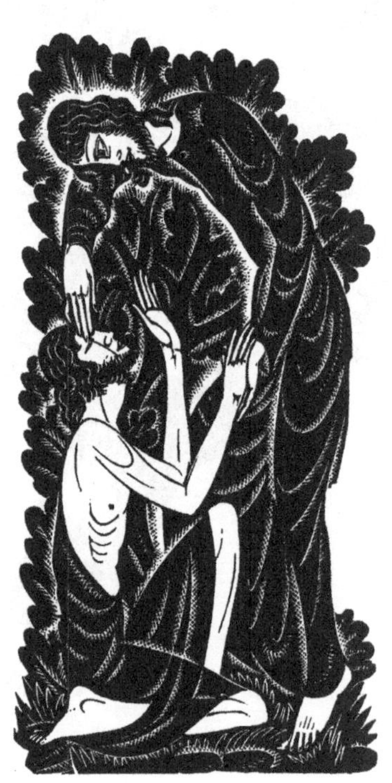

138 Bartimeus
1934
The Aldine Bible

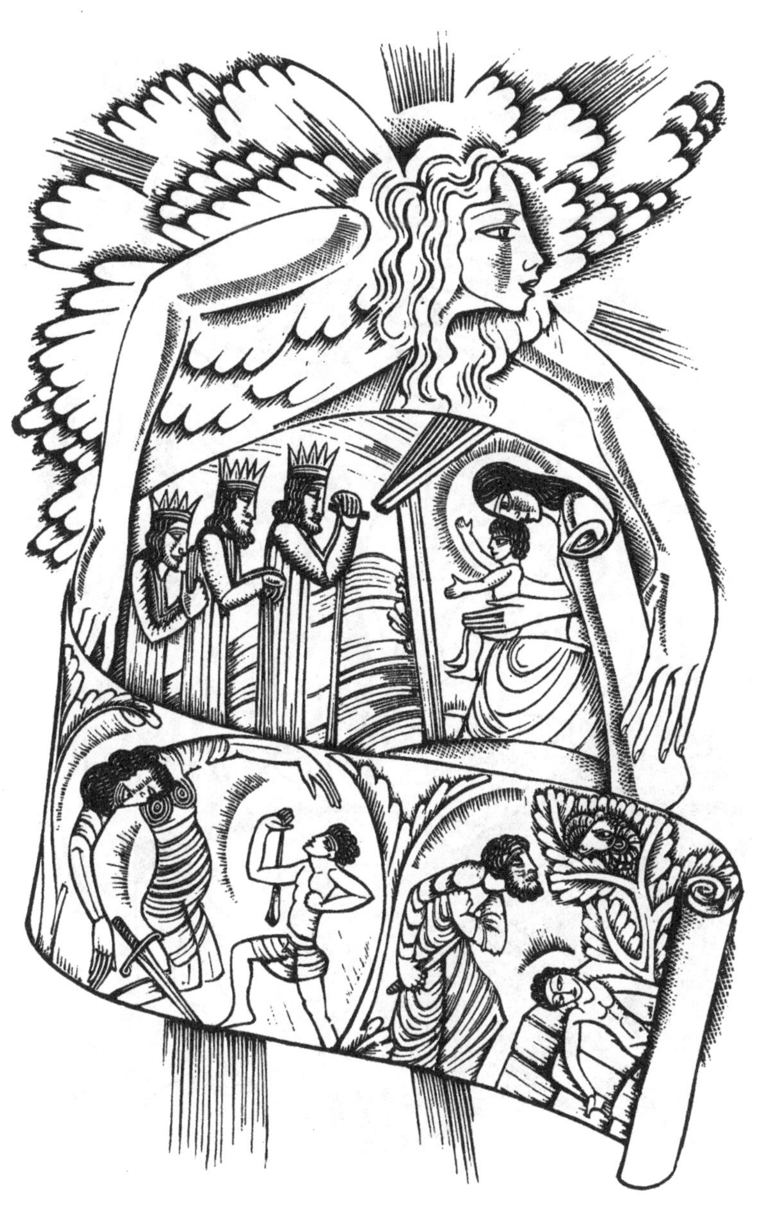

139 St Matthew
1934
The Aldine Bible, Vol. I

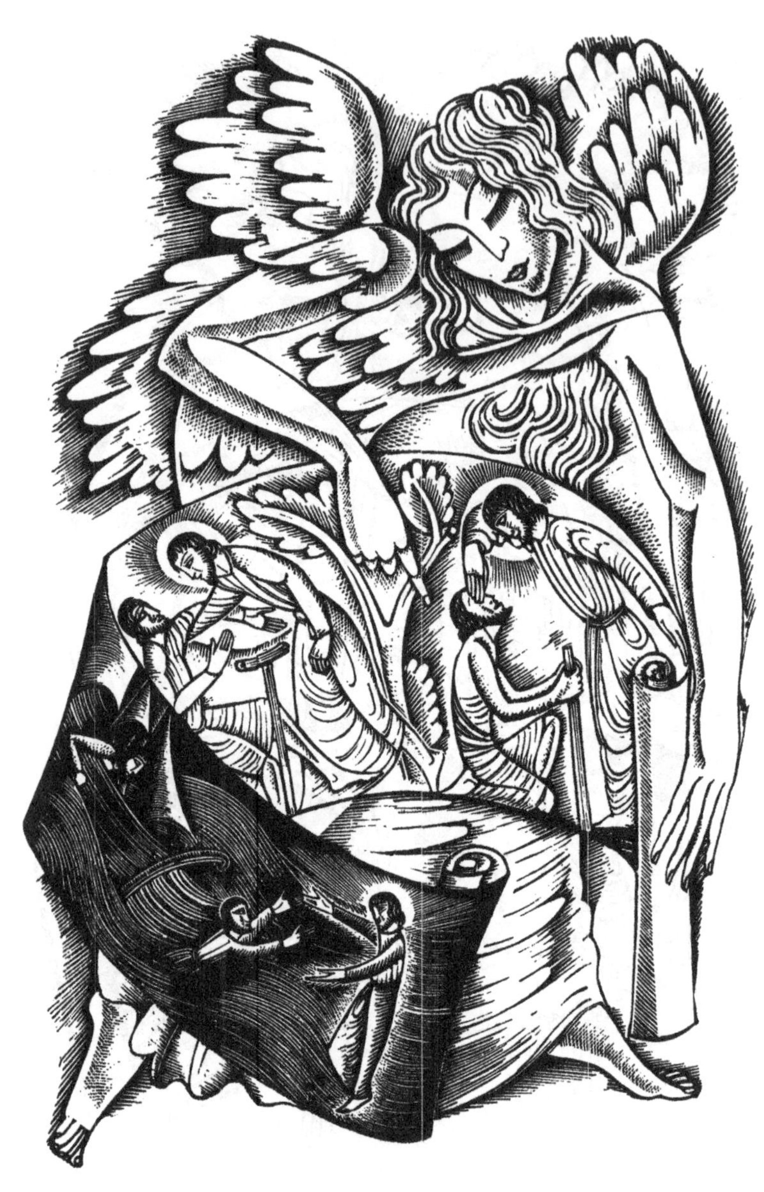

140 St Mark
1934
The Aldine Bible, Vol. I

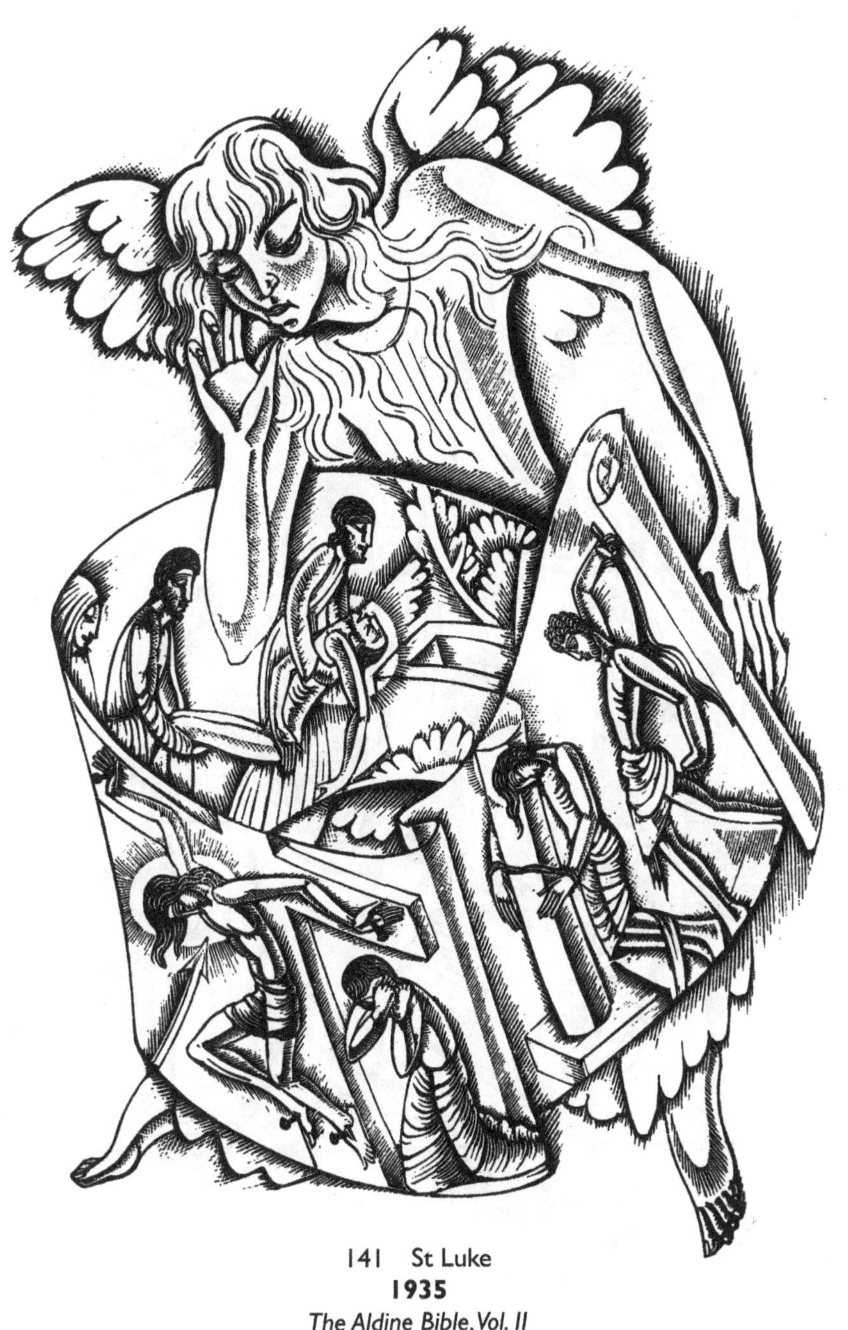

141 St Luke
1935
The Aldine Bible, Vol. II

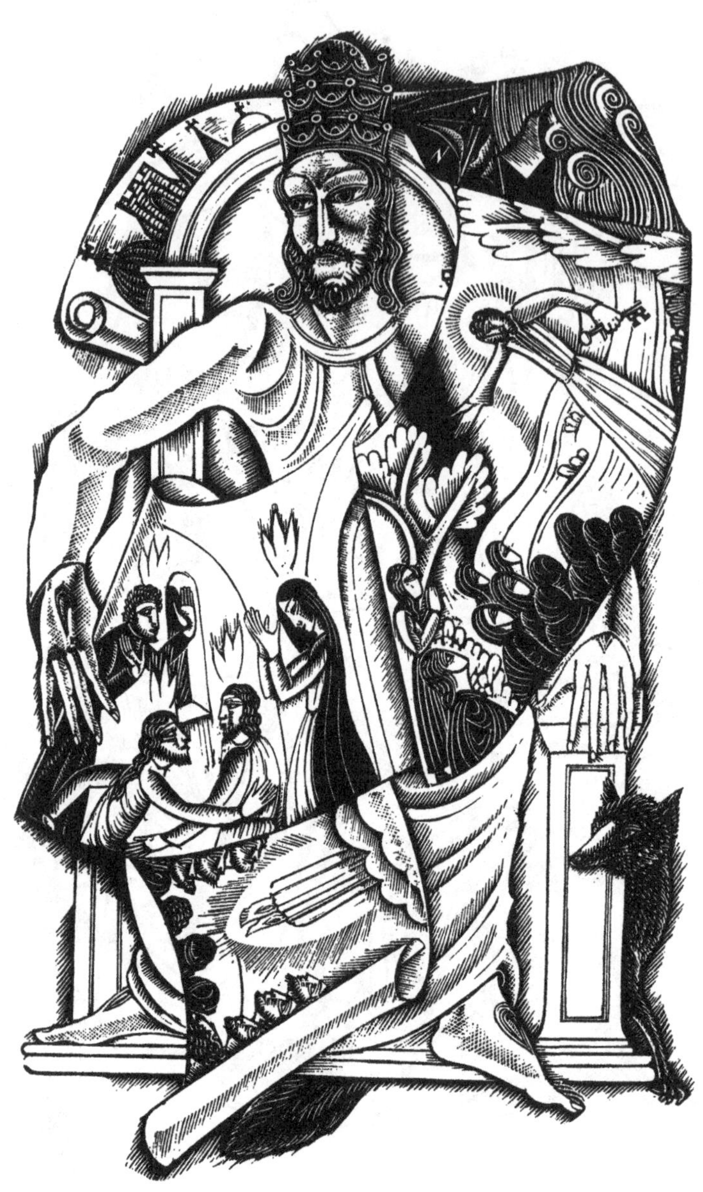

142 The Acts of the Apostles
1935
The Aldine Bible, Vol. II

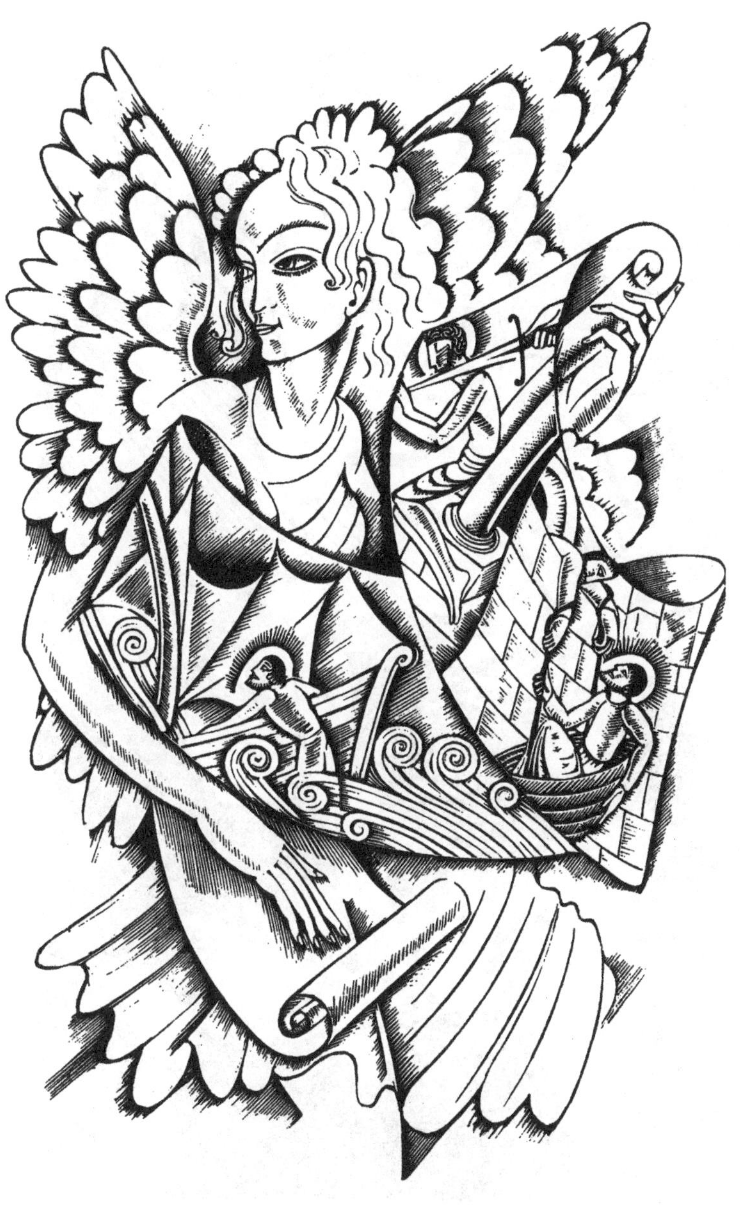

143 Woman with Ship
1935
The Aldine Bible, Vol. III

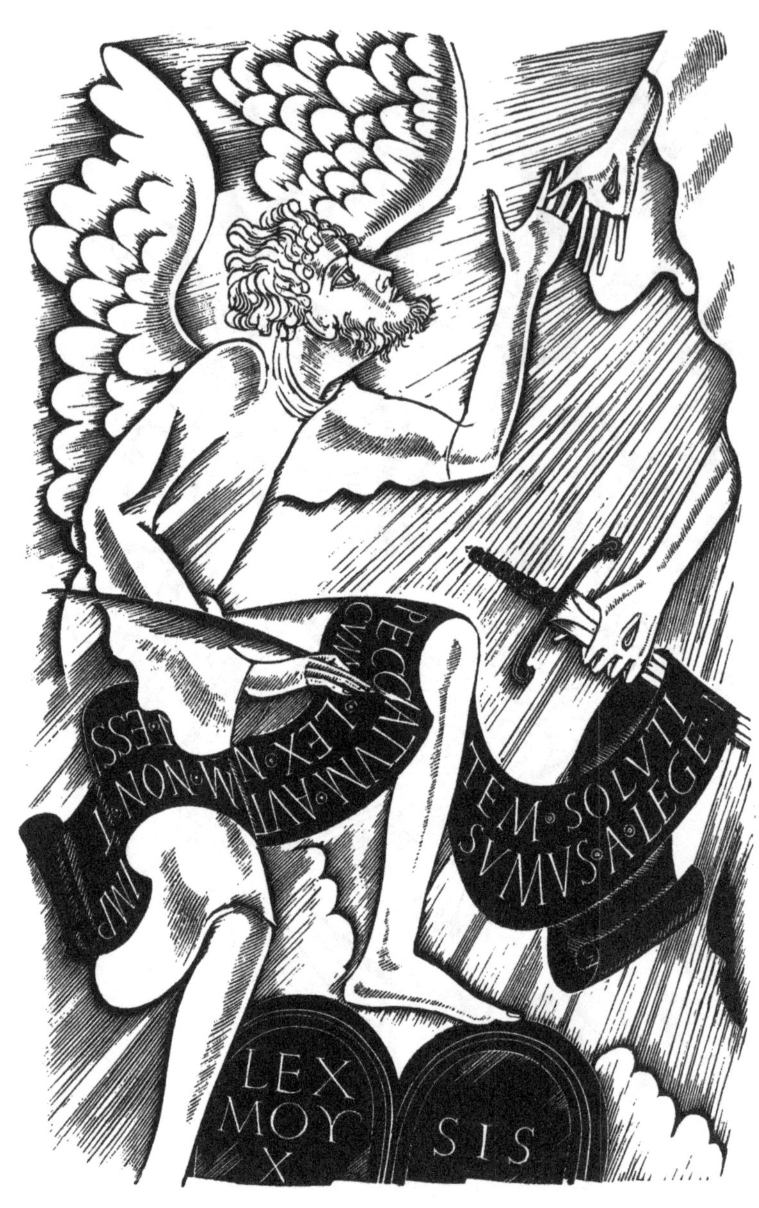

144 St Paul
1935
The Aldine Bible, Vol. III

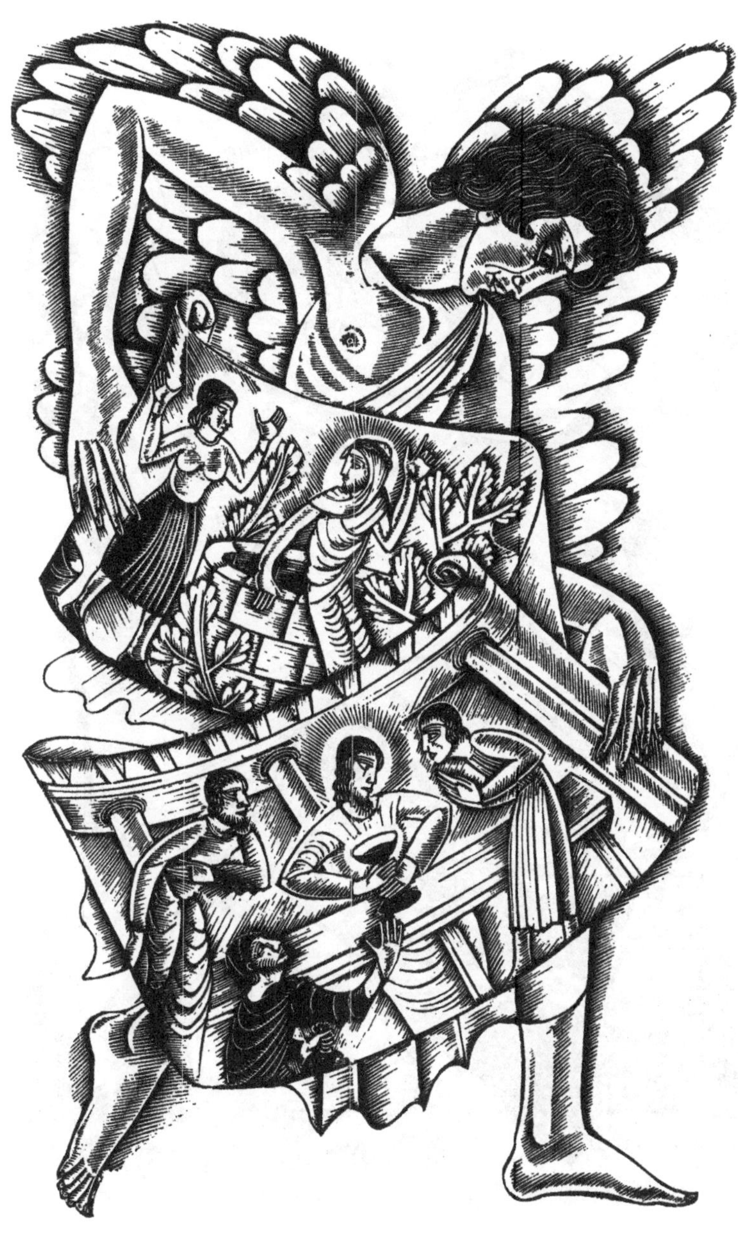

145 St John
1936
The Aldine Bible, Vol. IV

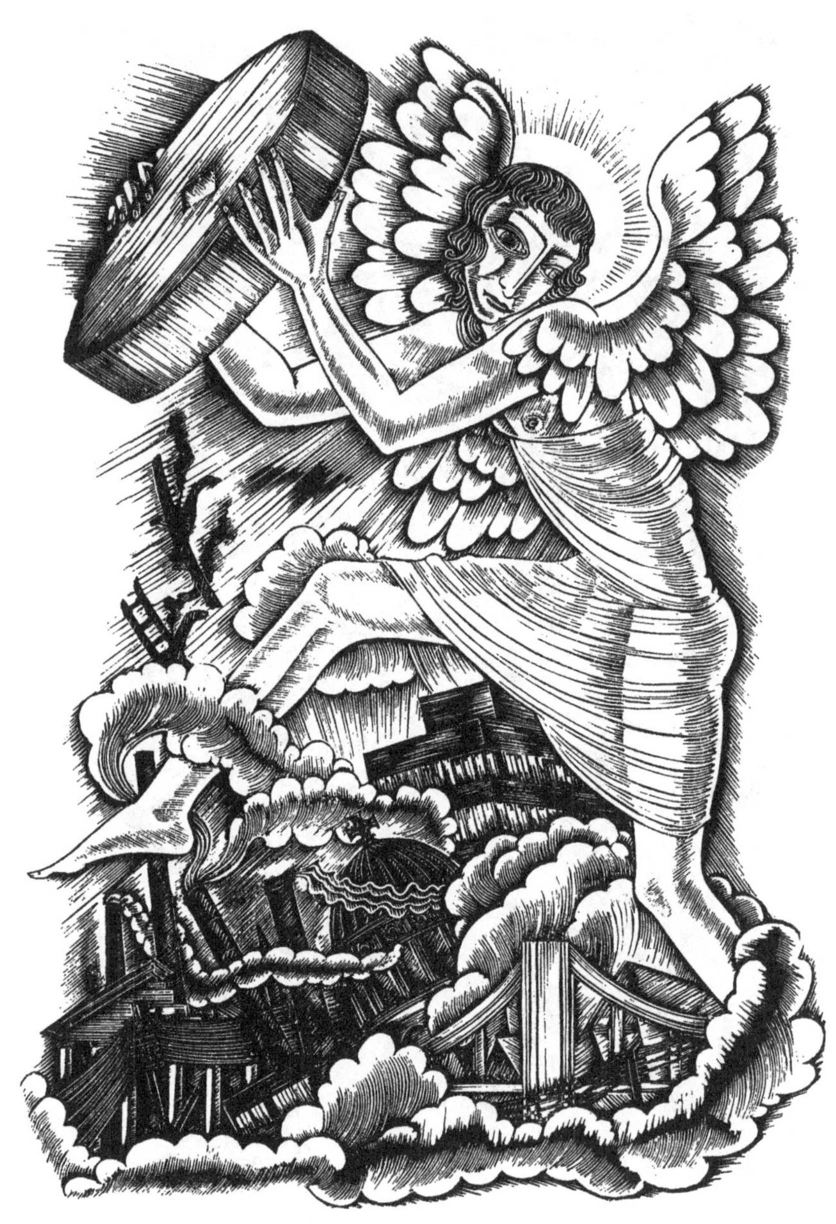

146 Apocalypse
1936
The Aldine Bible, Vol. IV

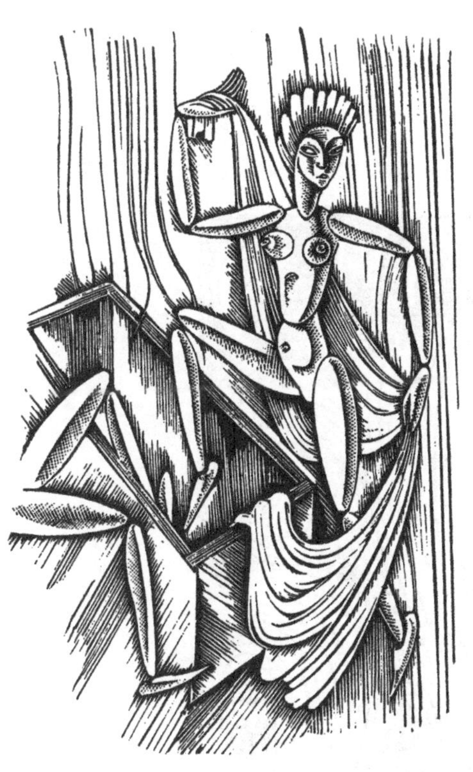

147 Marionette
1934
The Constant Mistress

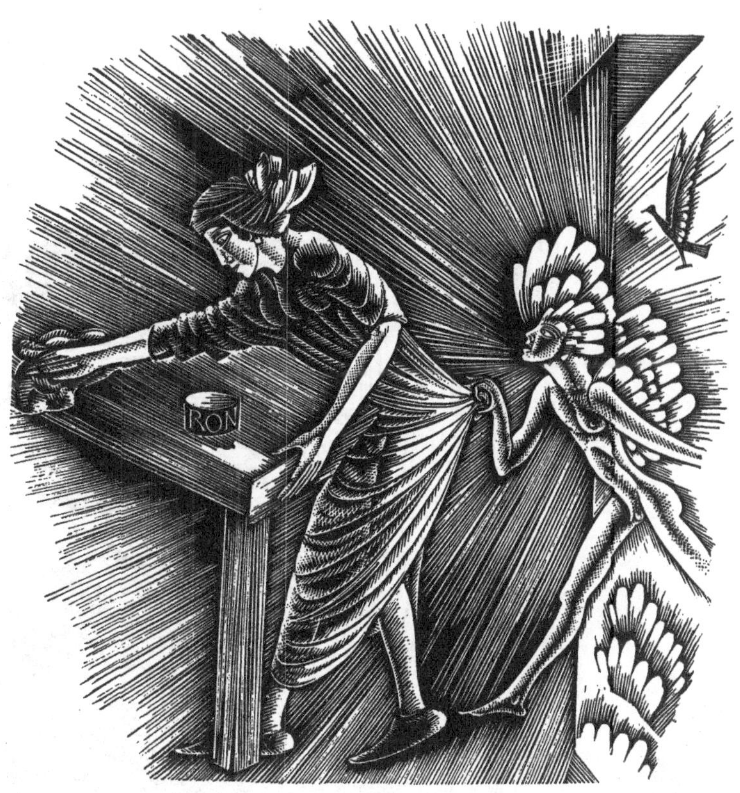

148 The Spring Cleaner
1934
The Constant Mistress

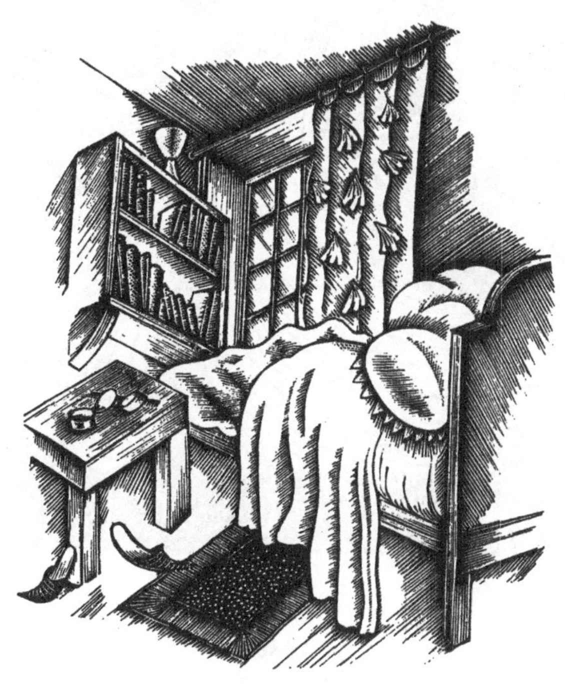

149 The Empty Bed (1st state)
1934
The Constant Mistress

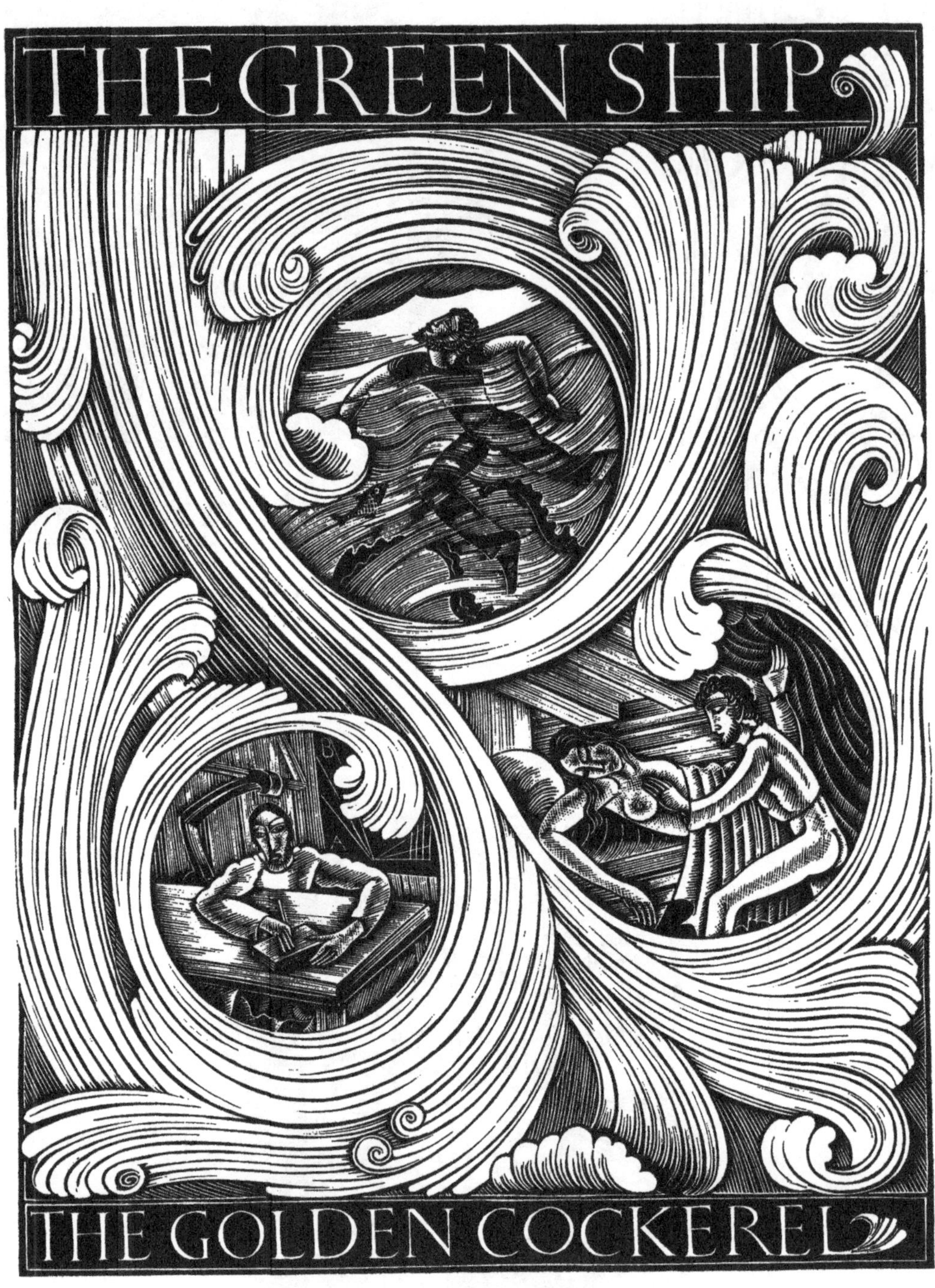

150 The Green Ship
1936
The Green Ship
(double title page)

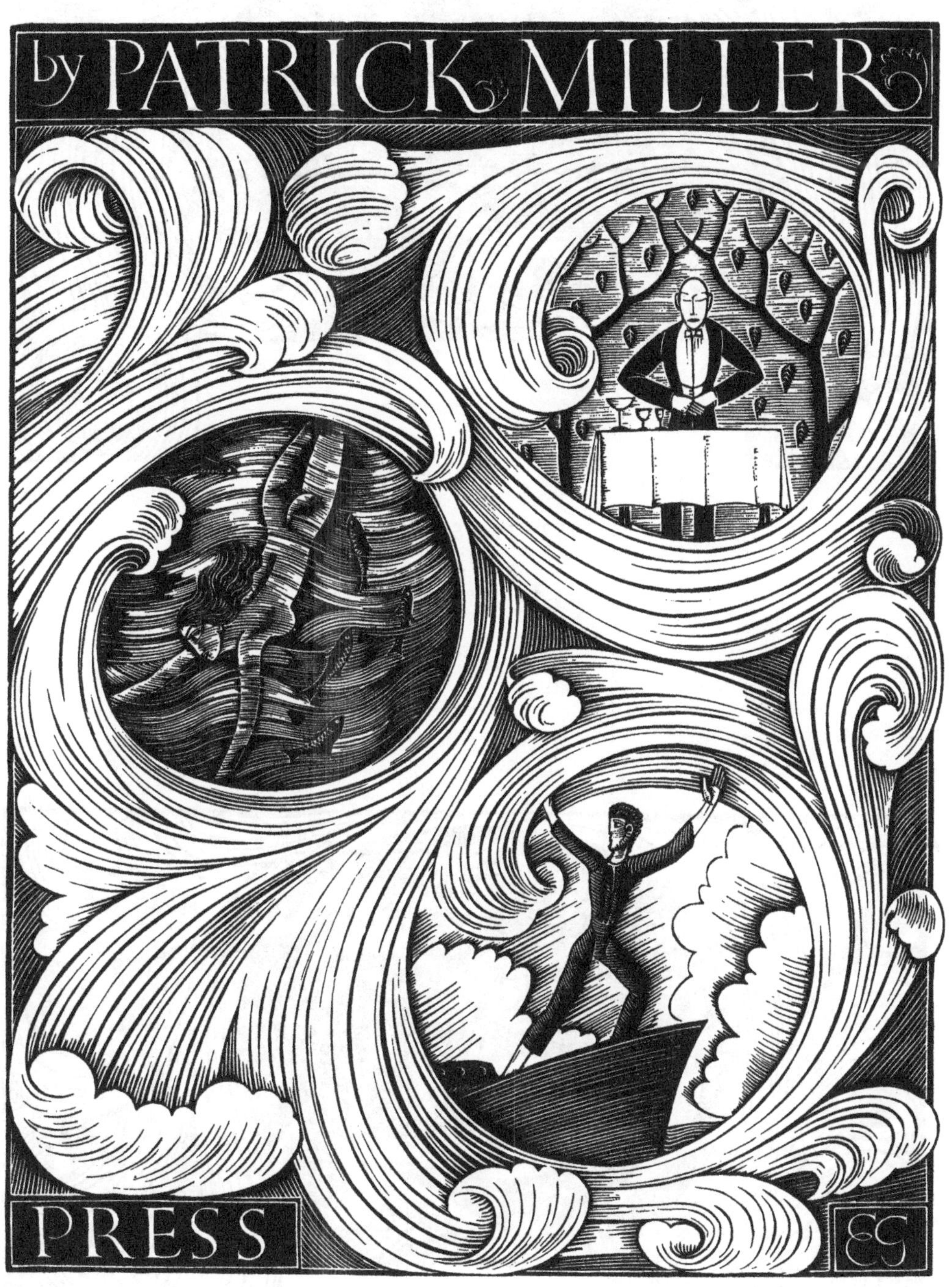

151 The Green Ship
1936
The Green Ship
(double title page)

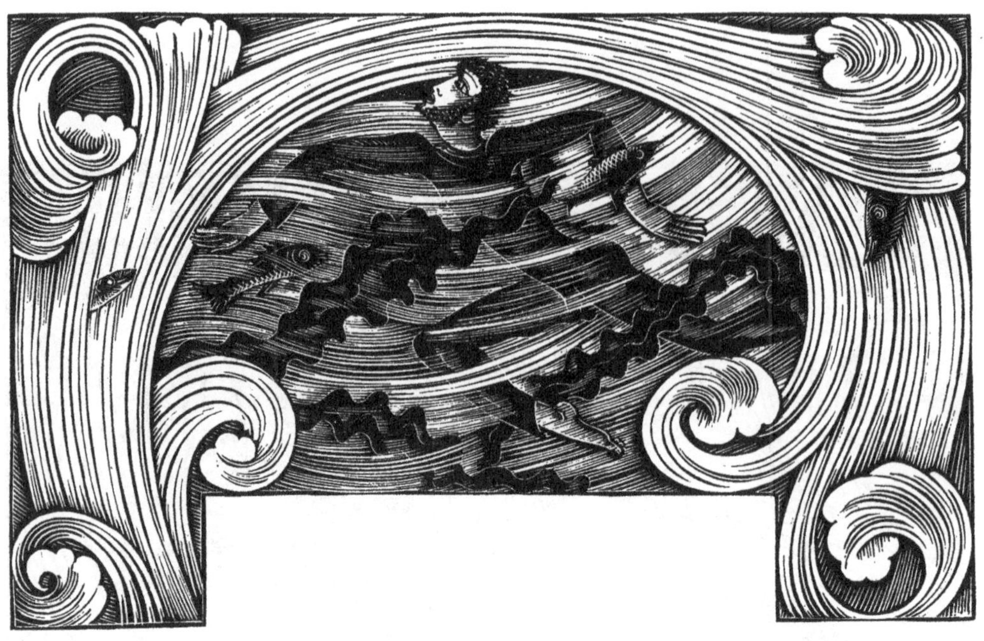

152 Man Swimming
1936
The Green Ship

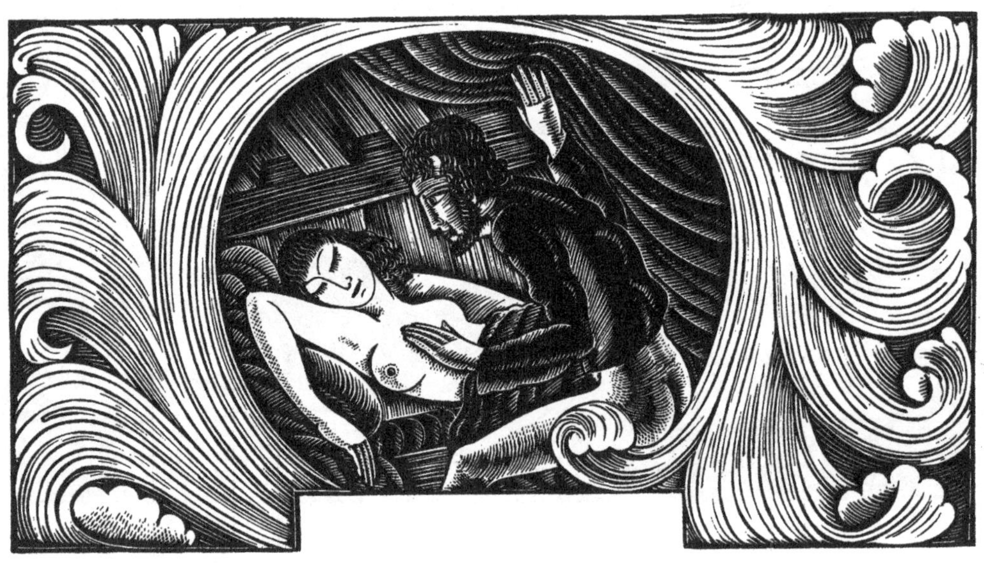

153 Woman Asleep
1936
The Green Ship

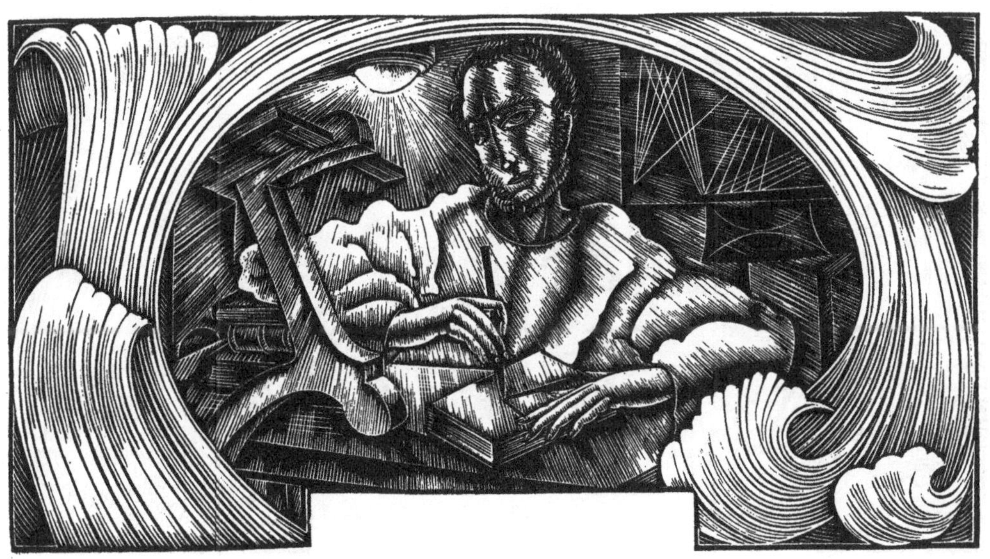

154 Mr Scribner
1936
The Green Ship

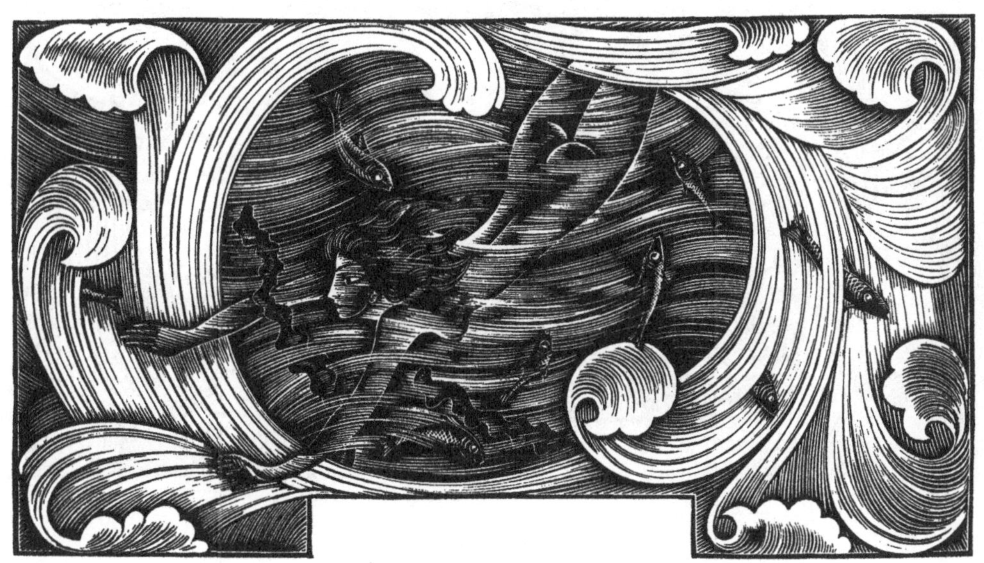

155 Woman Diving
1936
The Green Ship

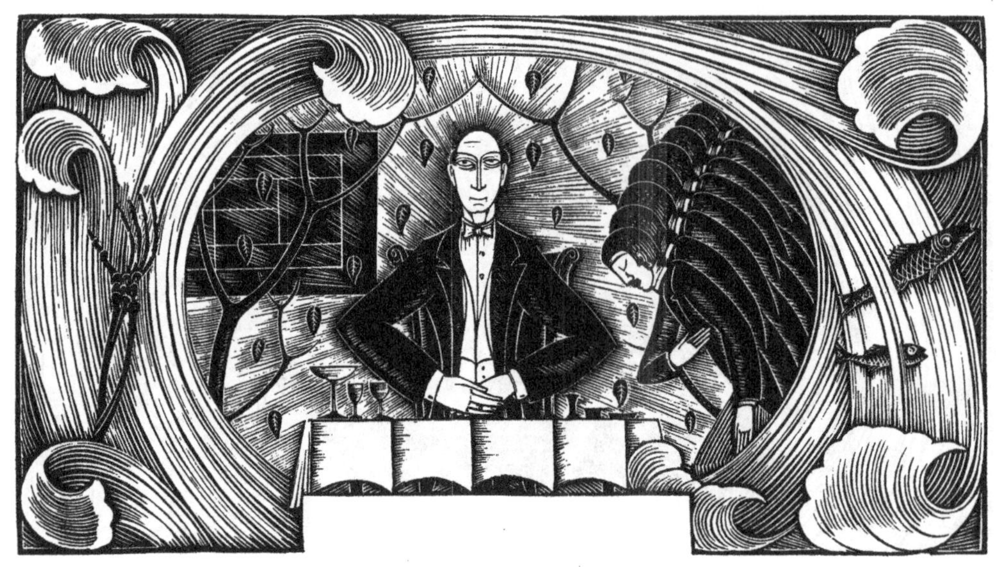

156 Mr Brown
1936
The Green Ship

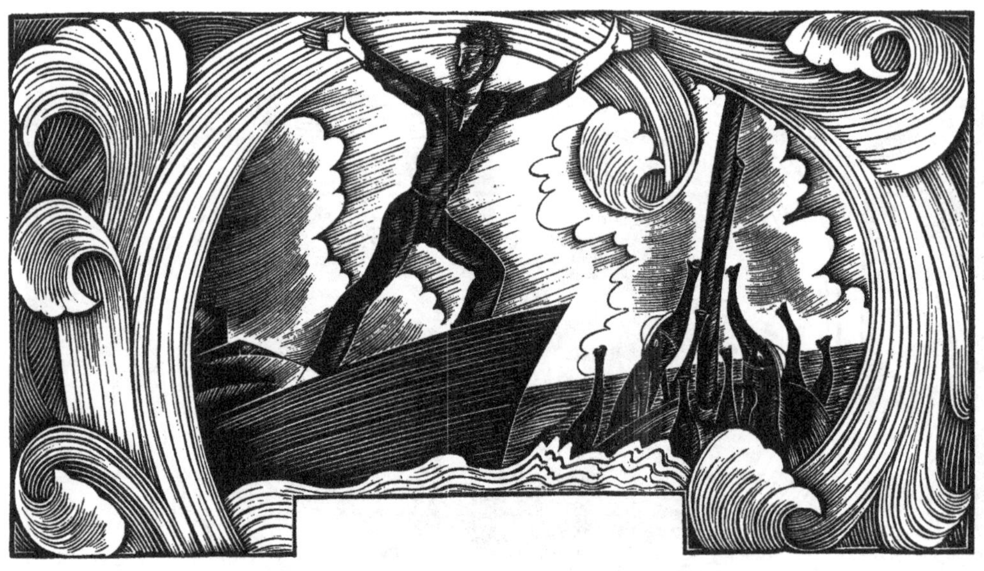

157 The Dying Patriot
1936
The Green Ship

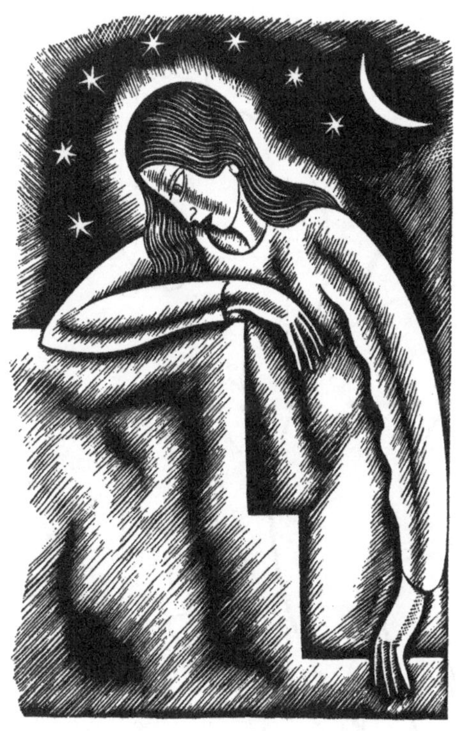

158 Mother and Stars and Moon
1936
Quia Amore Langueo

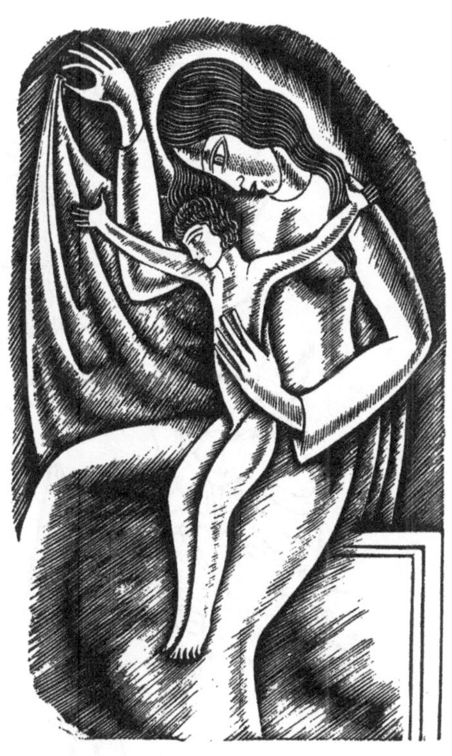

159 Mother and Child
1936
Quia Amore Langueo

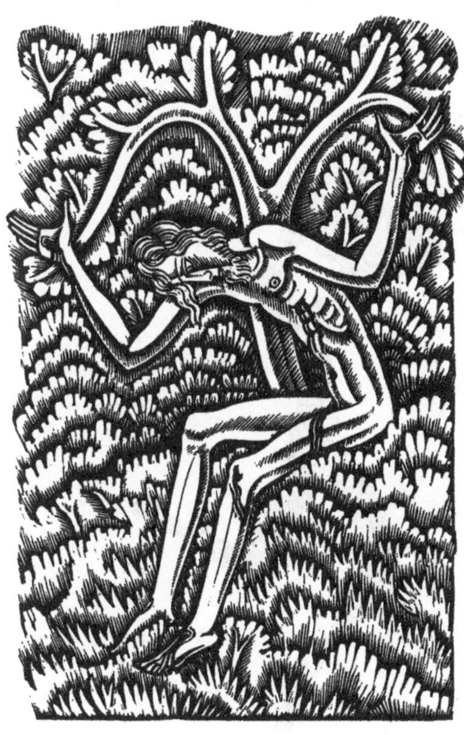

160 Christ Seated
1936
Quia Amore Langueo

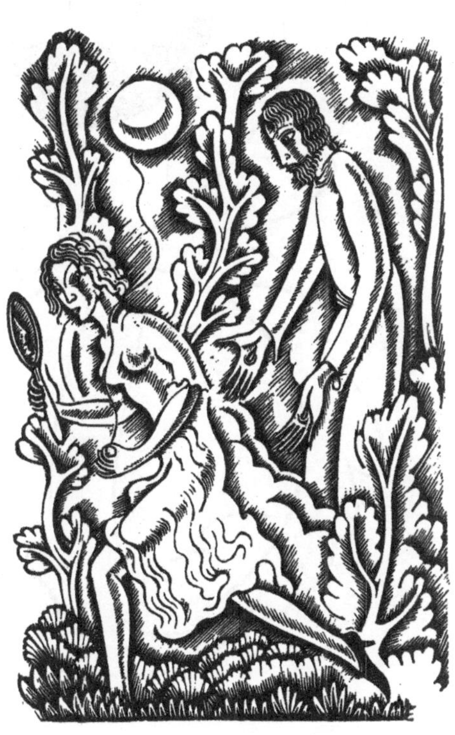

161 Girl with Mirror
1936
Quia Amore Langueo

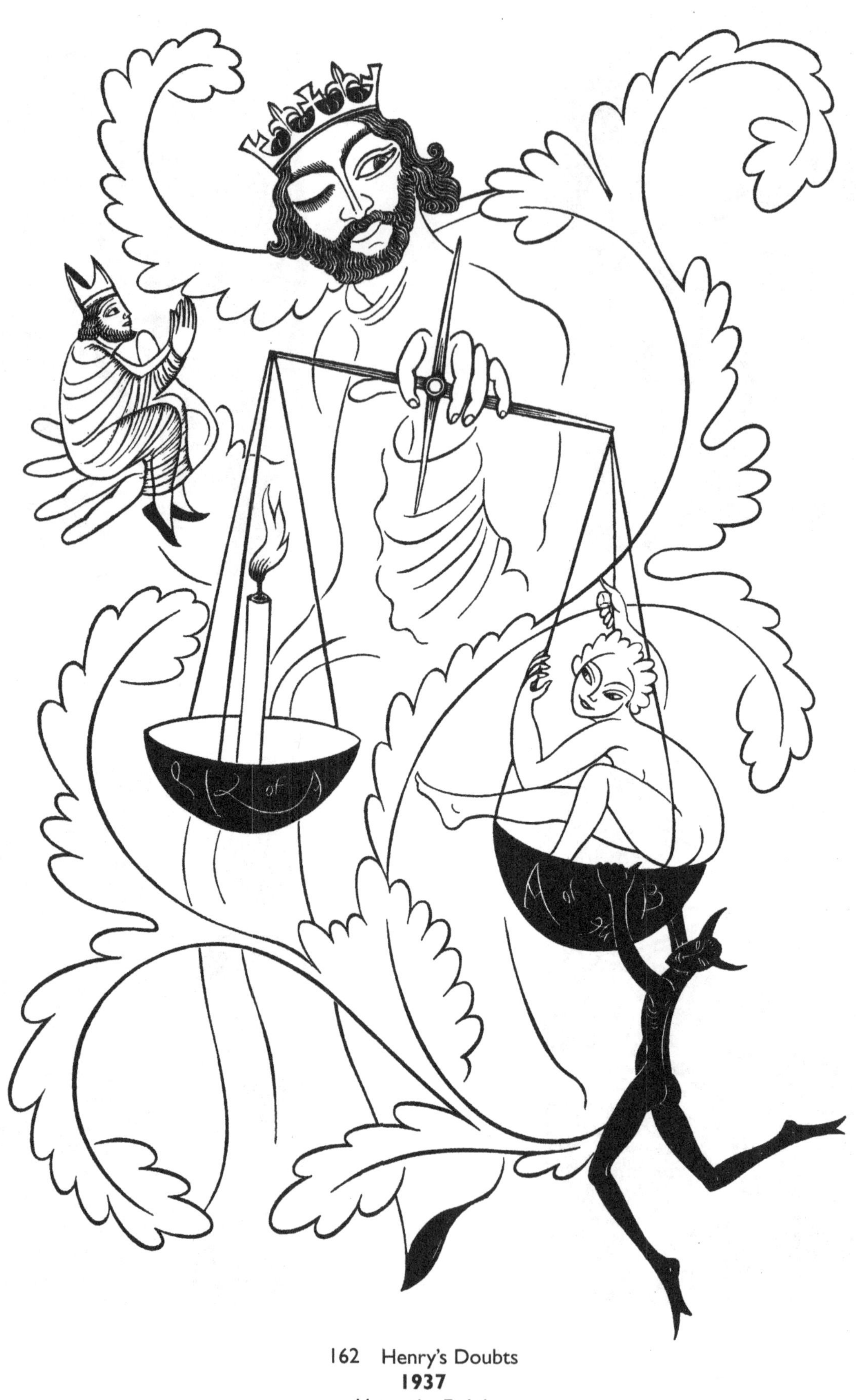

162 Henry's Doubts
1937
Henry the Eighth

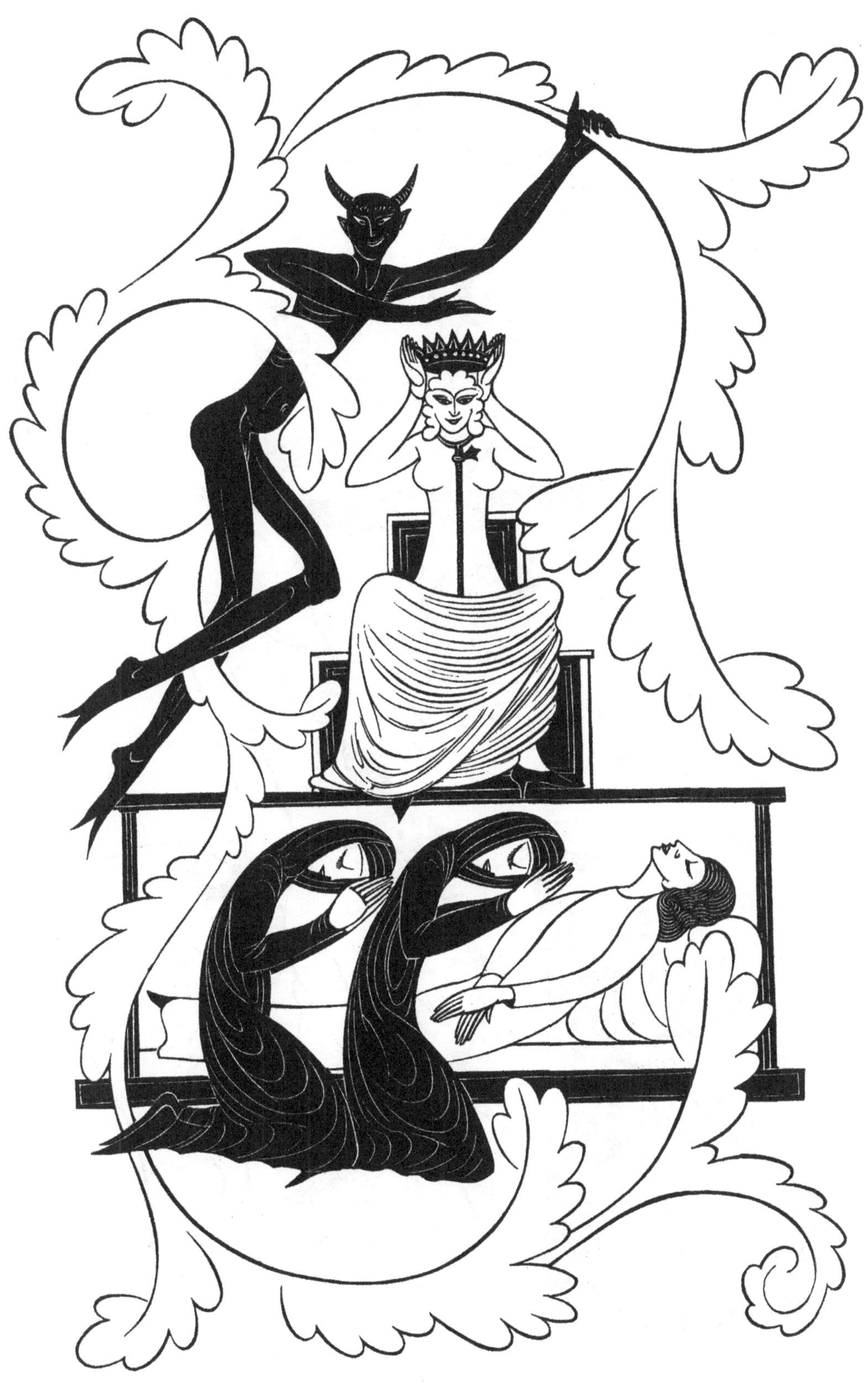

163 The Coronation of Anne
1937
Henry the Eighth

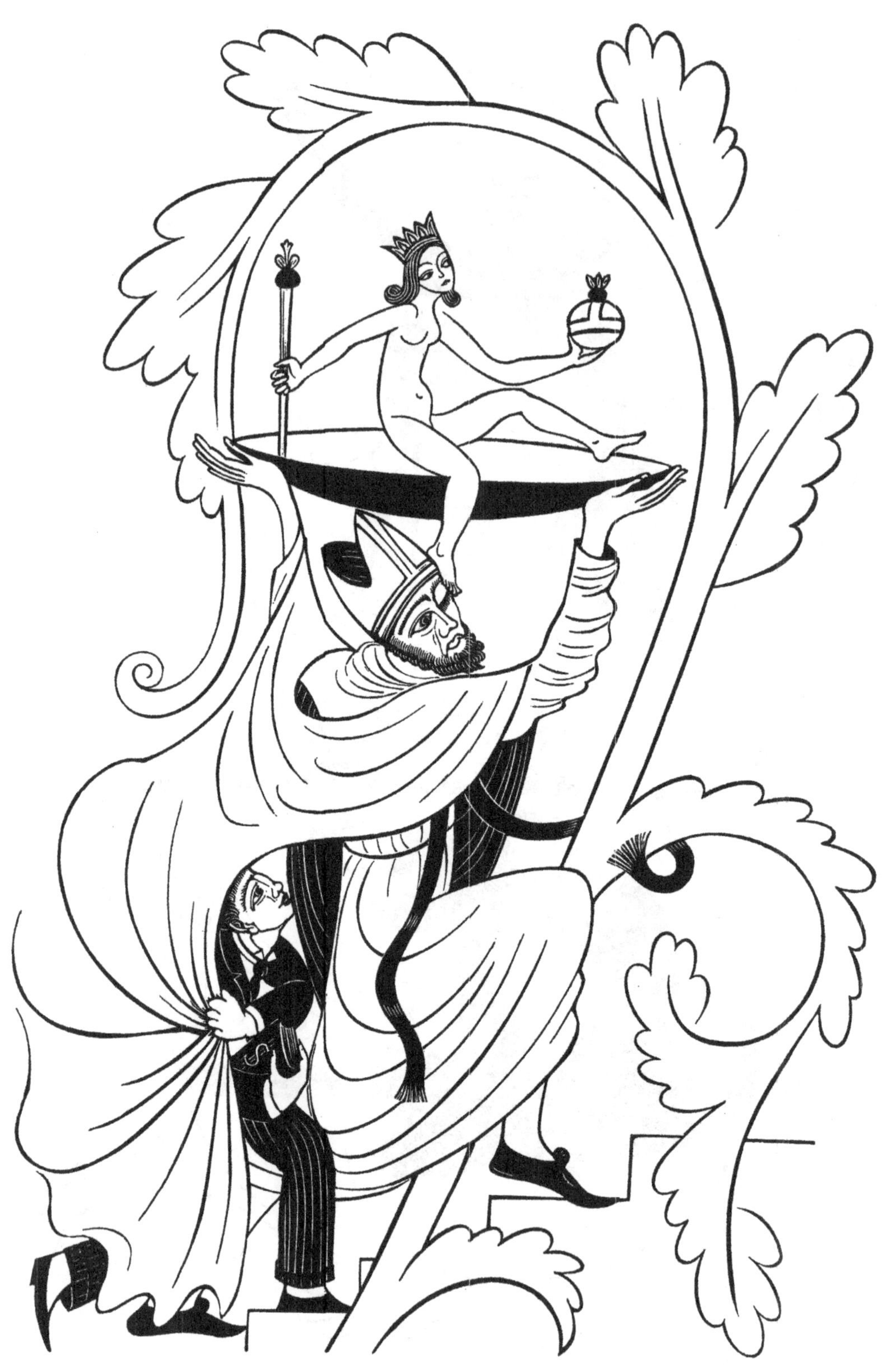

164 The Baptism of Elizabeth
1937
Henry the Eighth

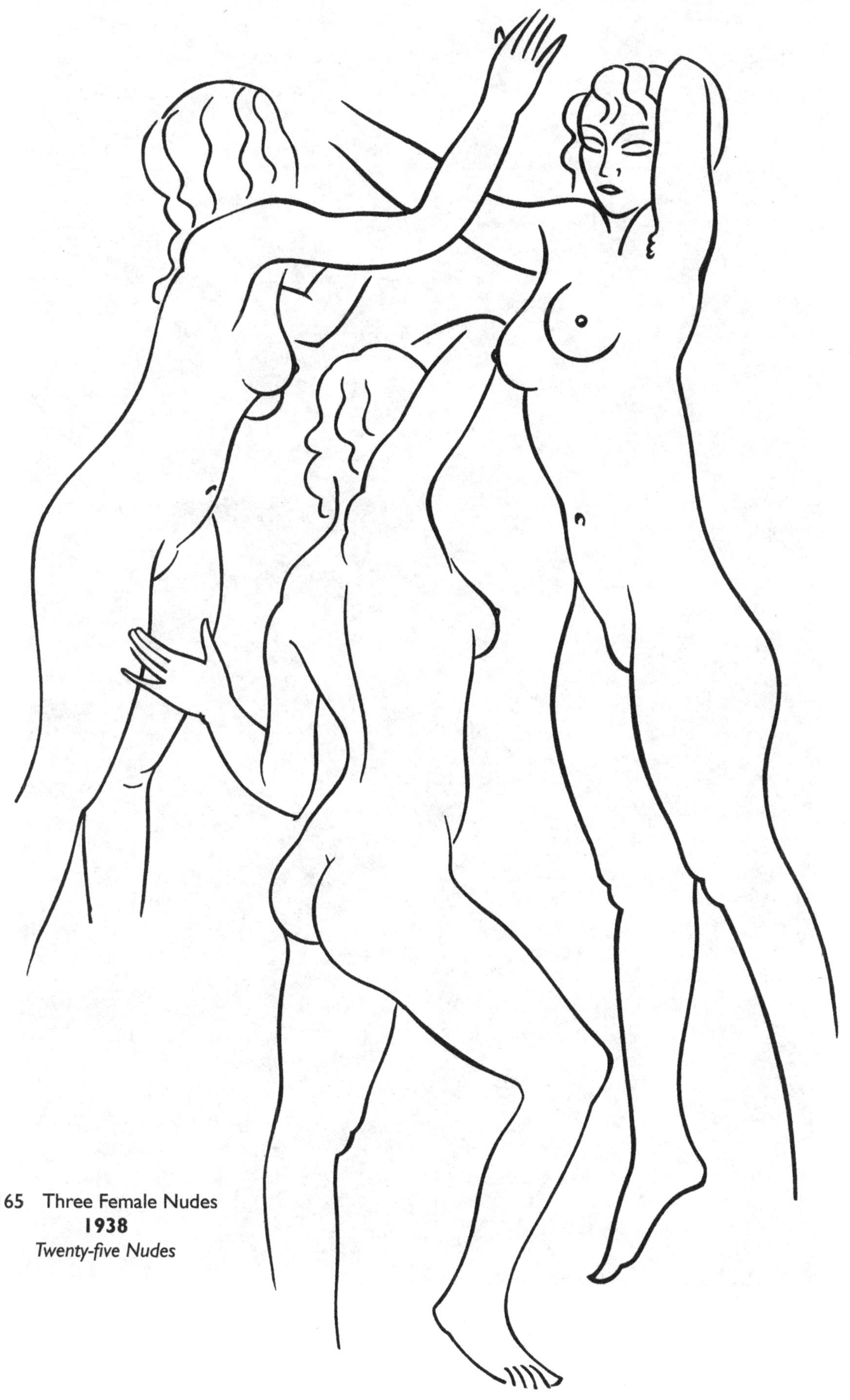

165 Three Female Nudes
1938
Twenty-five Nudes

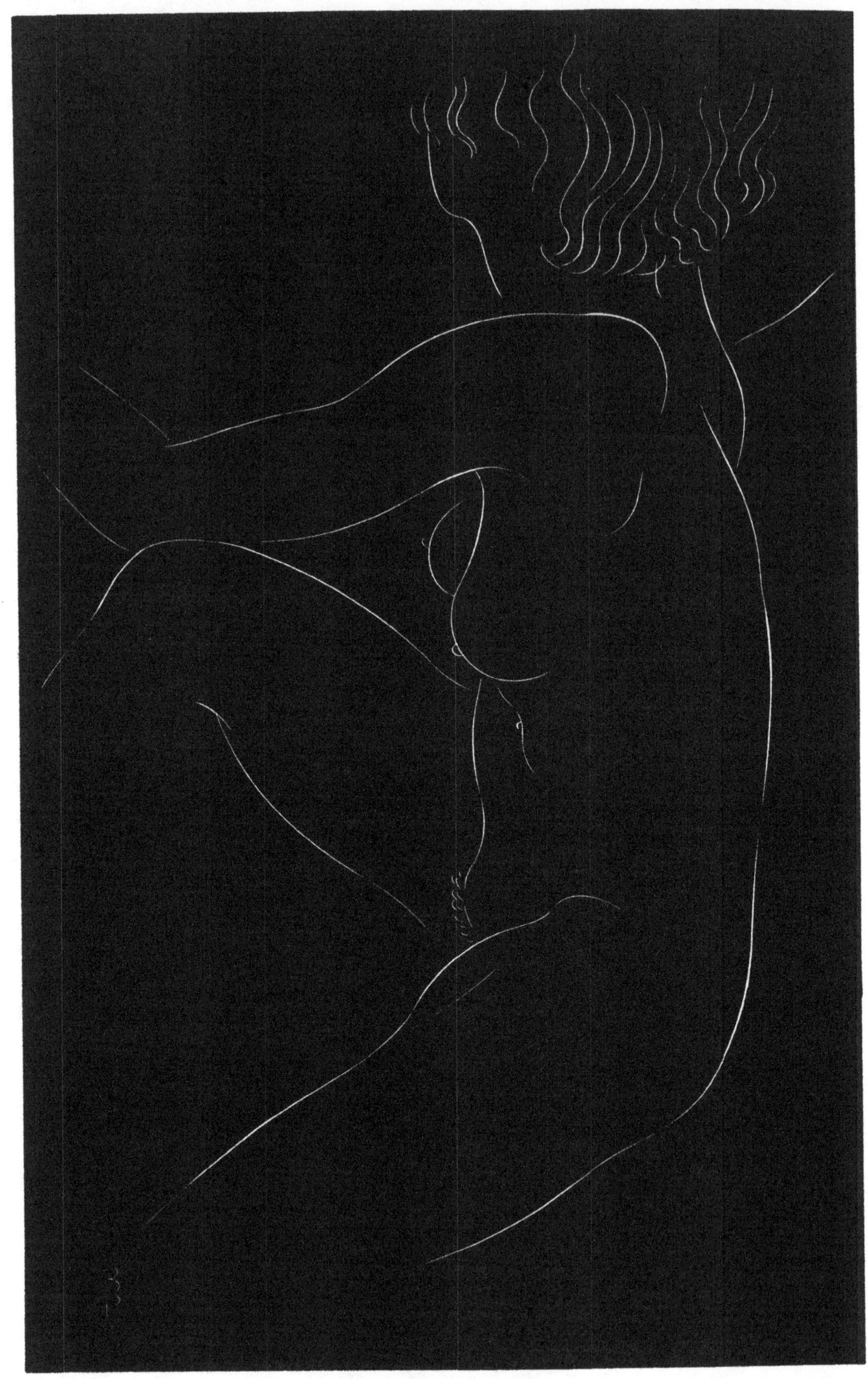

166 Female Nude, Seated
1937
Twenty-five Nudes

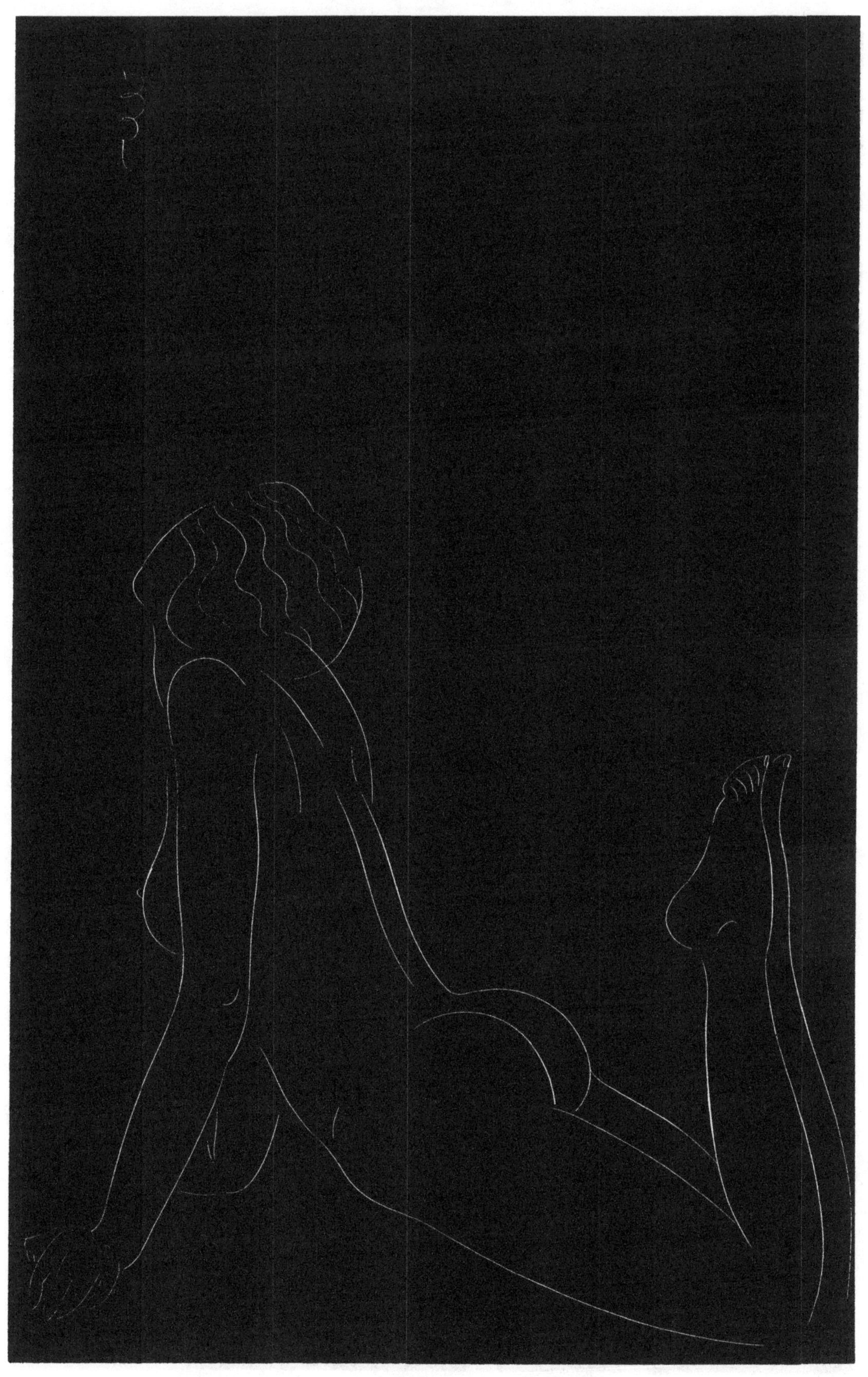

167 Female Nude, Kneeling
1937
Twenty-five Nudes

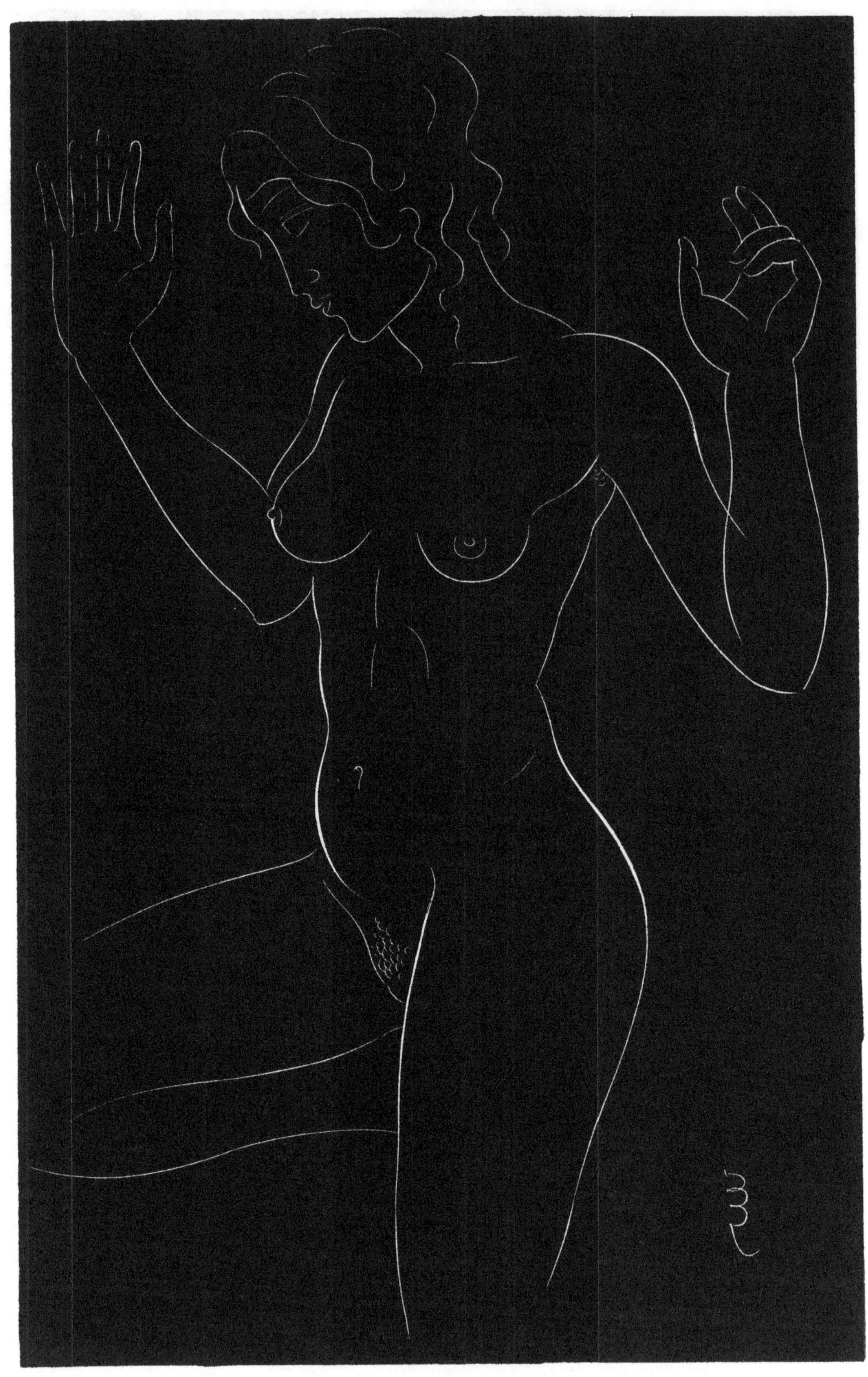

168 Female Nude, Standing
1937
Twenty-five Nudes

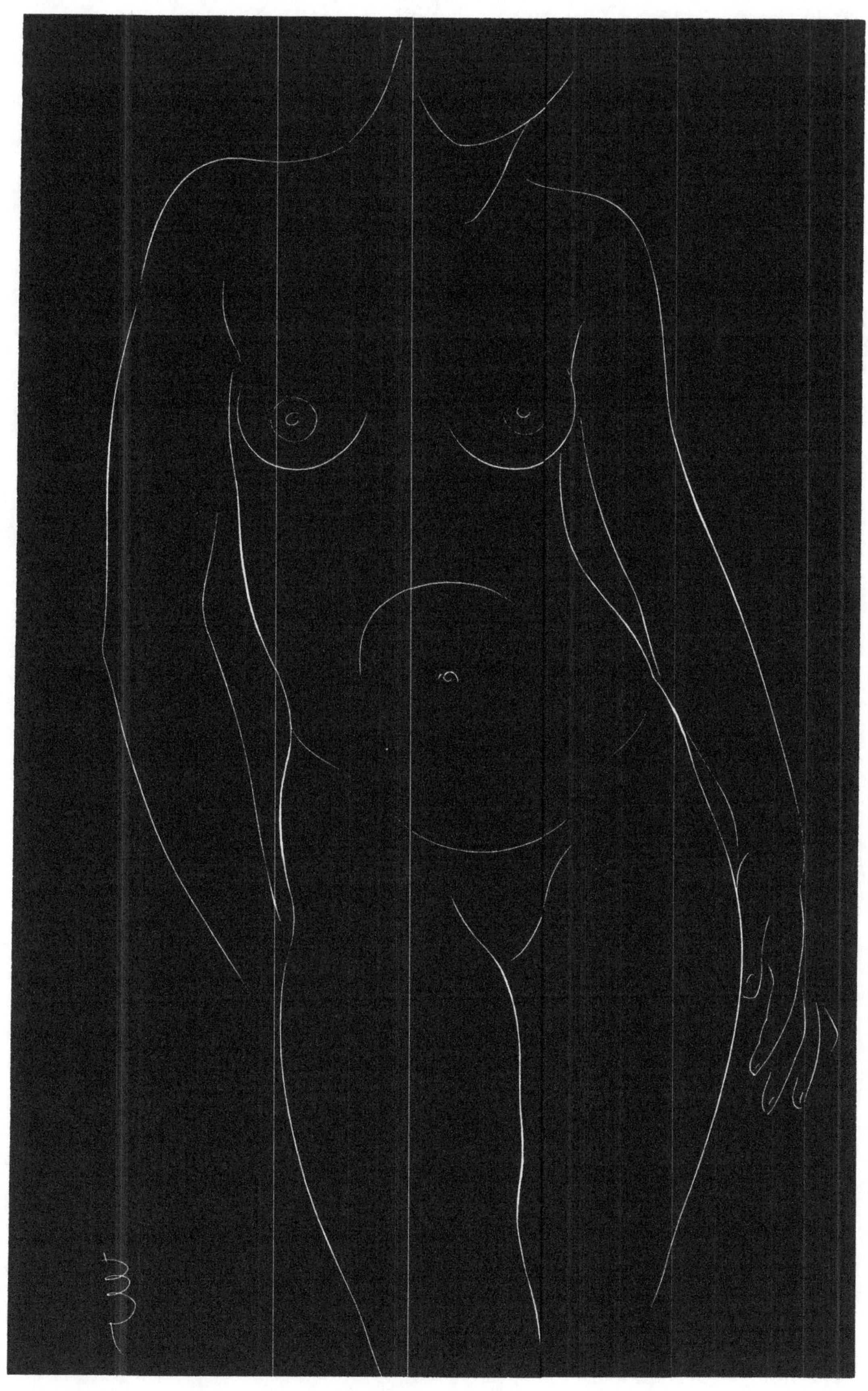

169 Female Nude, Standing
1937
Twenty-five Nudes

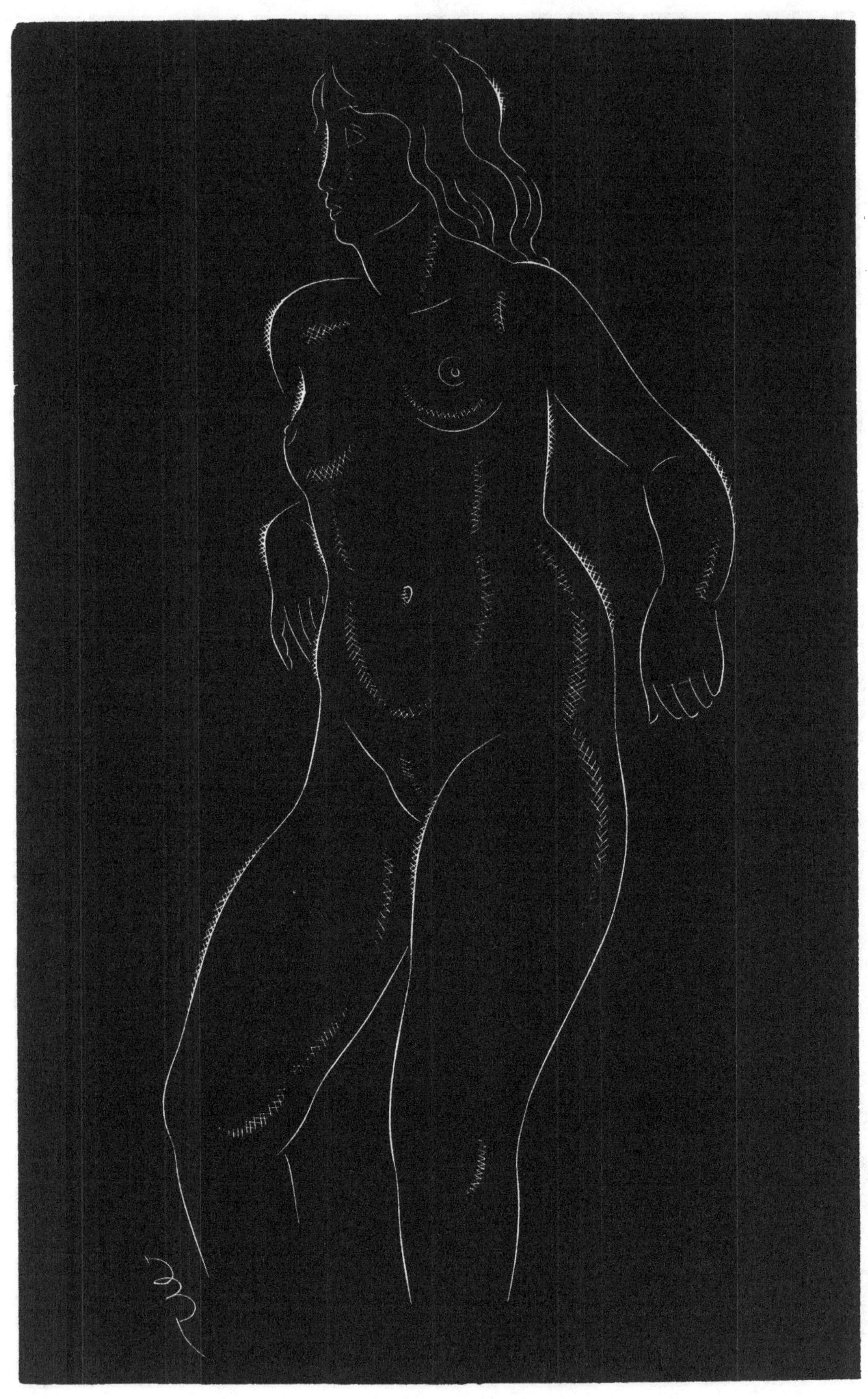

170 Female Nude, Reclining
1937
Twenty-five Nudes

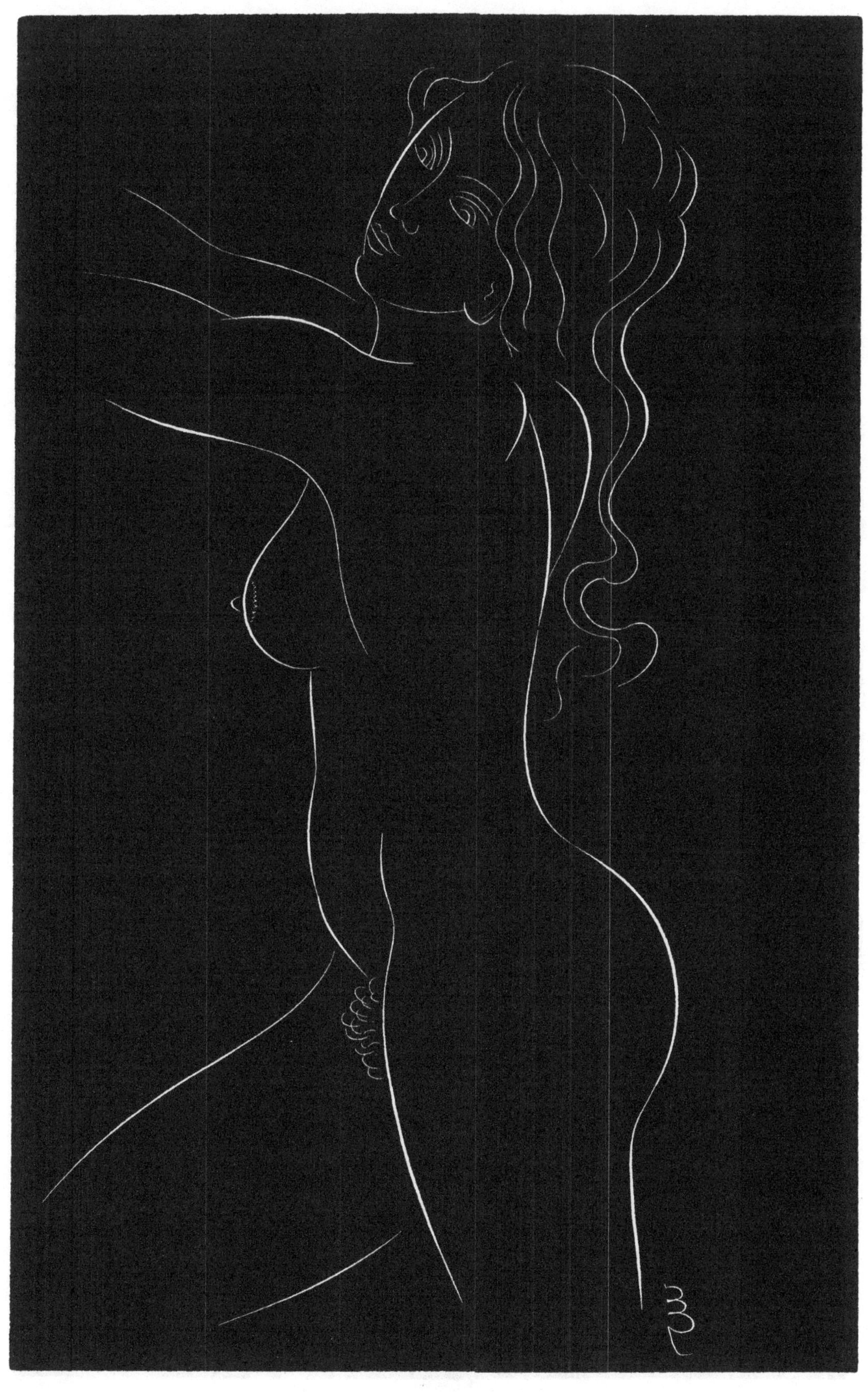

171 Female Nude, Standing
1937
Twenty-five Nudes

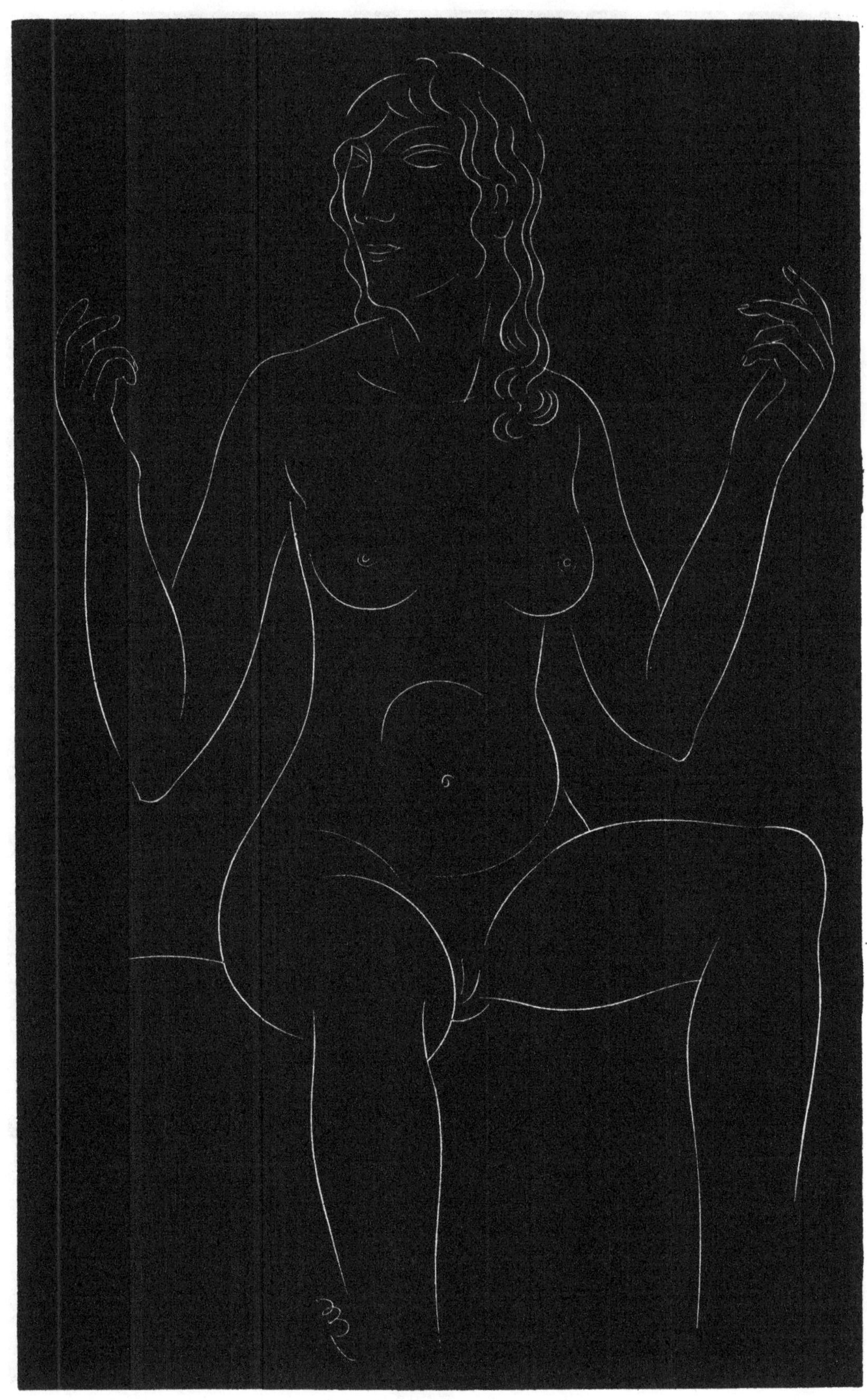

172 Female Nude, Seated
1937
Twenty-five Nudes

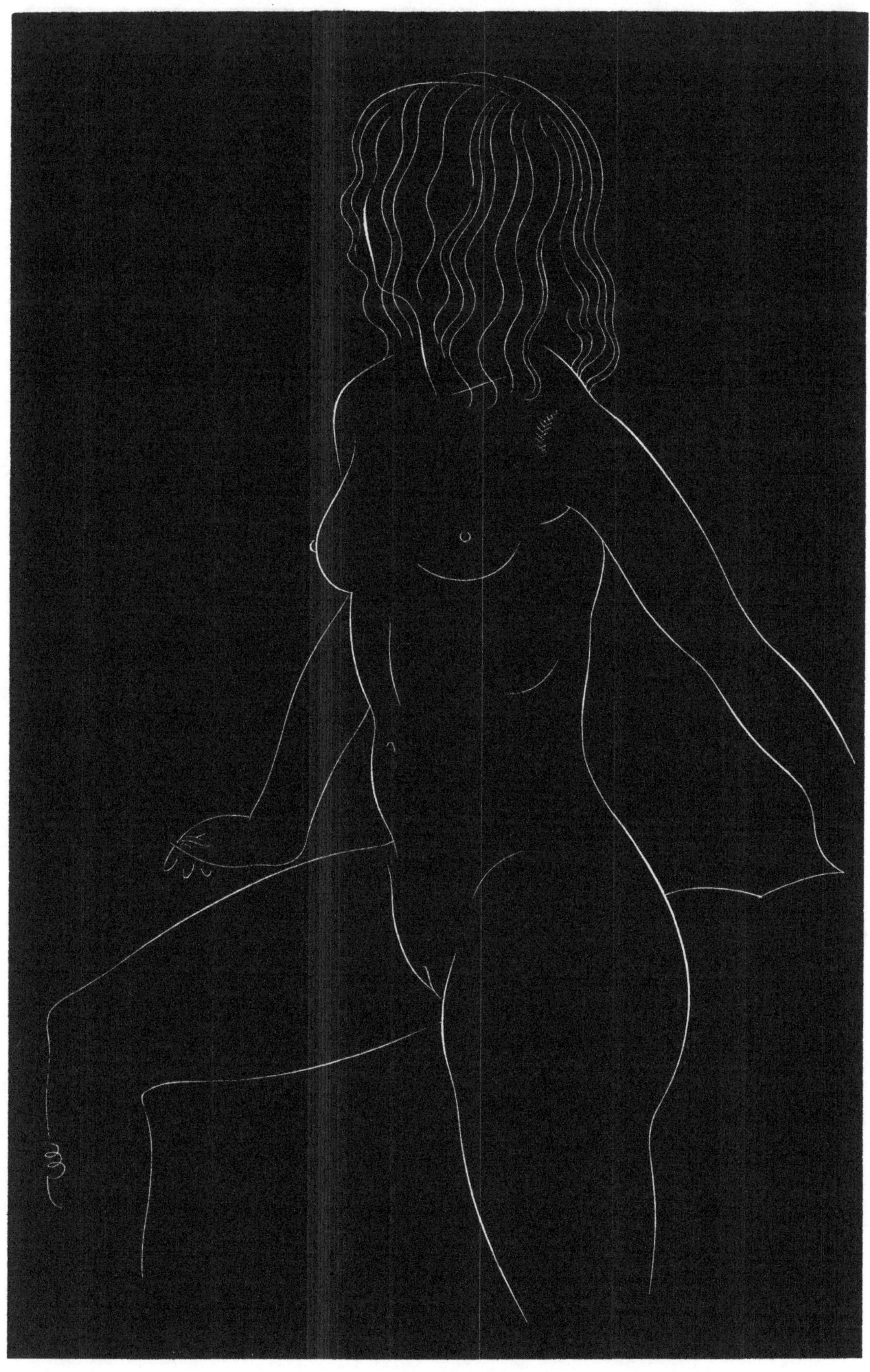

173 Female Nude, Seated
1937
Twenty-five Nudes

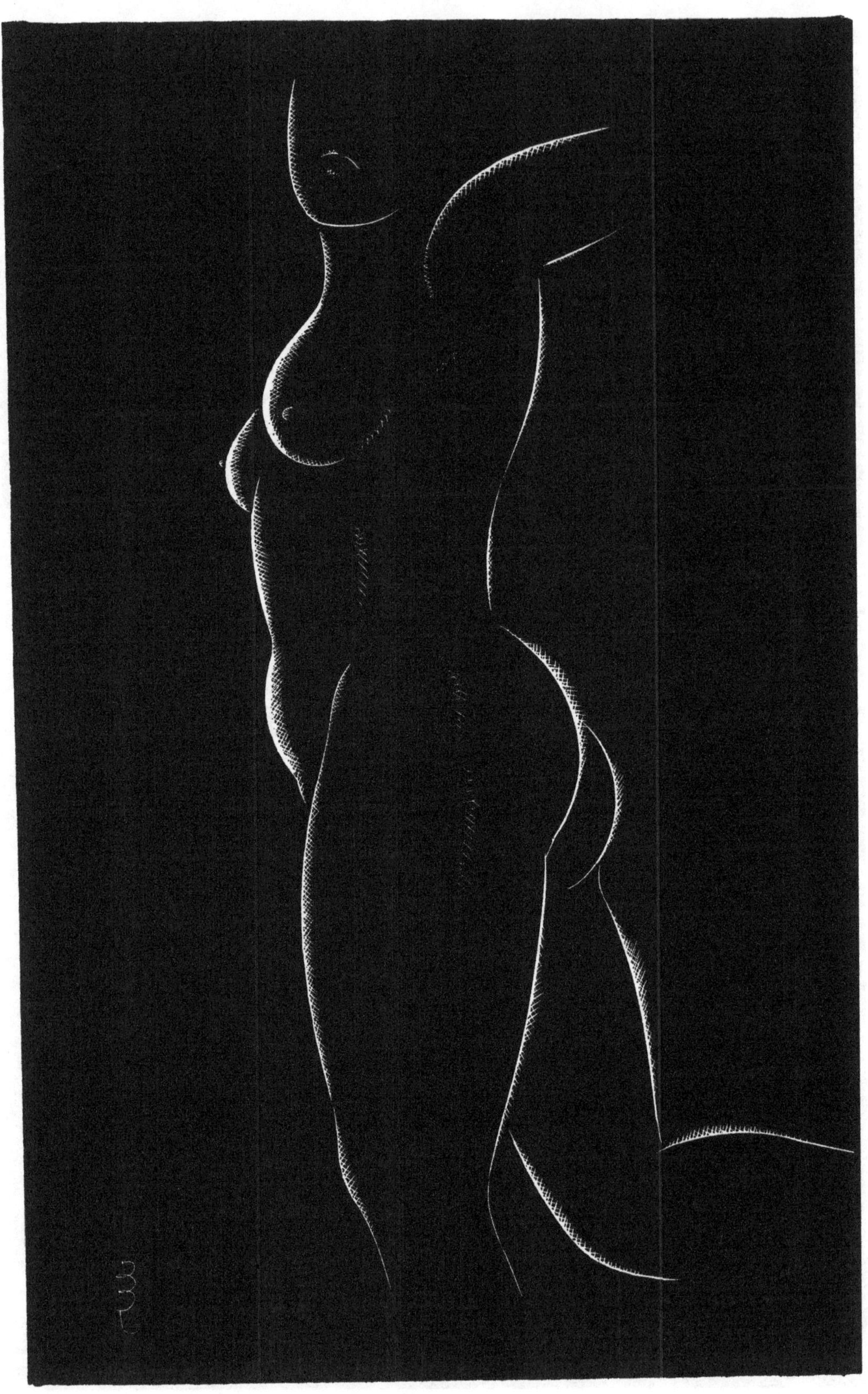

174 Female Nude, Standing
1937
Twenty-five Nudes

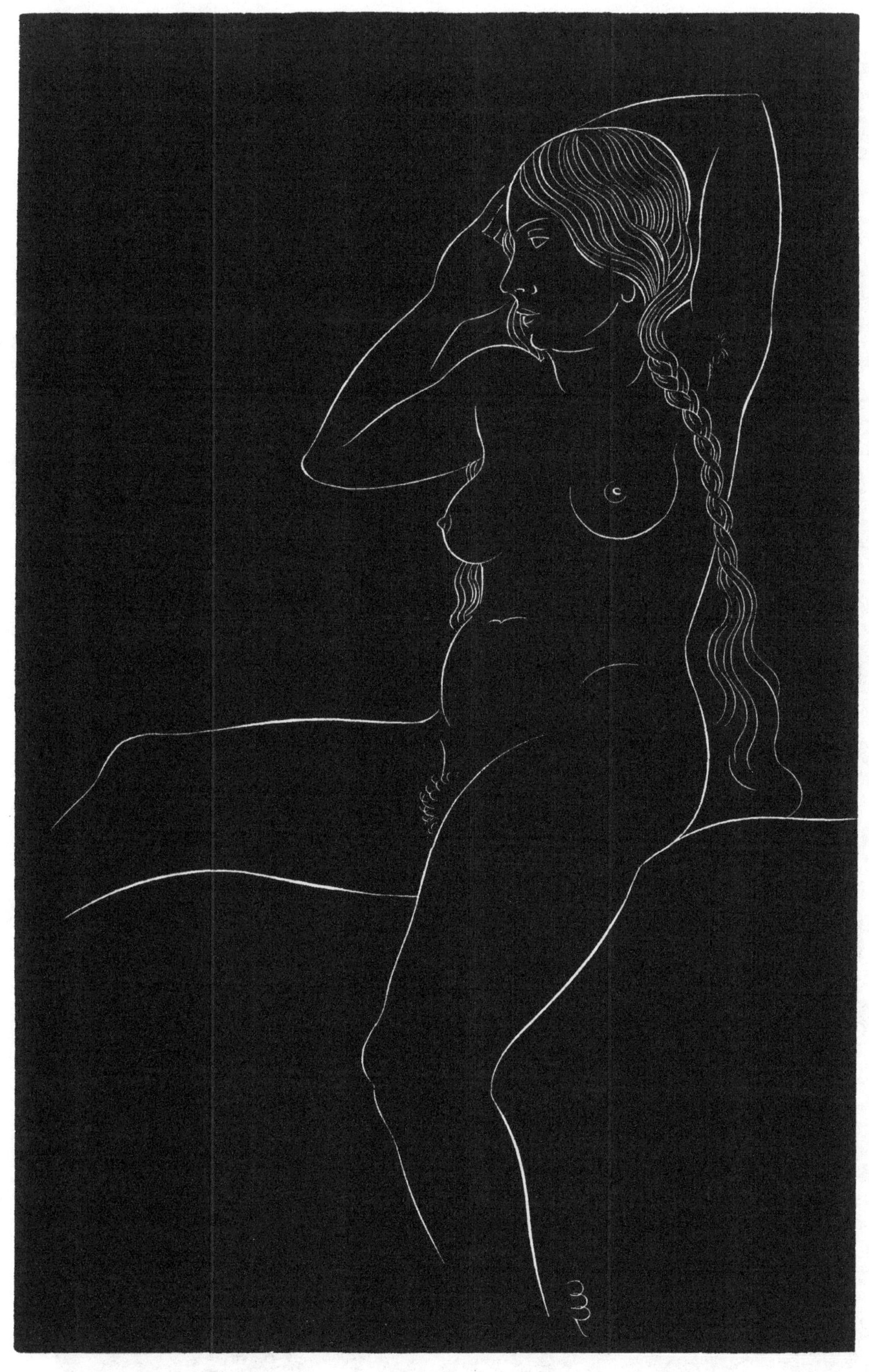

175 Female Nude, Seated
1937
Twenty-five Nudes (discarded)

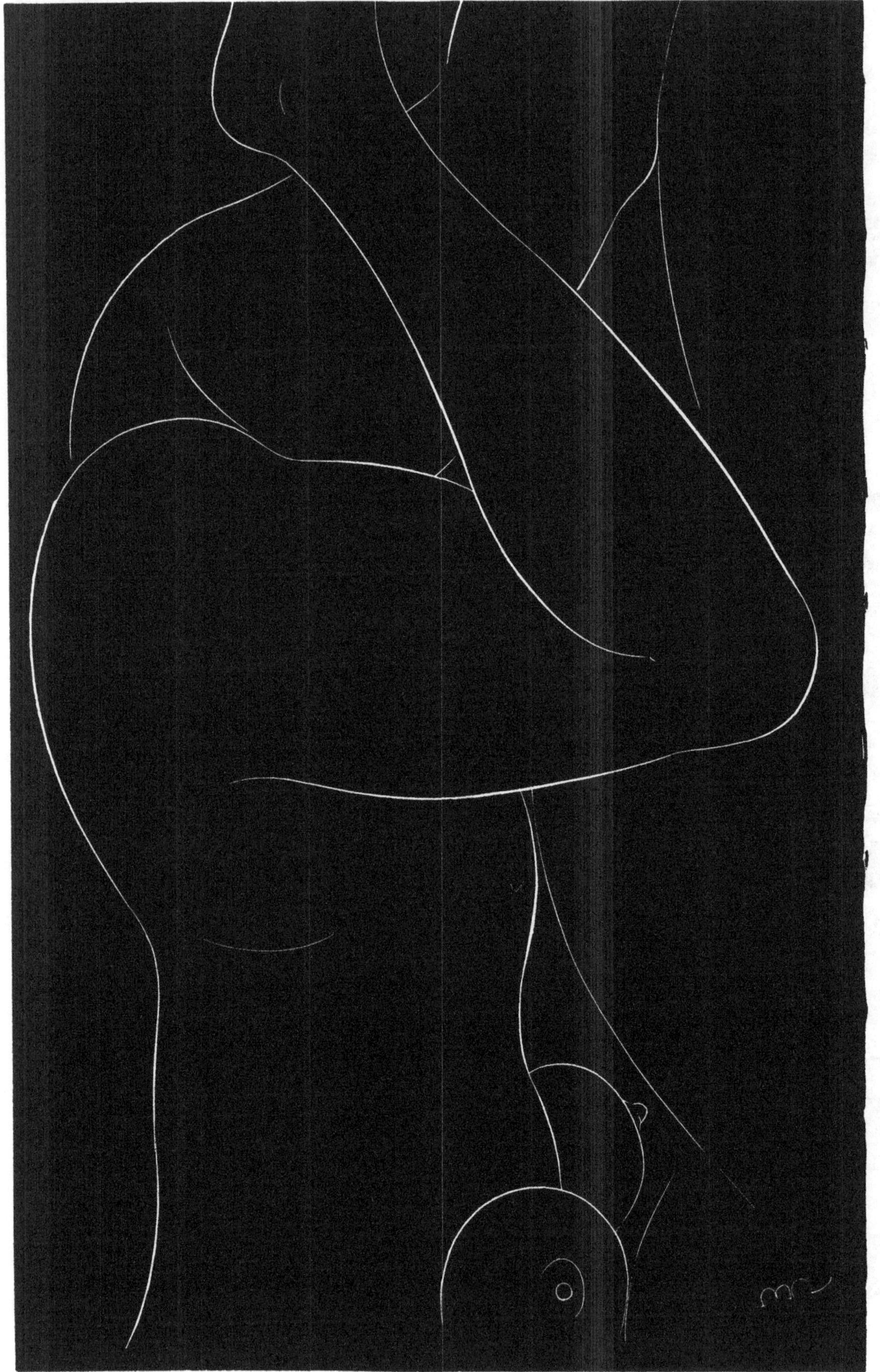

176 Female Nude, Lying
1937
Twenty-five Nudes

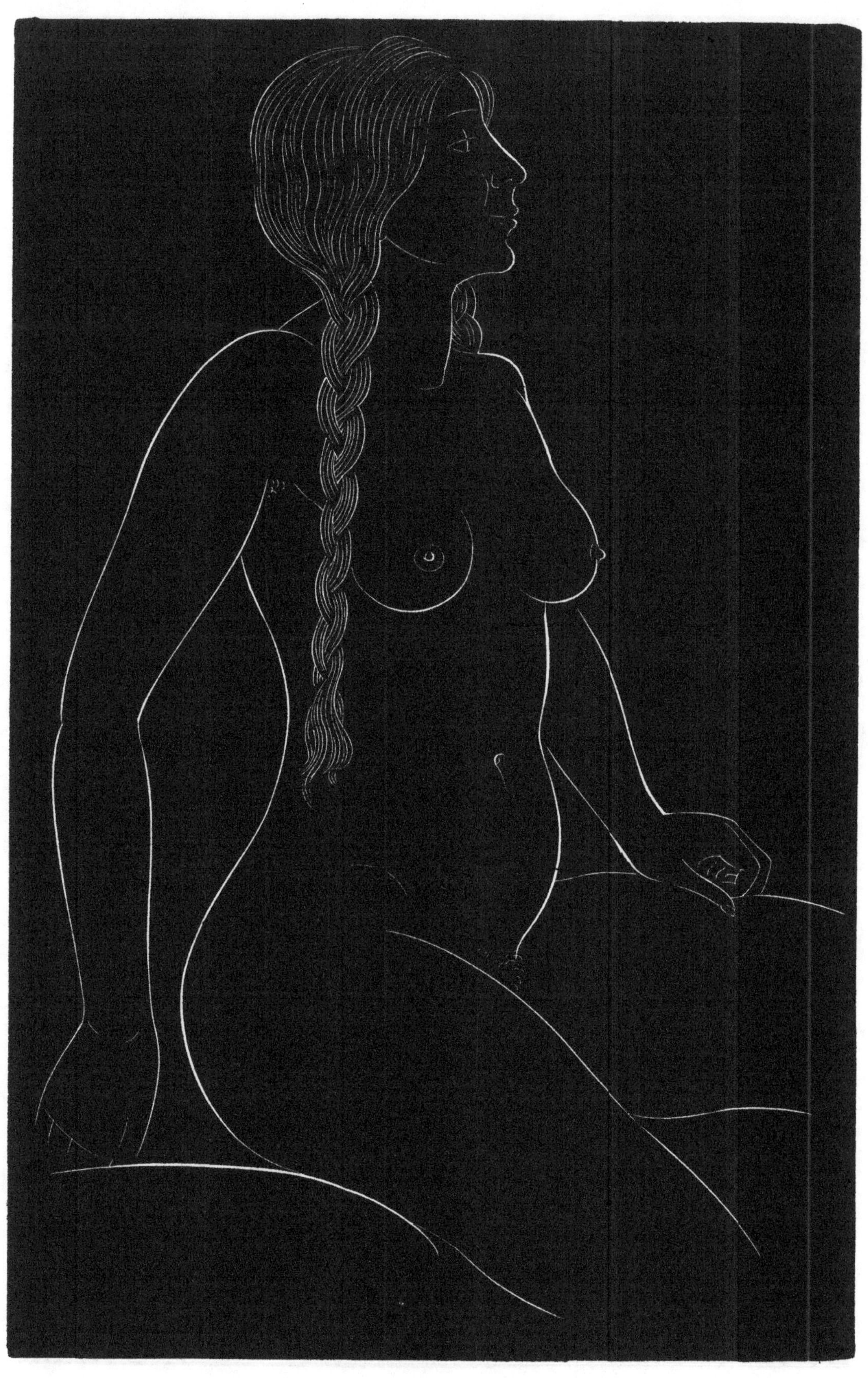

177 Female Nude, Seated
1937
Twenty-five Nudes

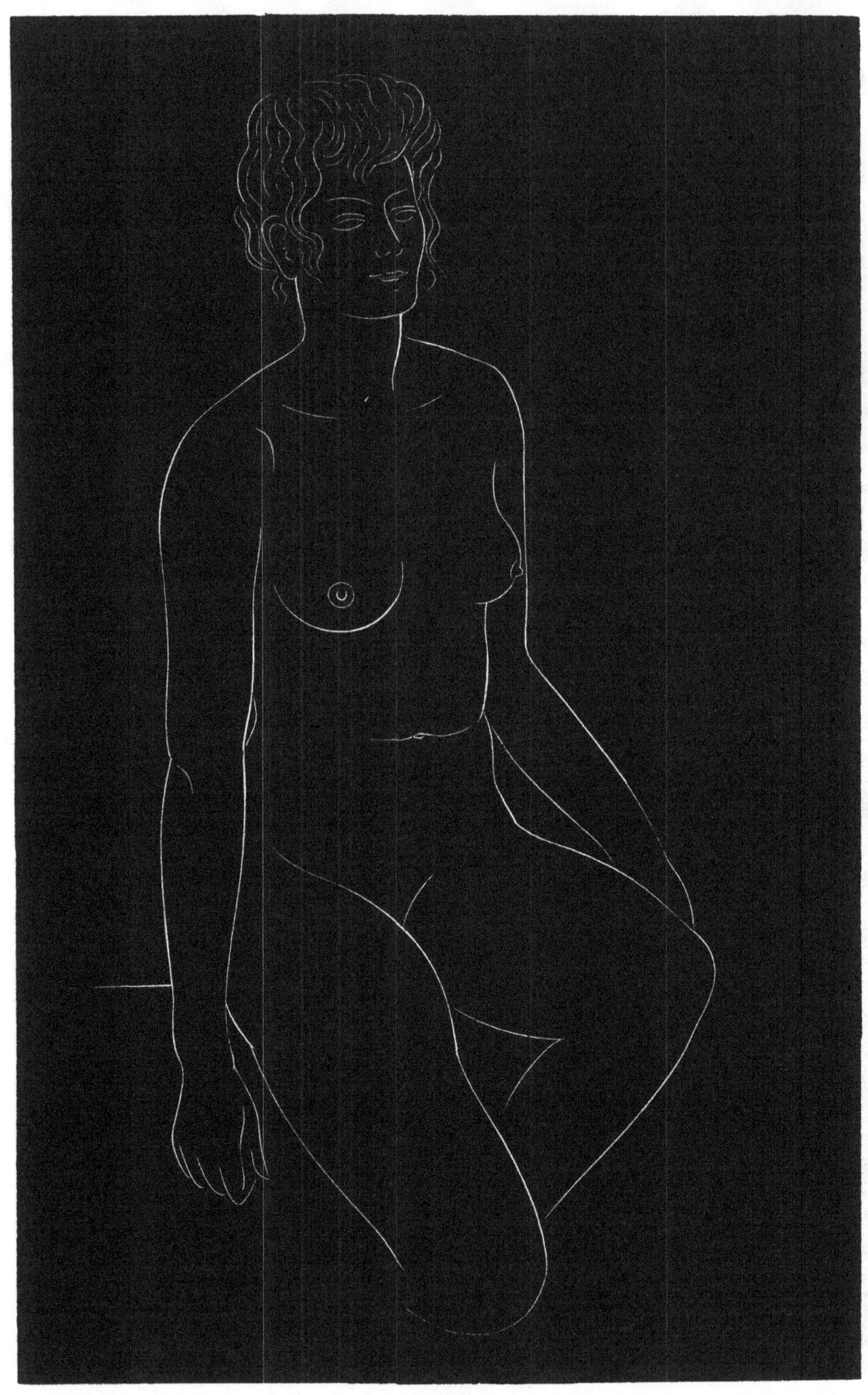

178 Female Nude, Seated
1937
Twenty-five Nudes

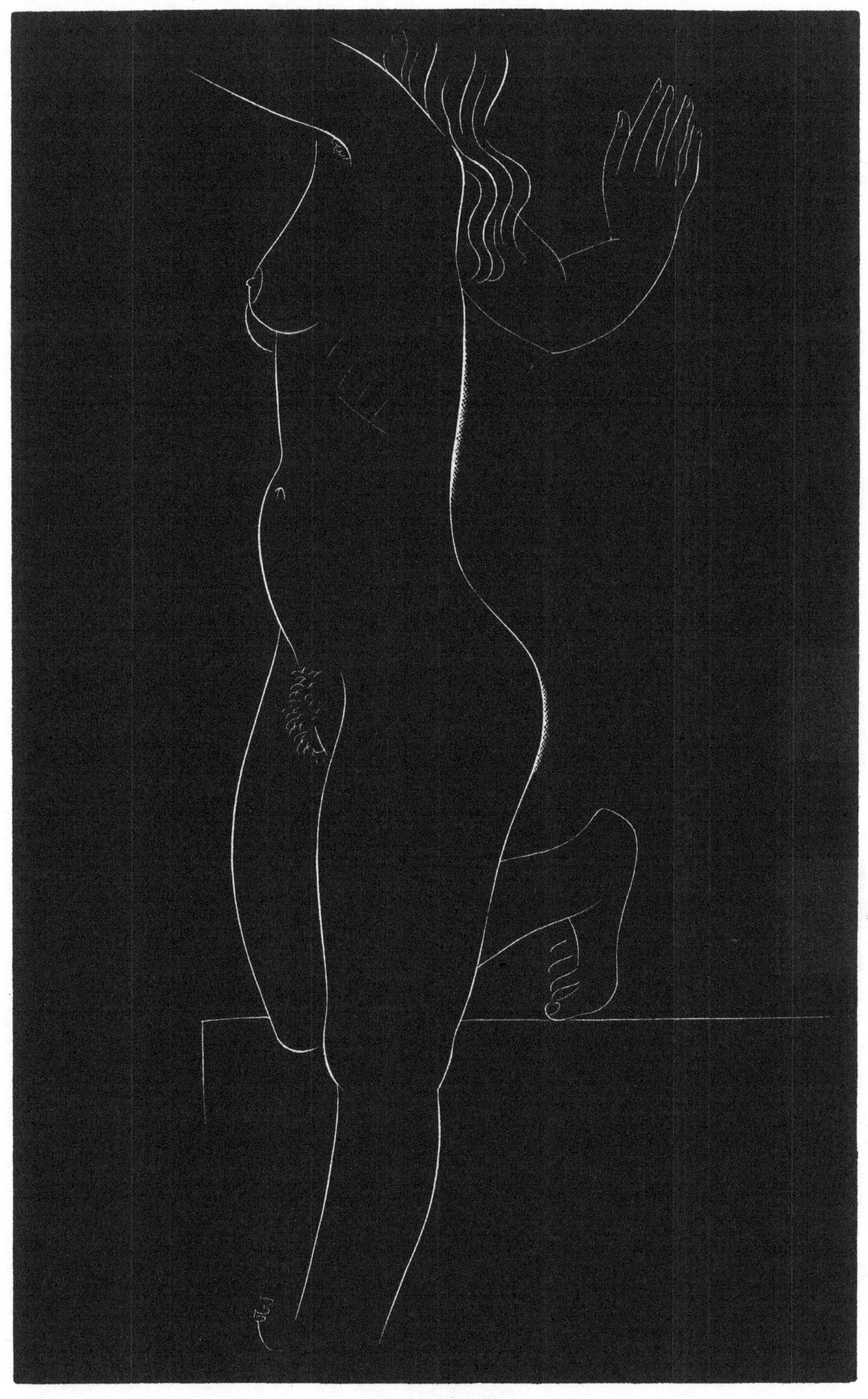

179 Female Nude, Seated
1937
Twenty-five Nudes

THE TRAVELS
OF FATHER JEAN
AMONG THE HURONS
CRIBED BY HIMSELF
ED FROM THE FRENCH

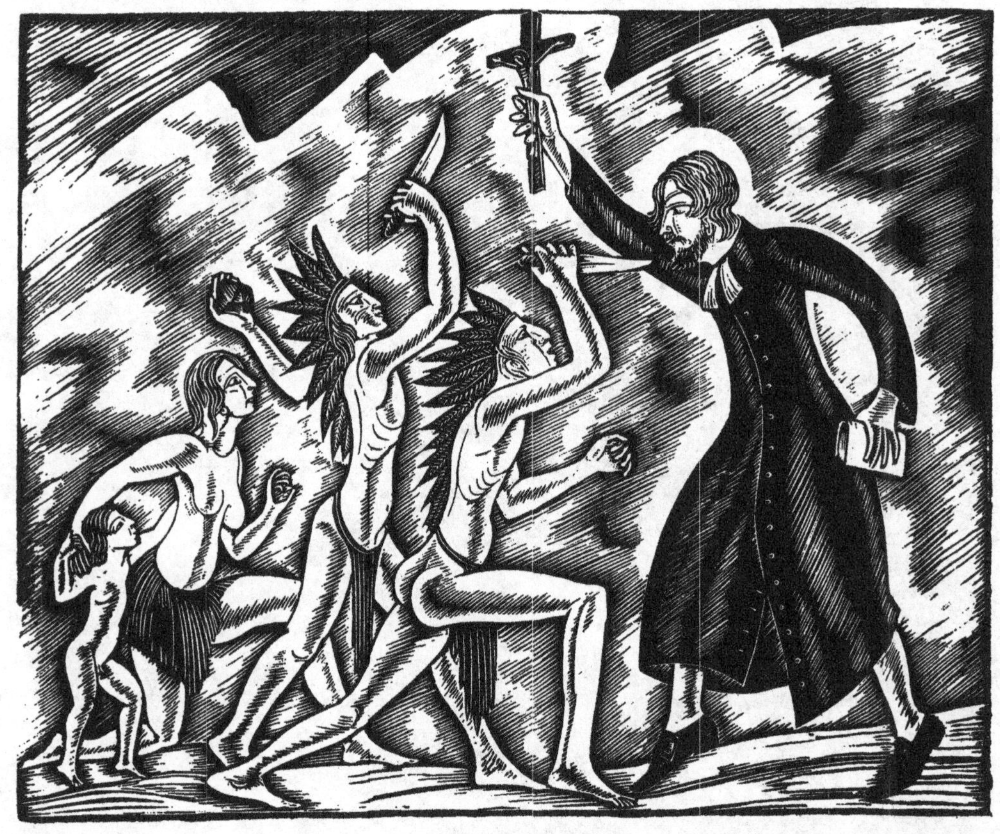

THE GOLDEN COCKEREL

180 The Attack
1938
The Travels & Sufferings of Father Jean de Brébeuf
[lettering engraved by Ralph Beedham]

&SUFFERINGS
DE BRÉBEUF +
OF CANADA AS DES-
EDITED &TRANSLAT-
AND LATIN BY THEO-
DORE BESTERMAN

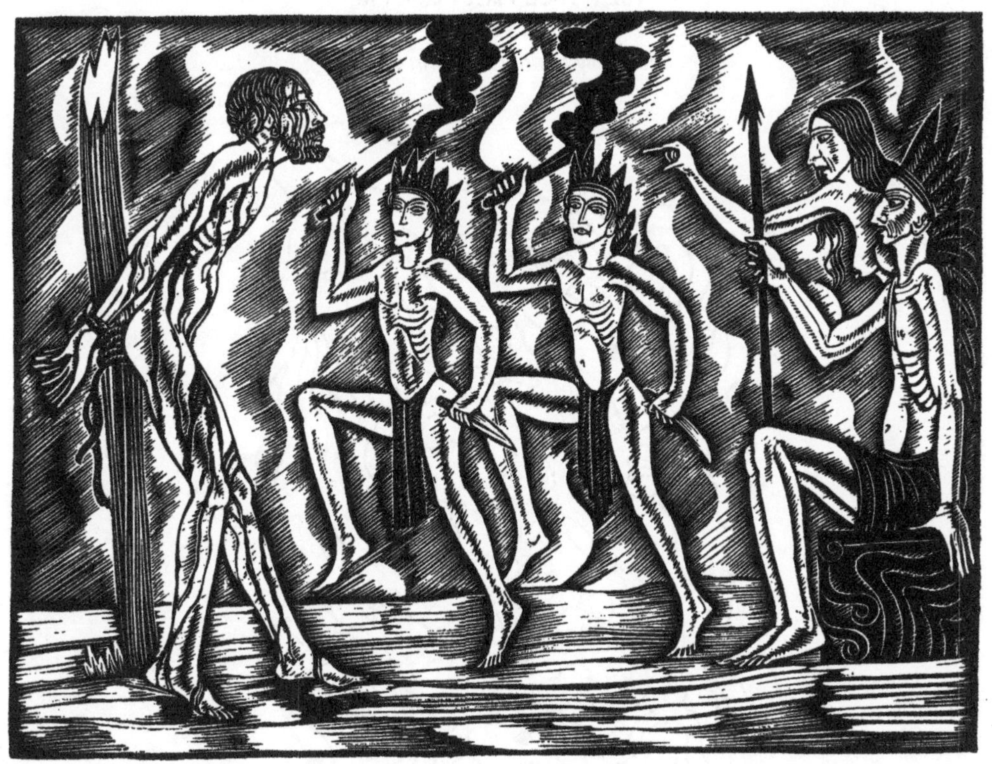

PRESS MCMXXXVIII

181 The Martyrdom
1938
The Travels & Sufferings of Father Jean de Brébeuf
[lettering engraved by Ralph Beedham]

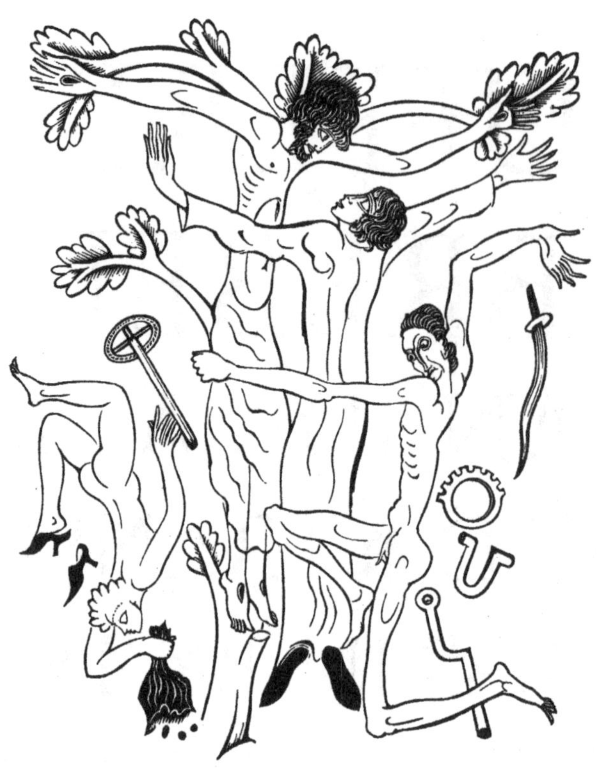

182 Thou Hast Made Me
1938
The Holy Sonnets of John Donne

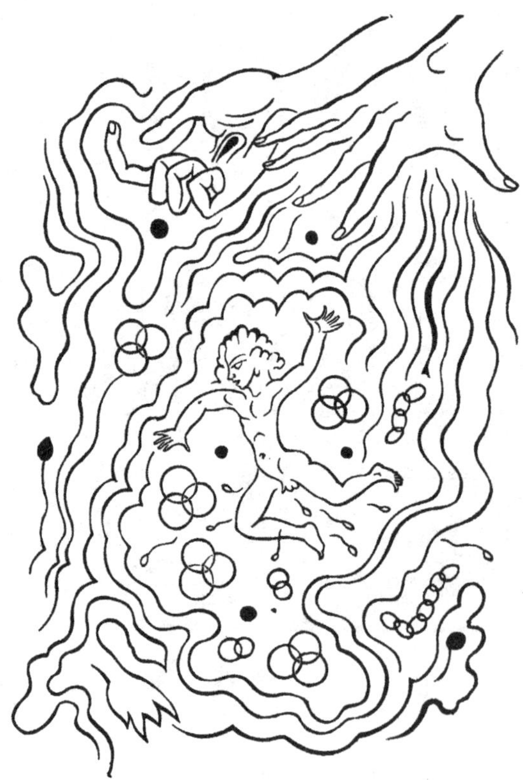

183 I Am a Little World
1938
The Holy Sonnets of John Donne

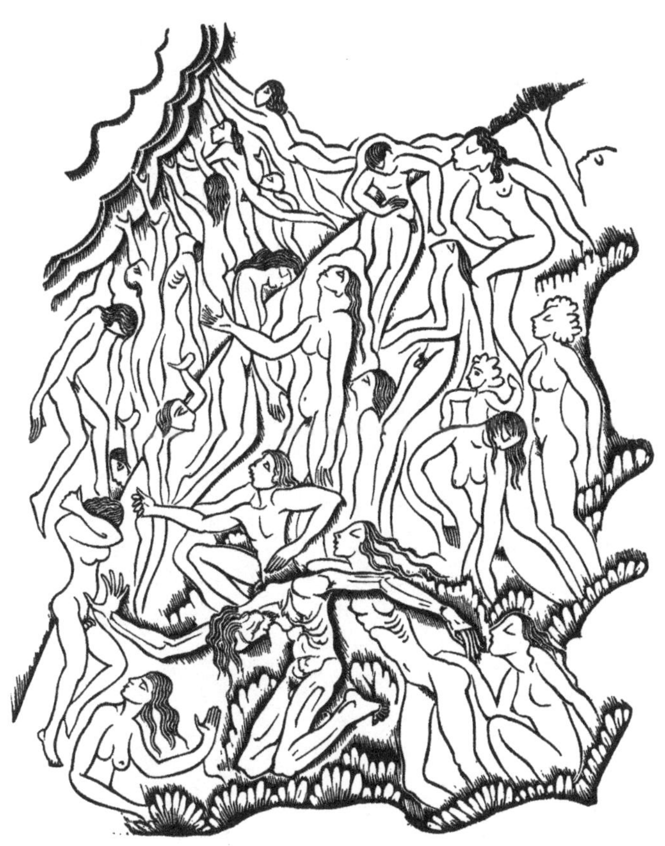

184 At the Round Earth's Imagin'd Corners
1938
The Holy Sonnets of John Donne

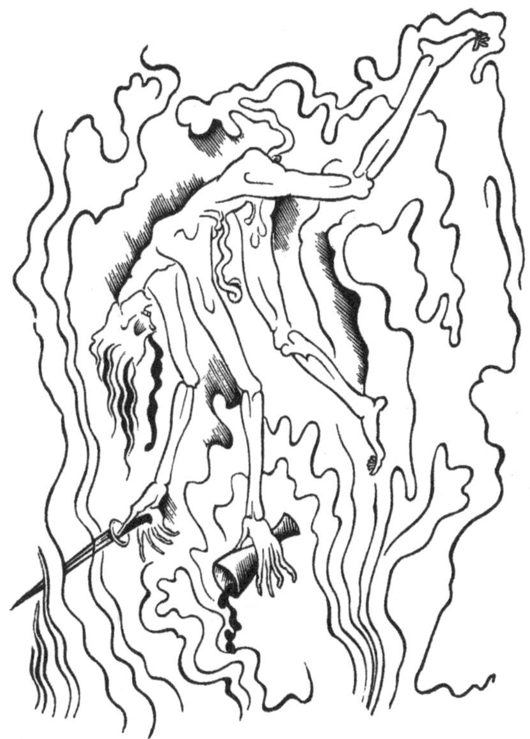

185 Death Be Not Proud
1938
The Holy Sonnets of John Donne

THE GAME

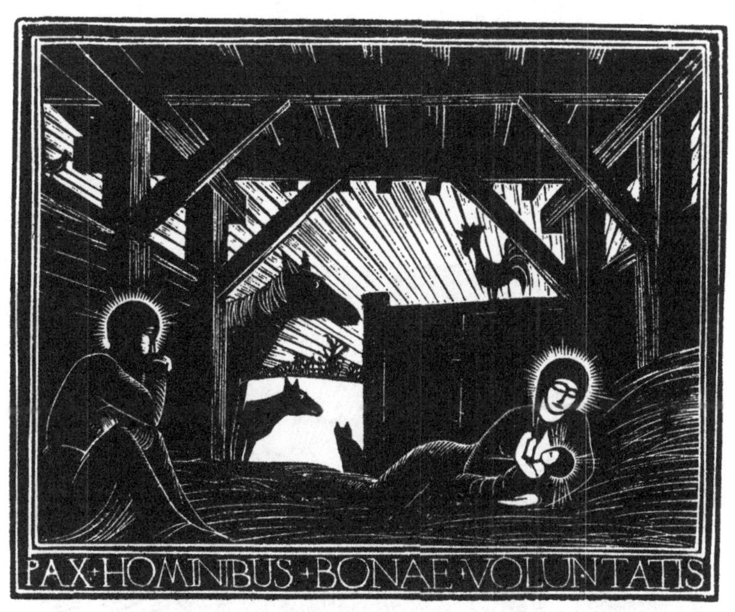

186 Christmas Gifts: Dawn
1916
The Game, Vol. I, No. 2

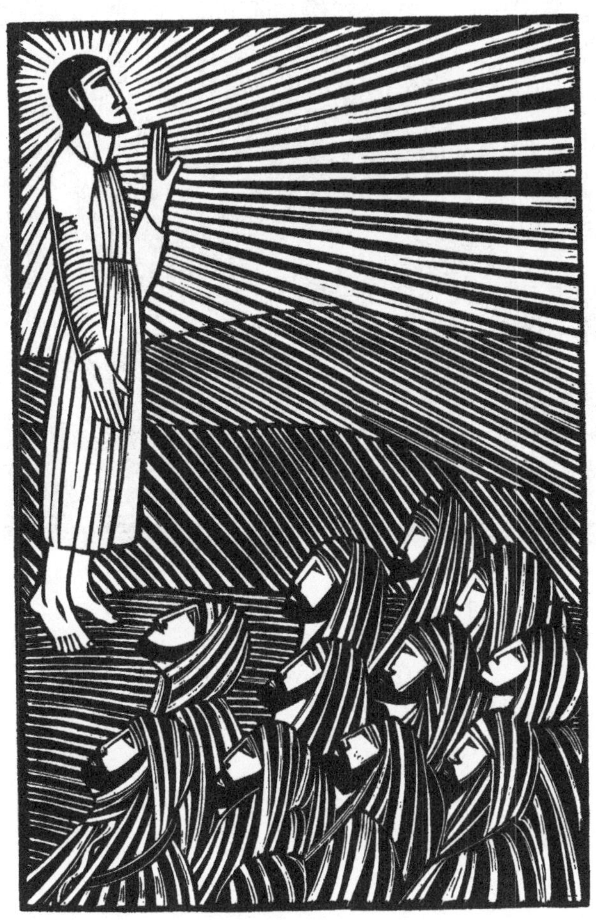

187 Ascension
1918
The Game, Vol. II, No. 2

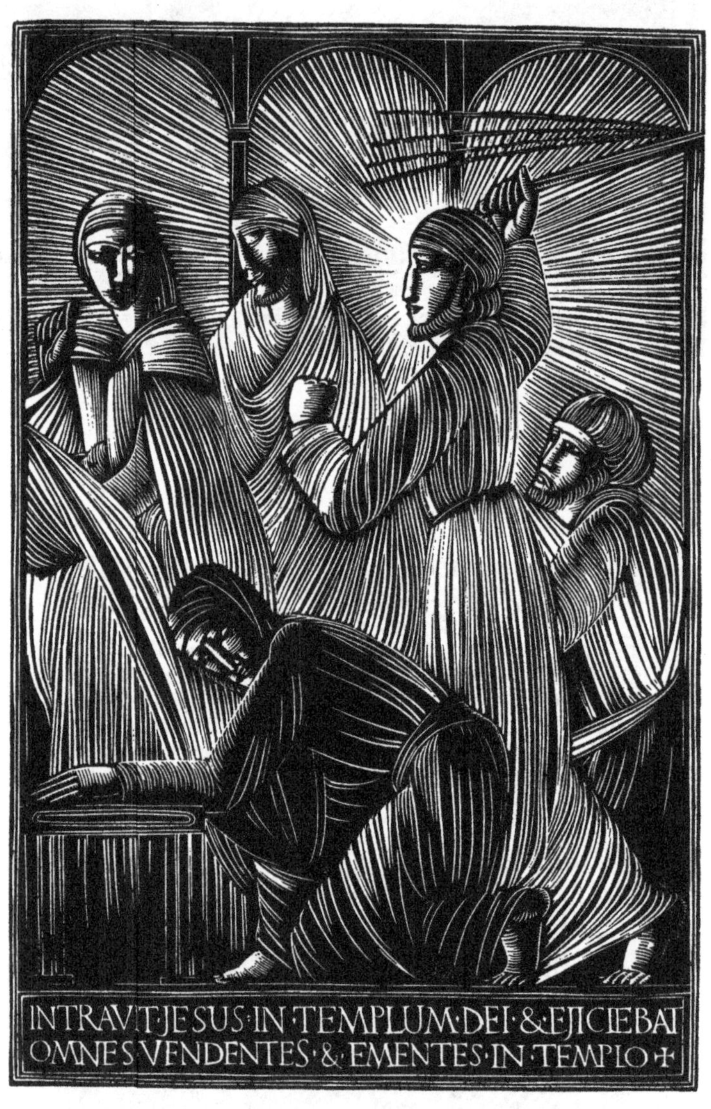

188 Christ and the Money-Changers
1919
The Game, Vol. III, No. 1

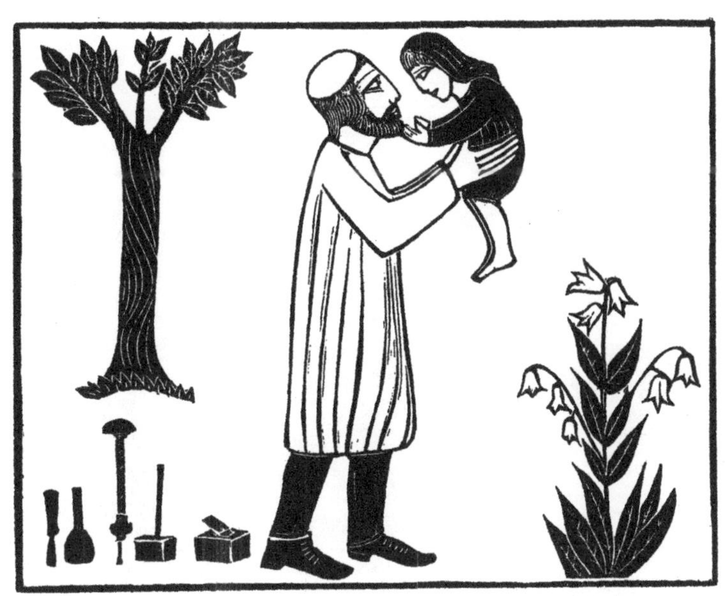

189 St Joseph
1921
The Game, Vol. IV, No. 3

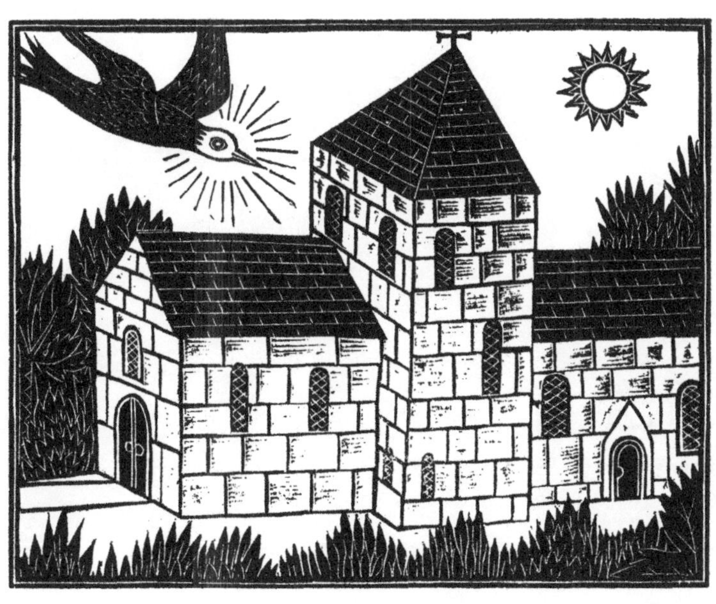

190 The Holy Ghost
The Game, Vol. IV, No. 4

Single Woodcuts & Engravings

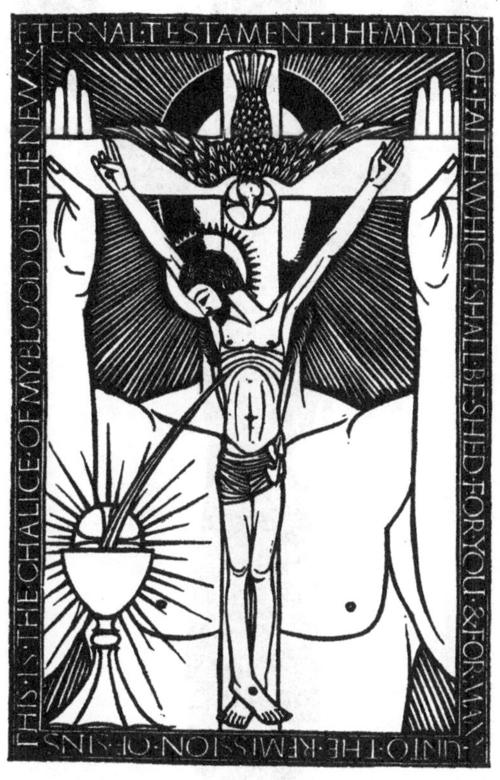

191 The Trinity with Chalice
1914

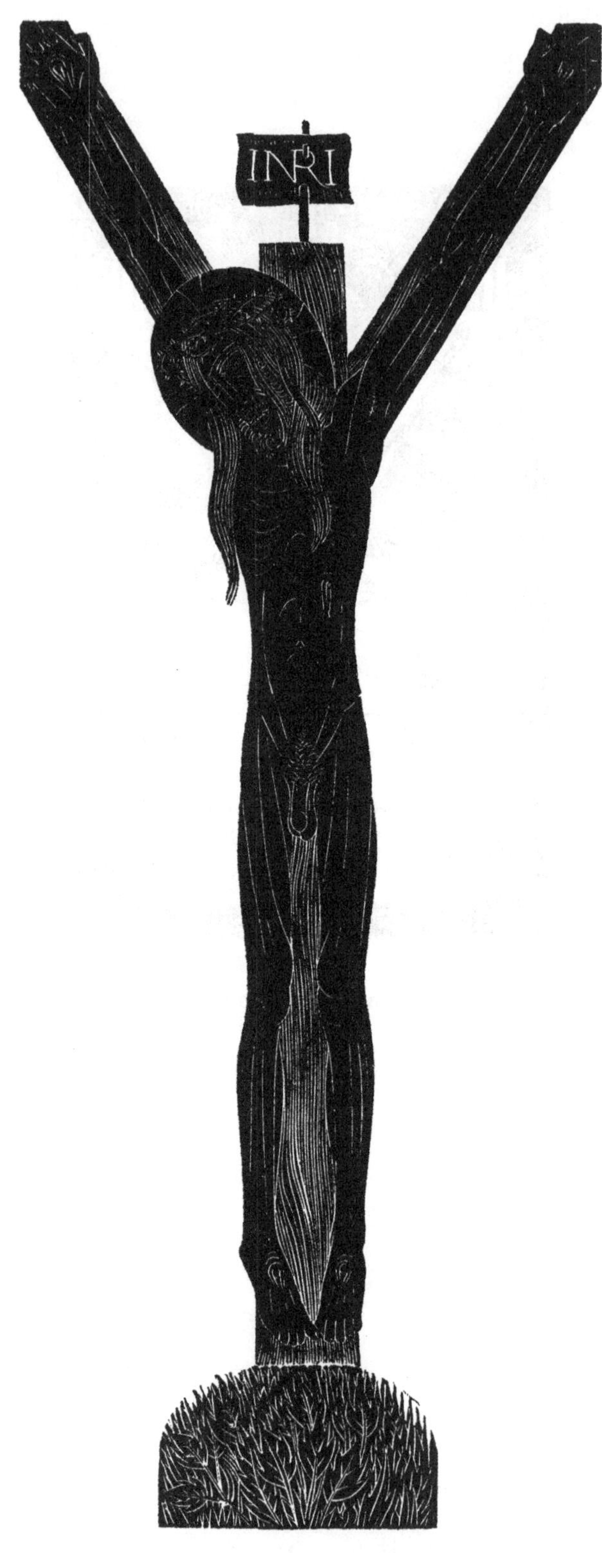

192 Crucifix with Crown of Thorns
(late state)
1922

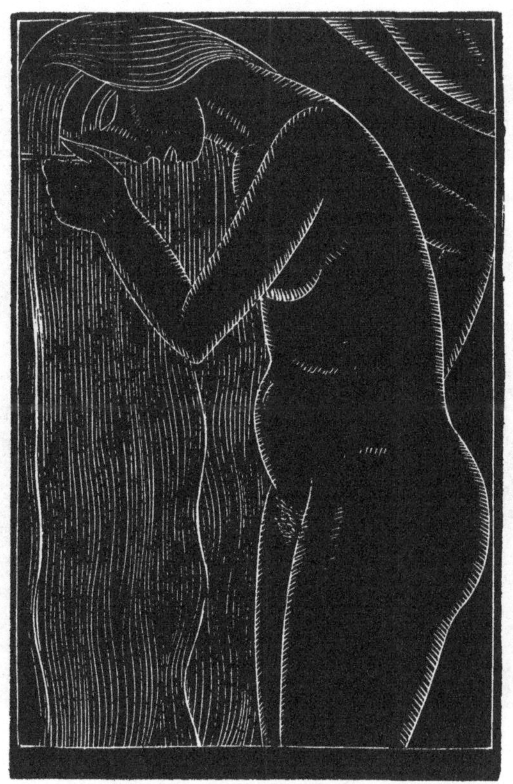

193 Hair Combing
(Petra, artist's daughter)
1922

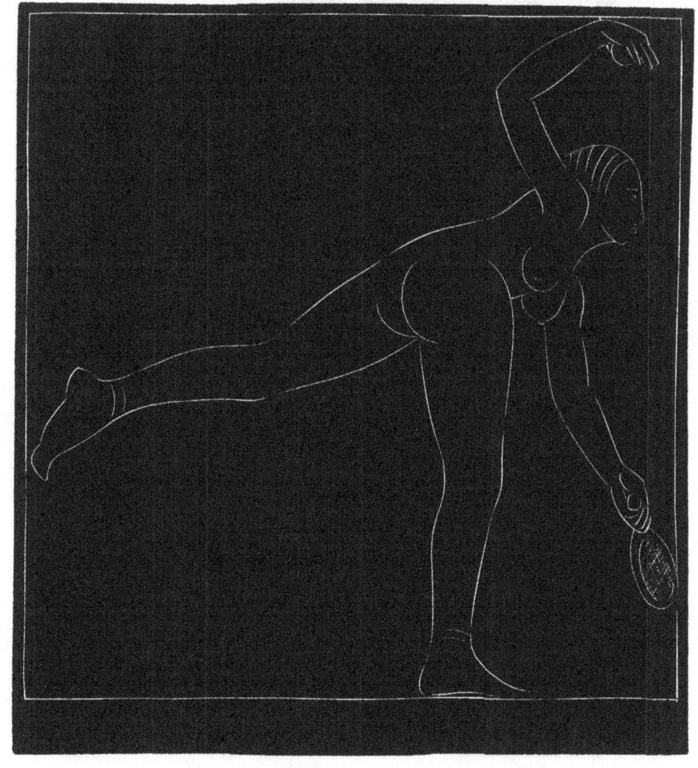

194 The Tennis Player
1923

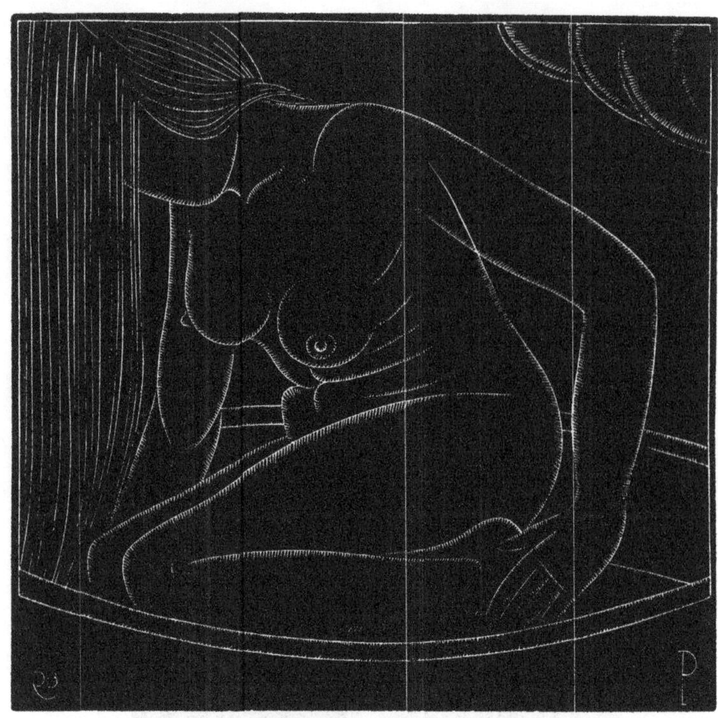

195 Girl in Bath, II (Petra)
1923

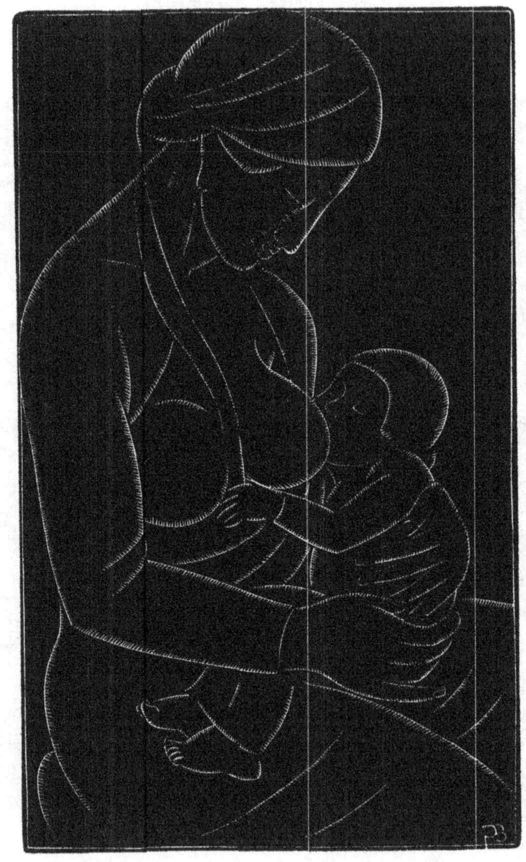

196 Mother and Child
1923

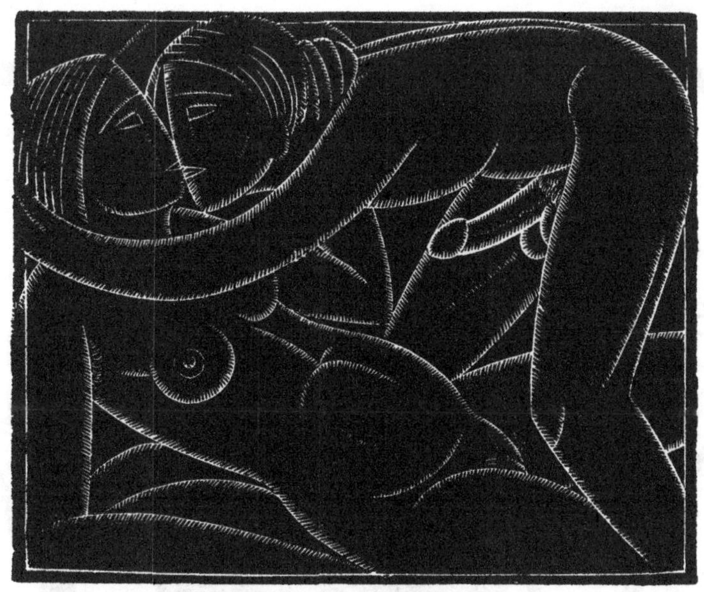

197 Lovers
(first state)
1924

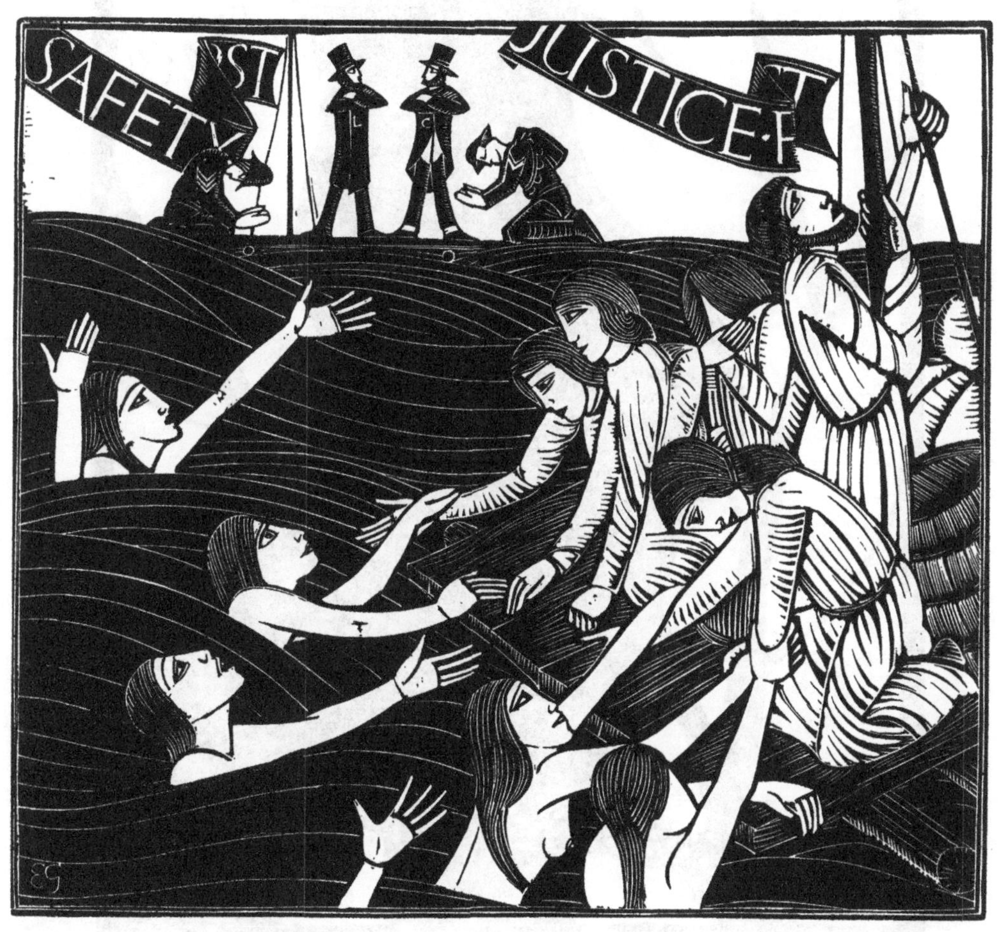

198 Safety First
1924
For 'The Labour Woman'

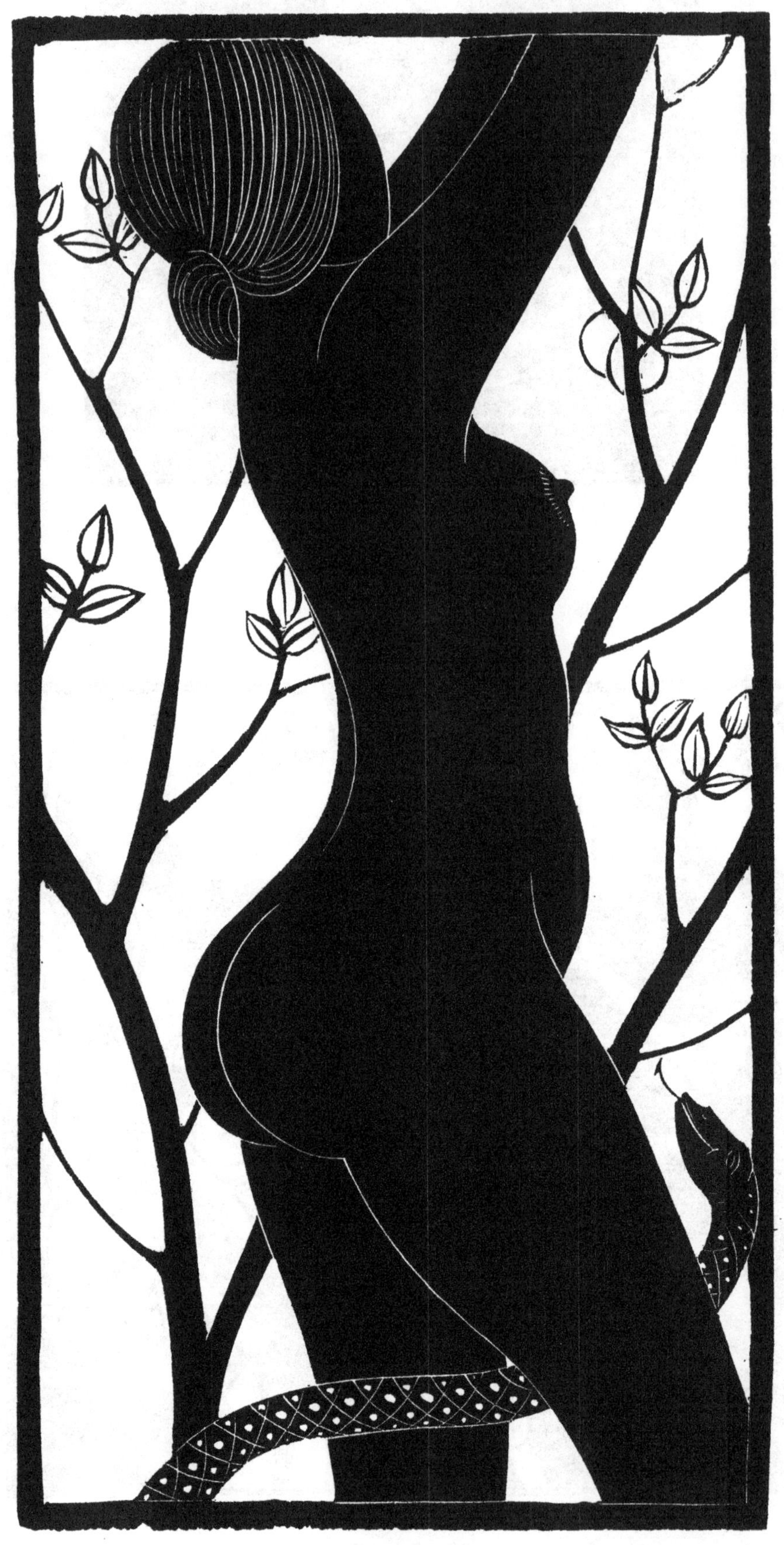

199 Eve
1926

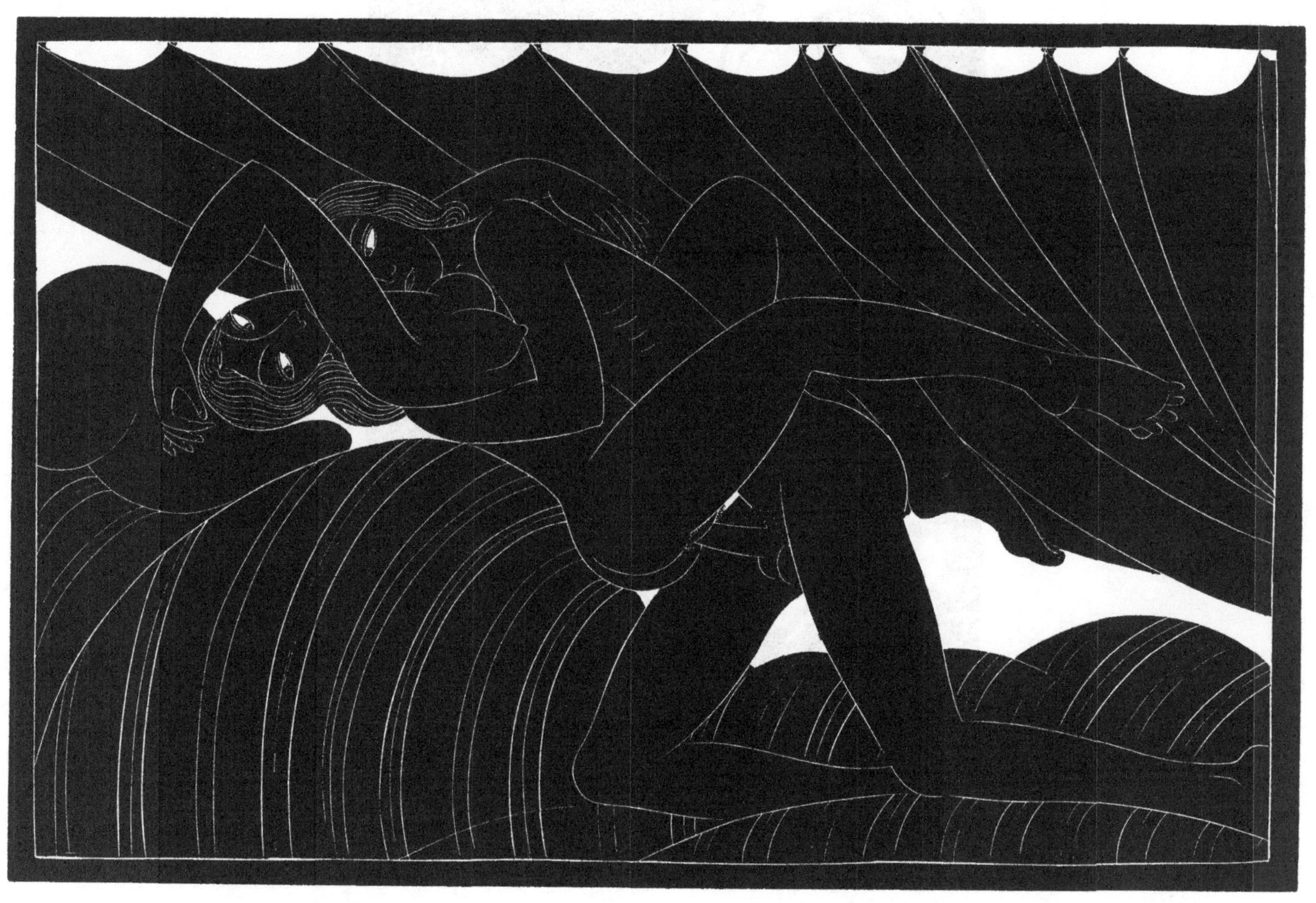

200 Lovers in Tent
1929

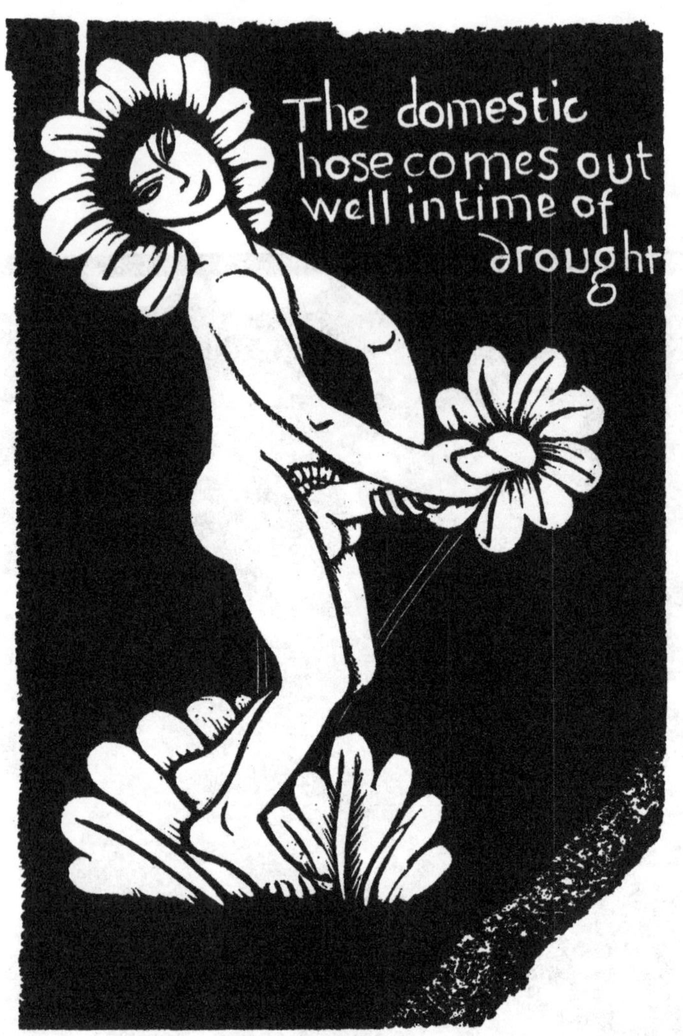

201 The Domestic Hose
(woodcut)
1929

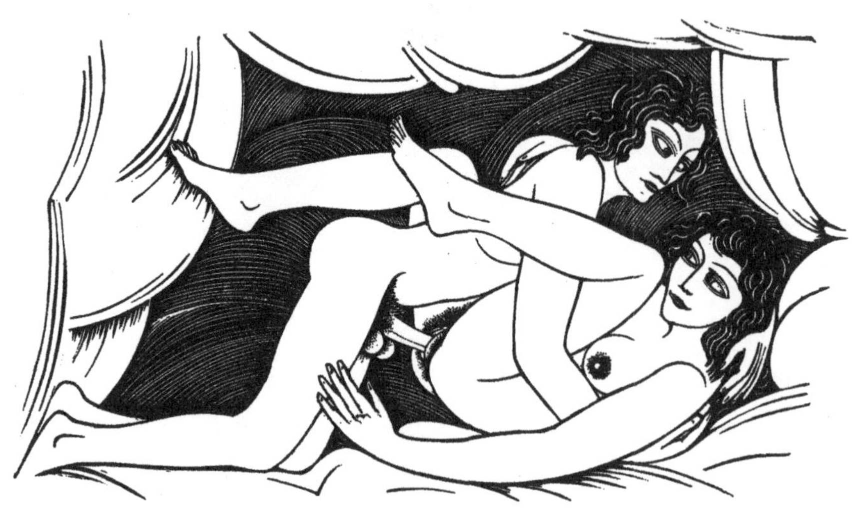

202 Lovers, The Raised Bottom
1934

Book-Plates

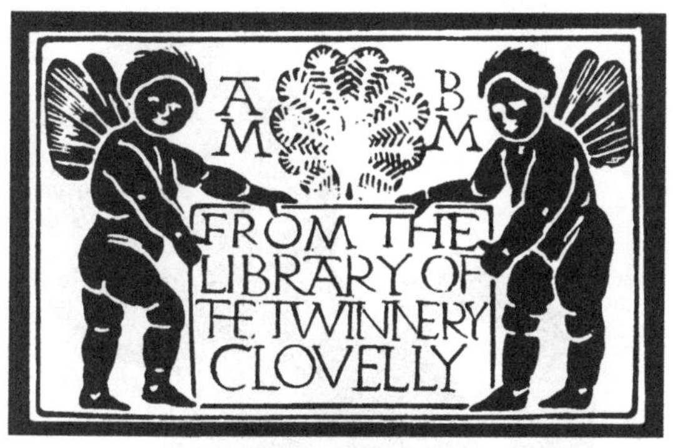

203 Book-Plate
1908

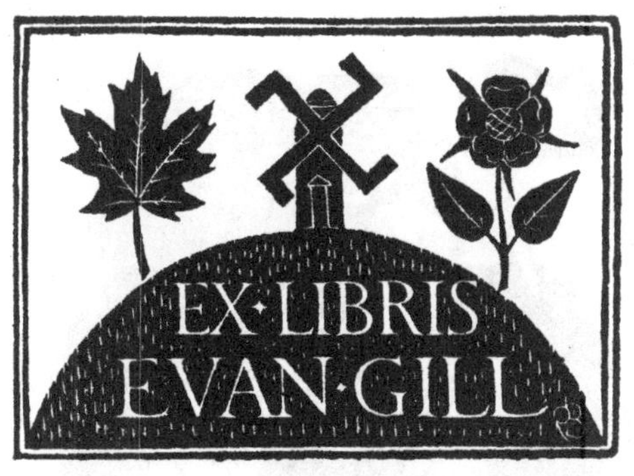

204 Book-Plate of Evan R. Gill
(later state)
1920

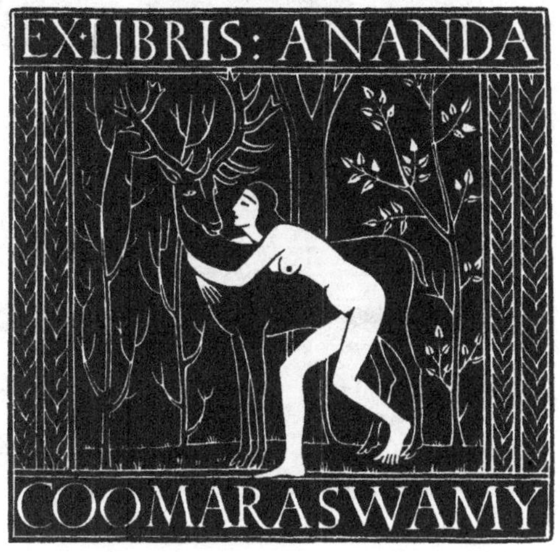

205 Girl with Deer
1920

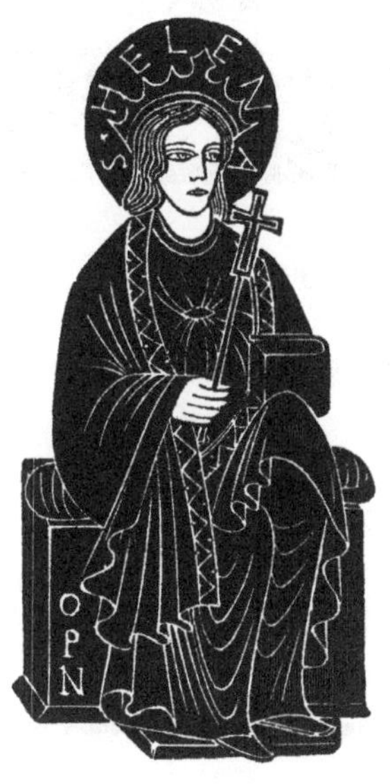

206 St Helena
1922

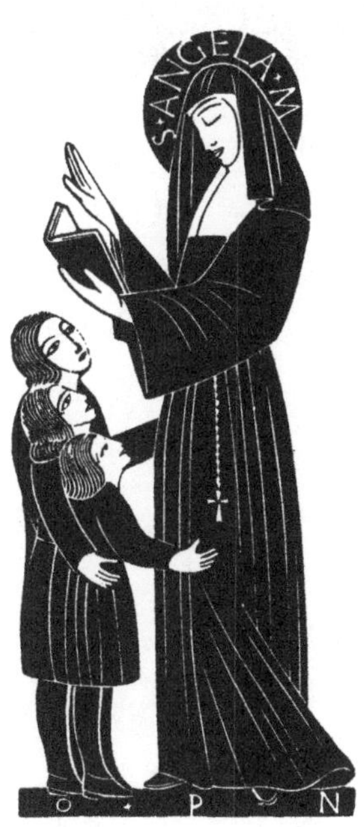

207 St Angela Merici
1922

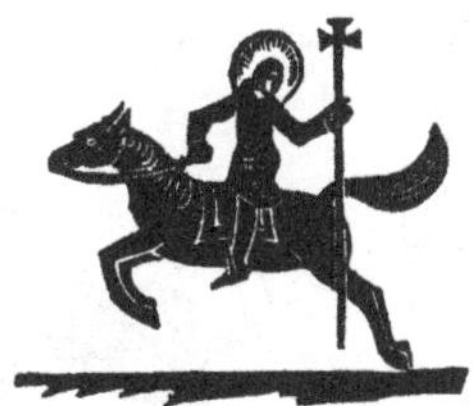

208 St Joan of Arc
1922

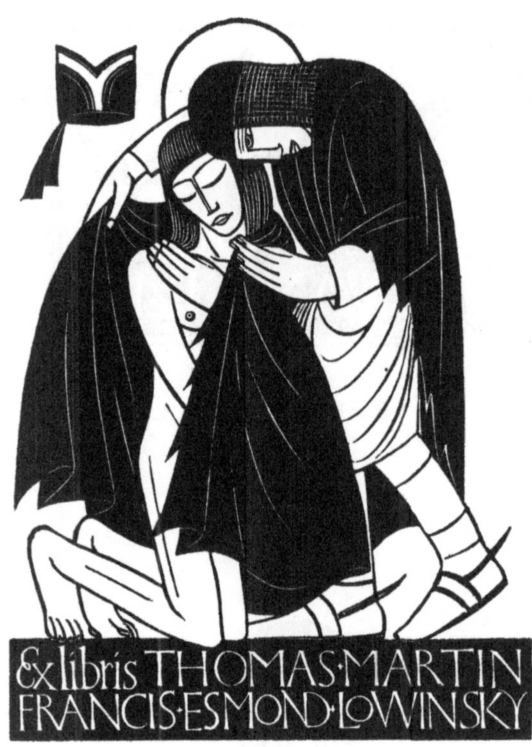

209 St Martin
1922
(after a drawing by David Jones)

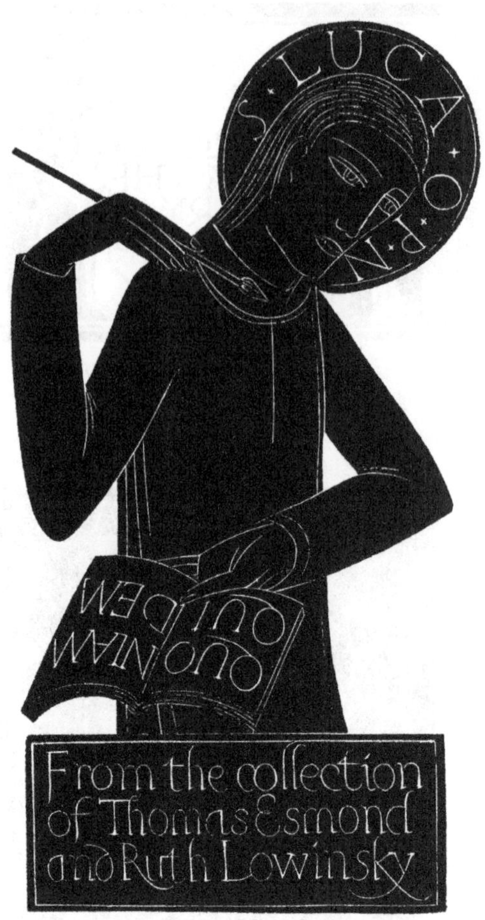

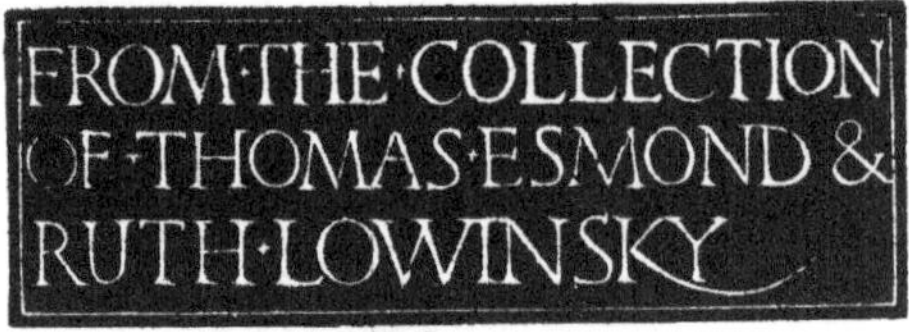

210 St Luke
1922

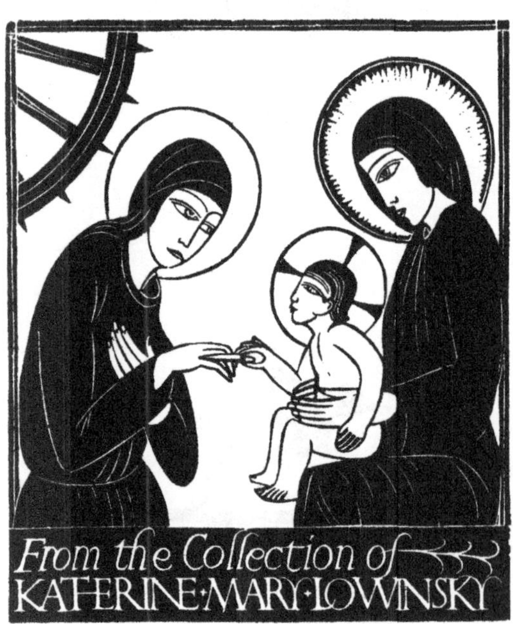

211 Marriage of St Catherine
1922

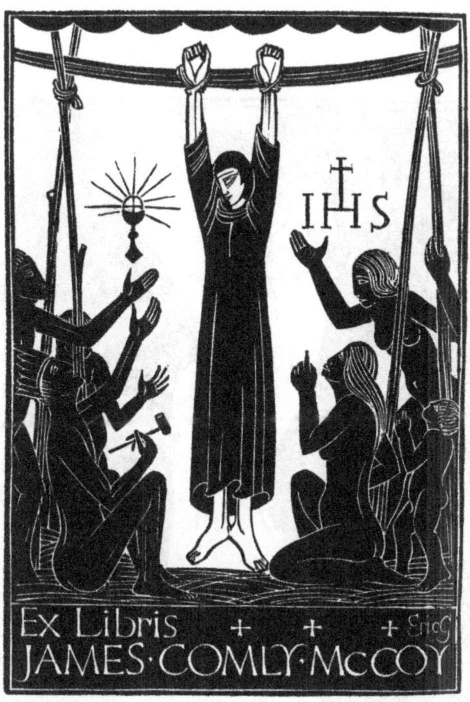

212 Jesuit Martyr
1923
(final state)

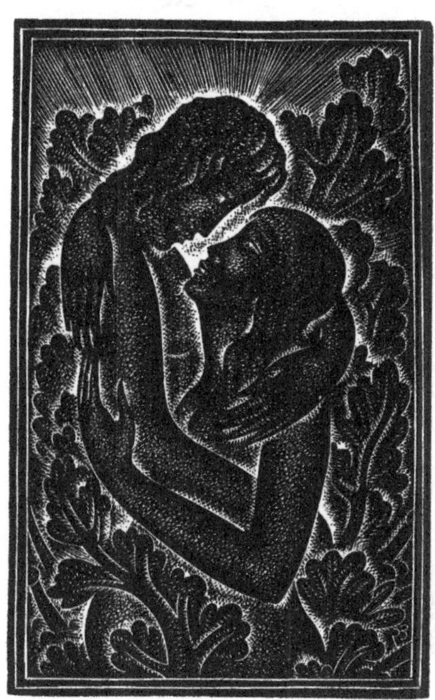

216 Lovers (The Pregnant Wife)
1932

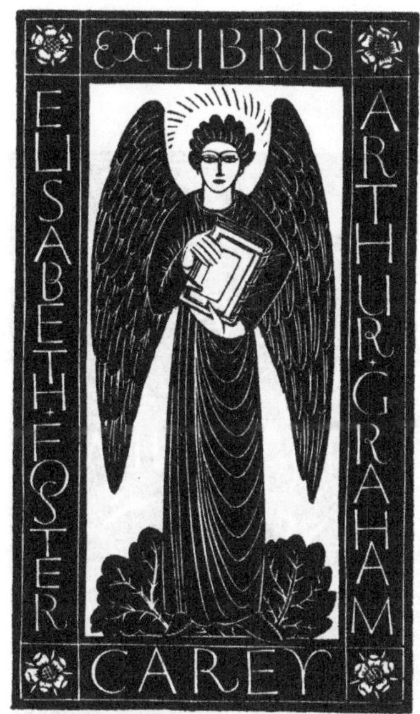

213 Angel Holding a Book
1928

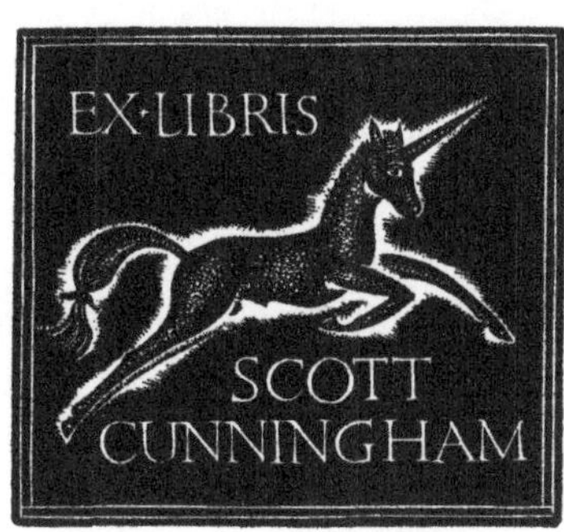

214 Unicorn
1931

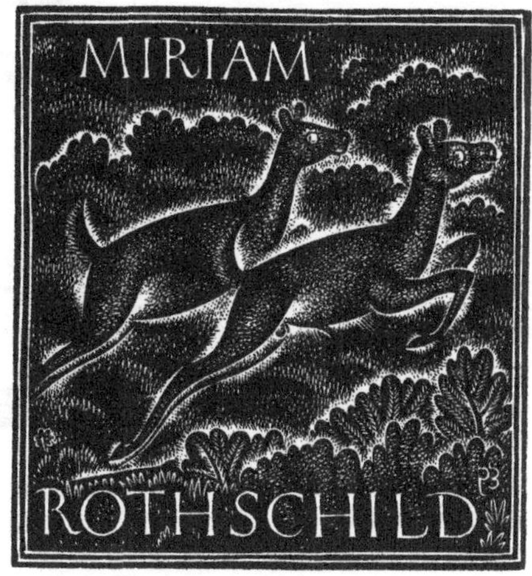

215 Two Deer
1932

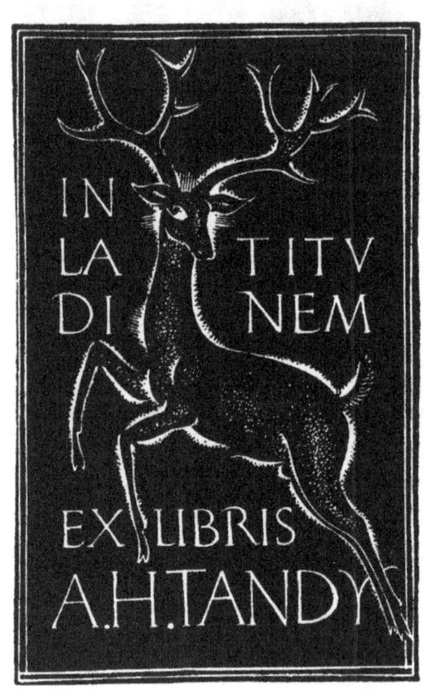

217 Stag
1932

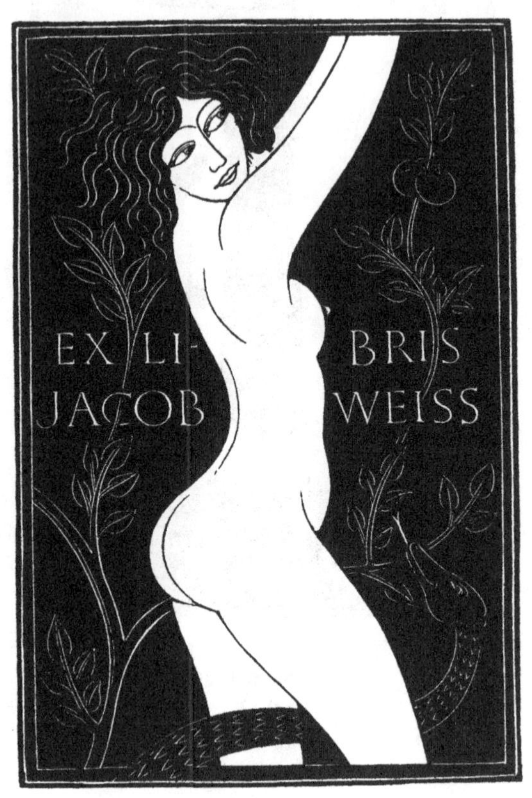

218 Eve
1935

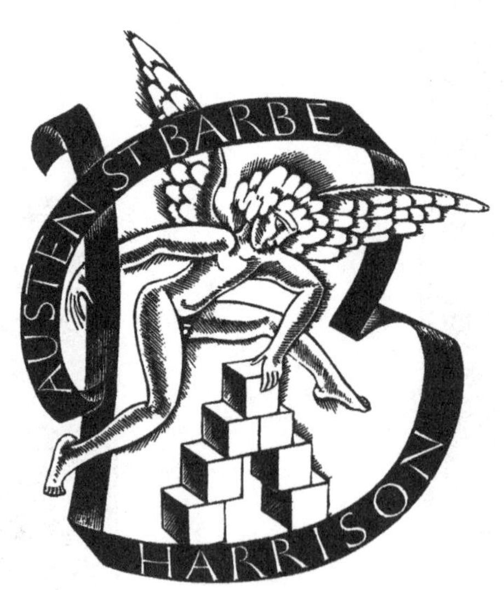

219 Cupid
1935

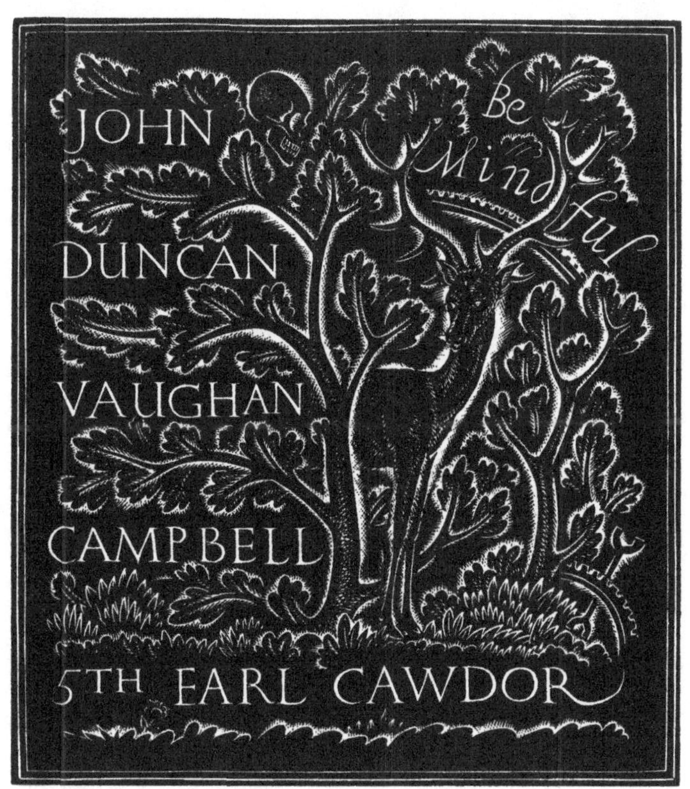

220 Book-Plate
1936

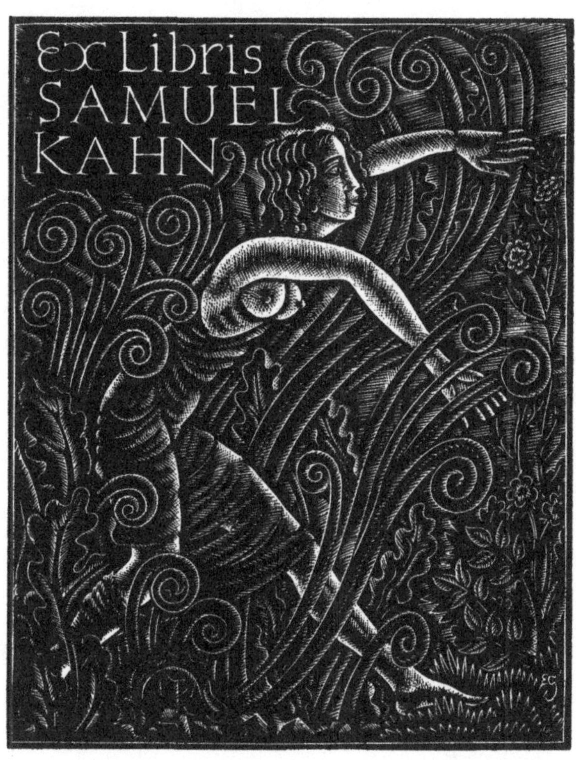

221 Woman Looking through Foliage
1936

Covers & Designs

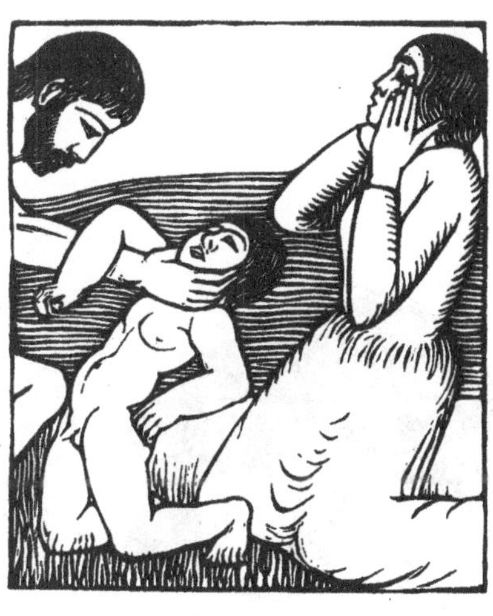

222 The Slaughter of the Innocents
1914

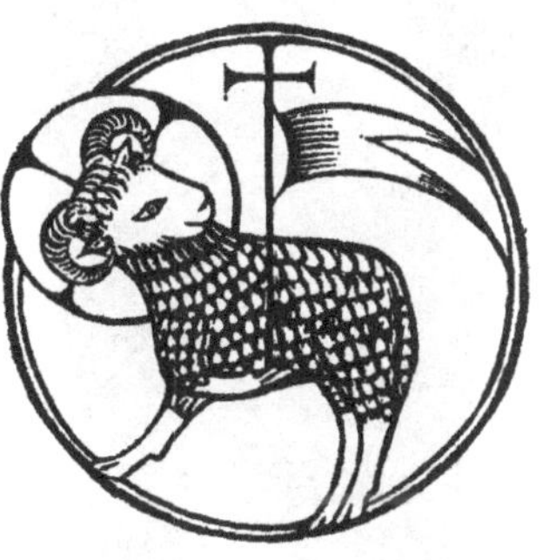

223 Paschal Lamb
1914

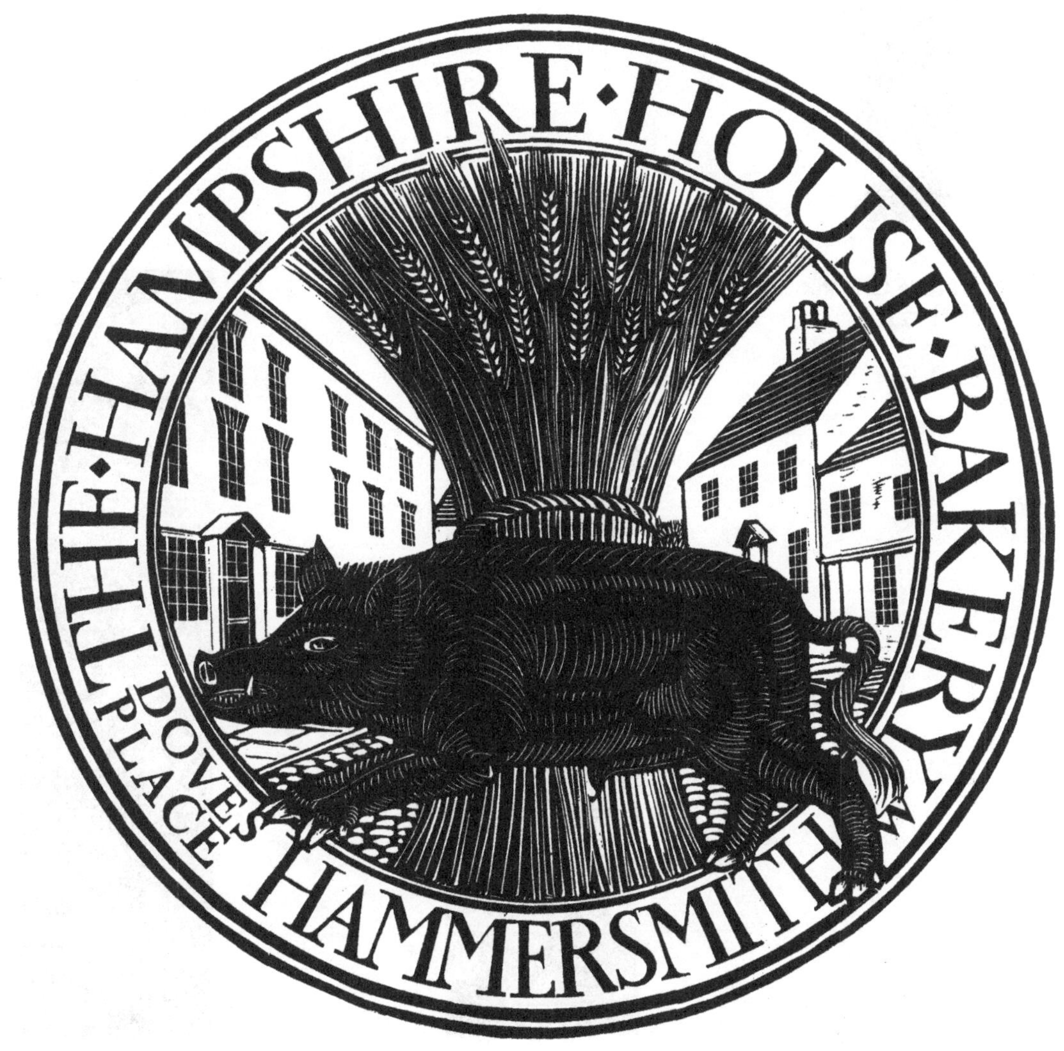

224 Hog and Wheatsheaf
1915

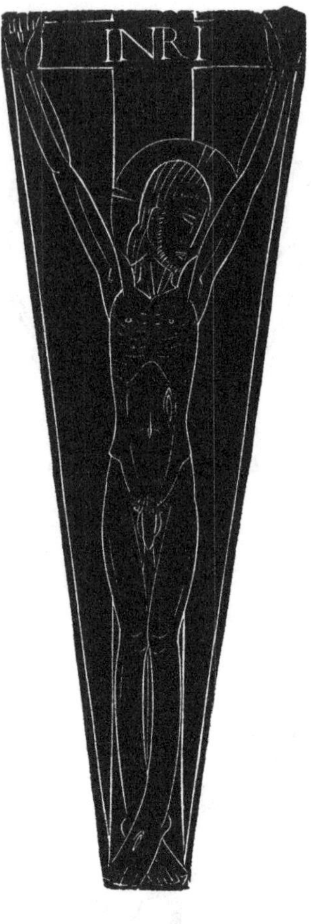

225 Nude Crucifix
1922

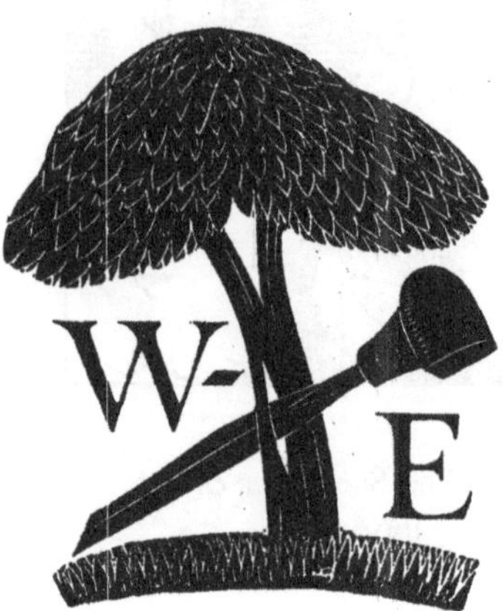

226 Tree and Burin
1921

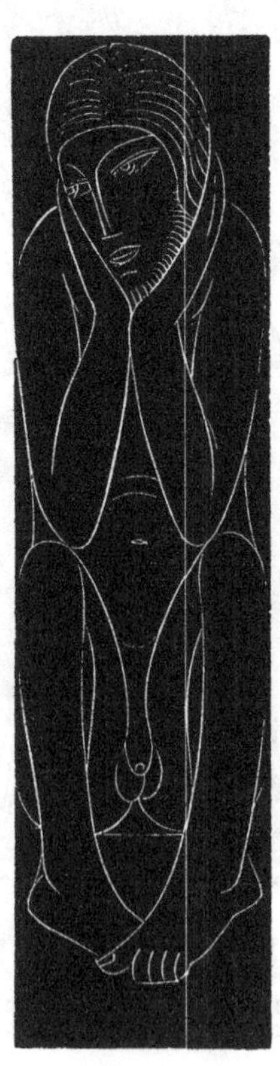

227 Adam
1923

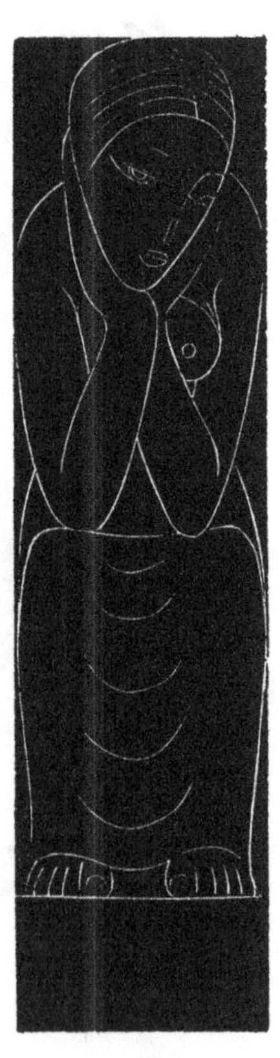

228 Eve
1923

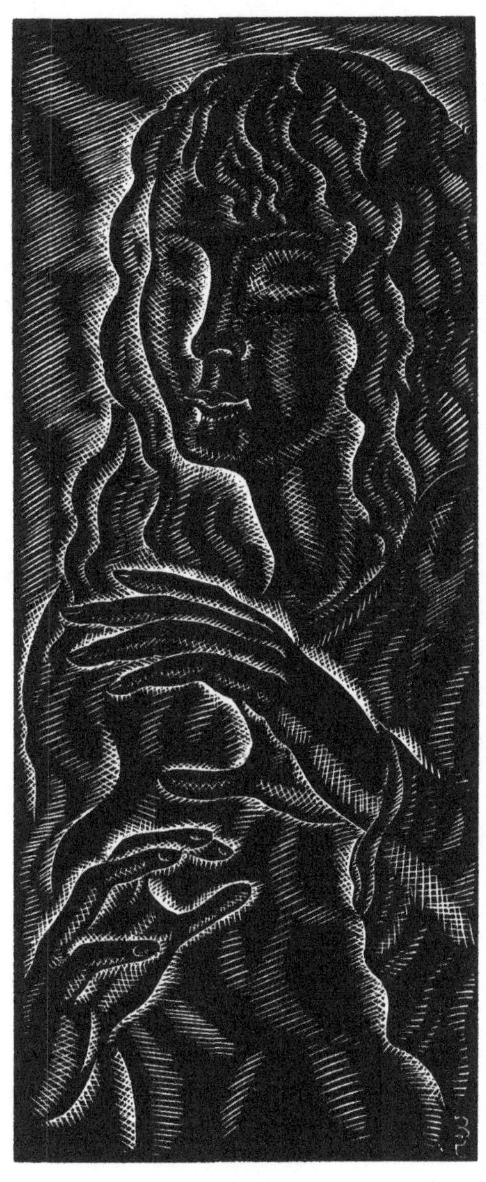

229 Blind Girl
1939

Christmas Cards

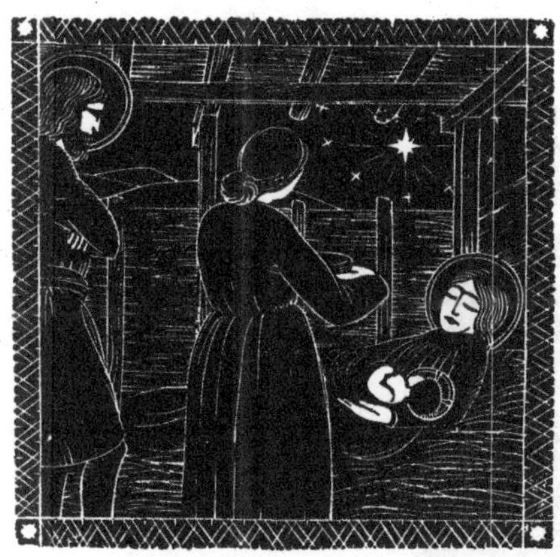

230 Nativity with Midwife, St Joseph Standing
1913

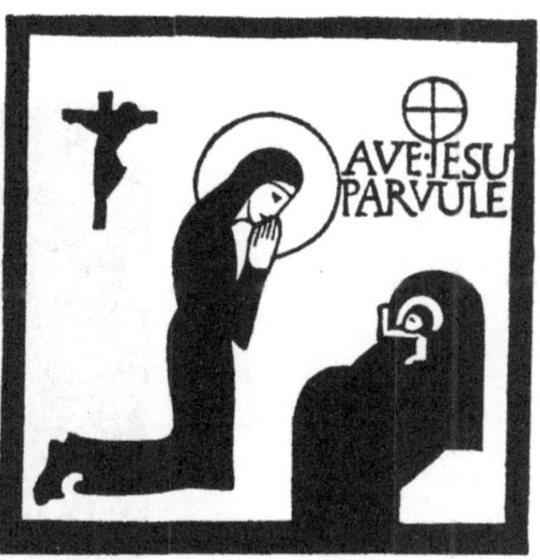

231 Madonna and Child, with Crucifix
1917

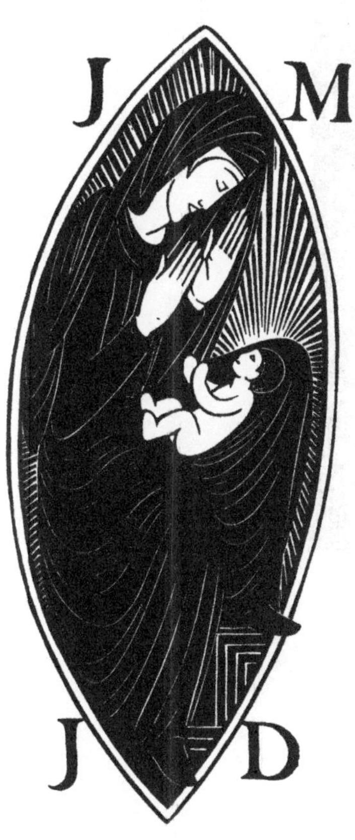

232 Madonna and Child in Vesica
1918

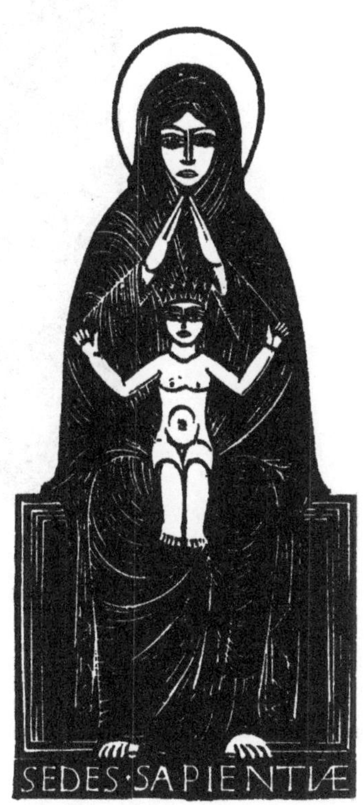

233 Madonna and Child with Arms Outstretched
1922

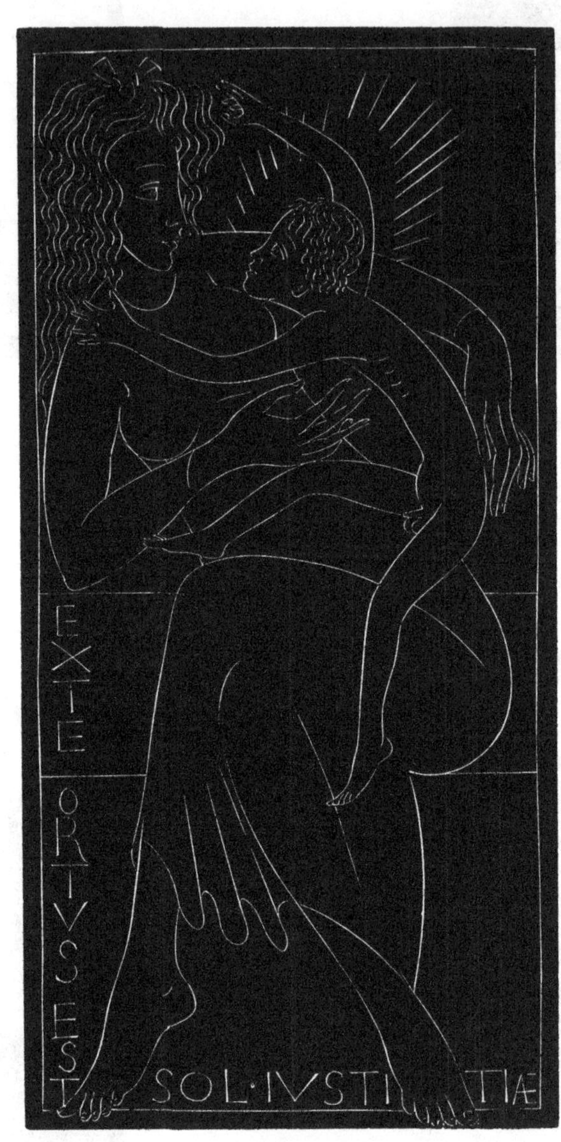

234 Virgin and Child
1931

Pamphlets, Cards & Posters

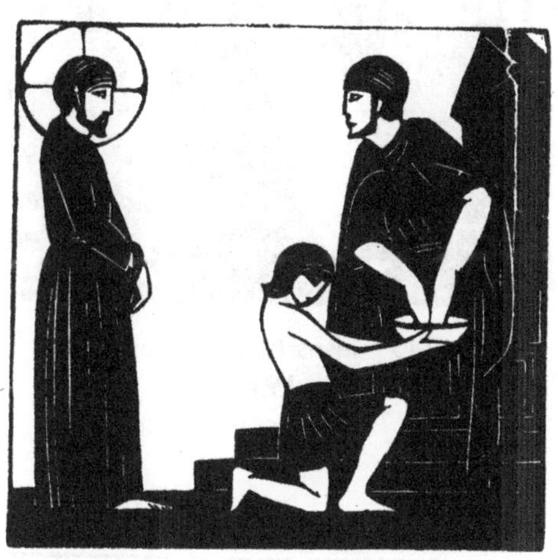

235 Jesus Is Condemned to Death
1917
The Way of the Cross

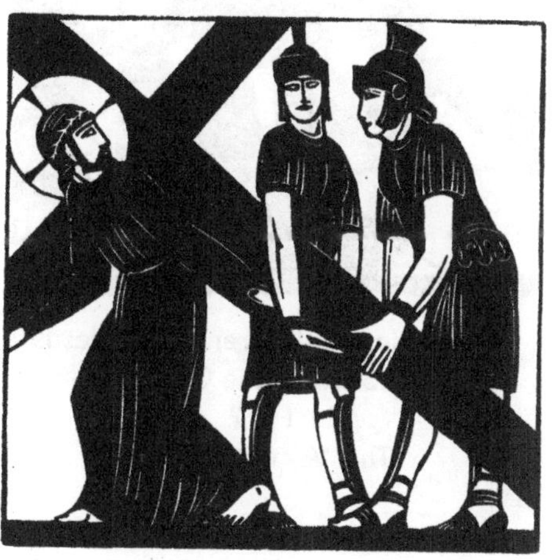

236 Jesus Receives His Cross
1917
The Way of the Cross

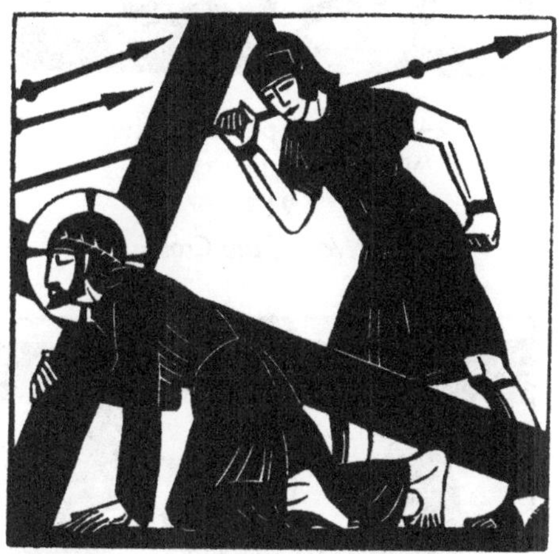

237 Jesus Falls the First Time
1917
The Way of the Cross

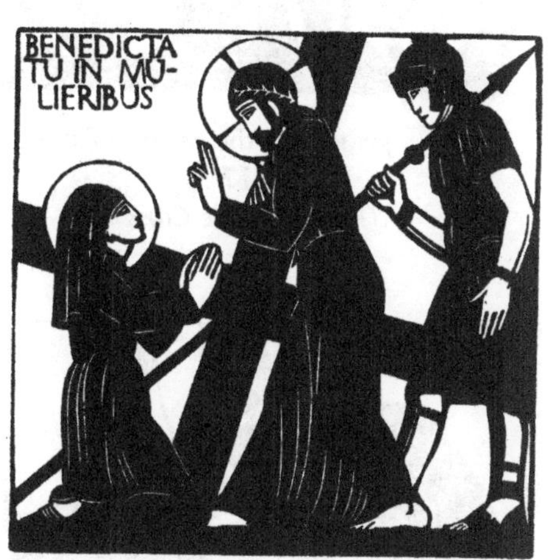

238 Jesus Meets His Mother
1917
The Way of the Cross

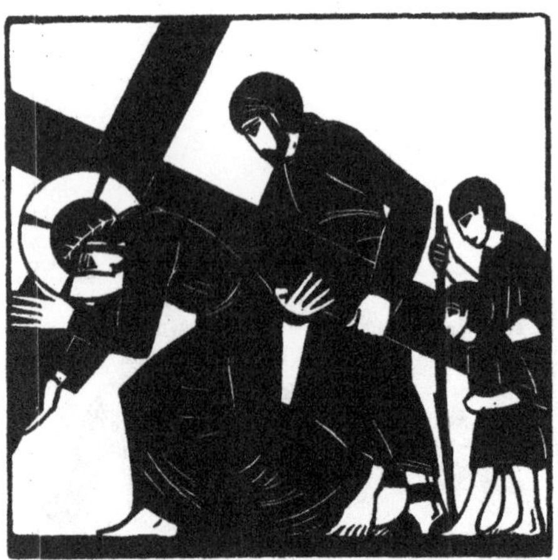

239 Simon of Cyrene Helps Jesus to Carry the Cross
1917
The Way of the Cross

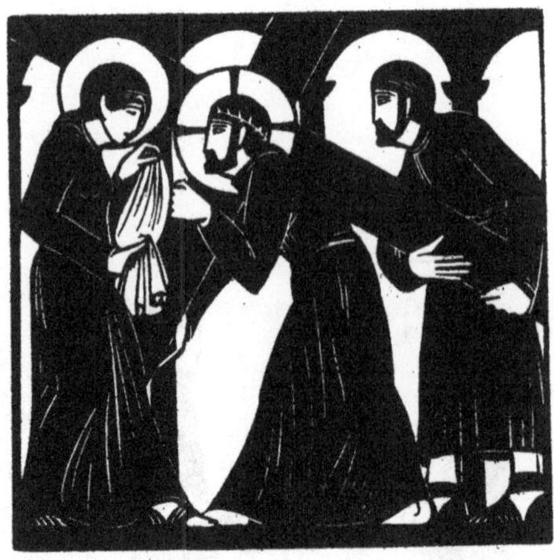

240 Jesus Meets Veronica
1917
The Way of the Cross

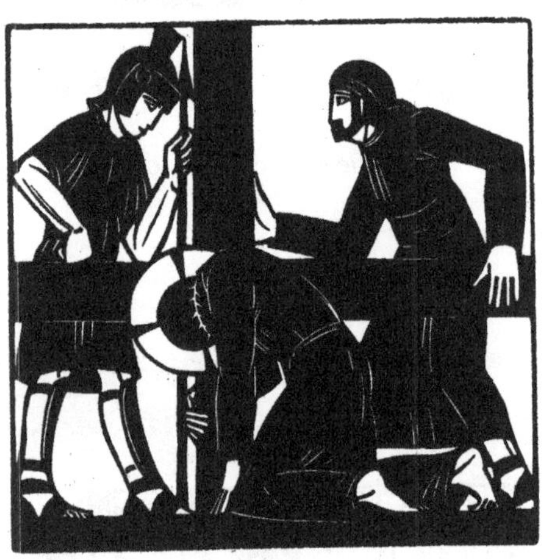

241 Jesus Falls the Second Time
1917
The Way of the Cross

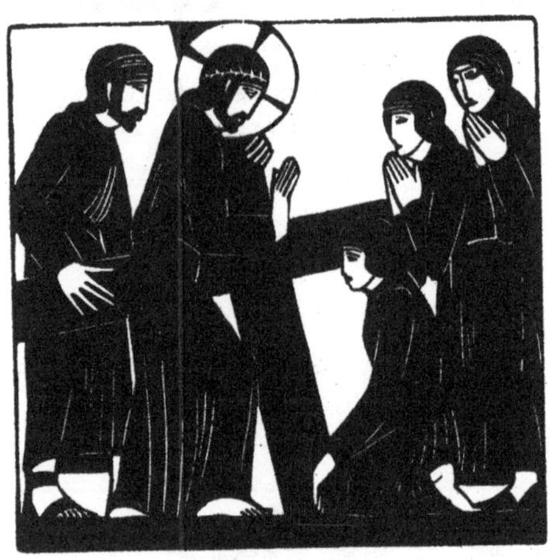

242 Jesus Speaks to the Women of Jerusalem
1917
The Way of the Cross

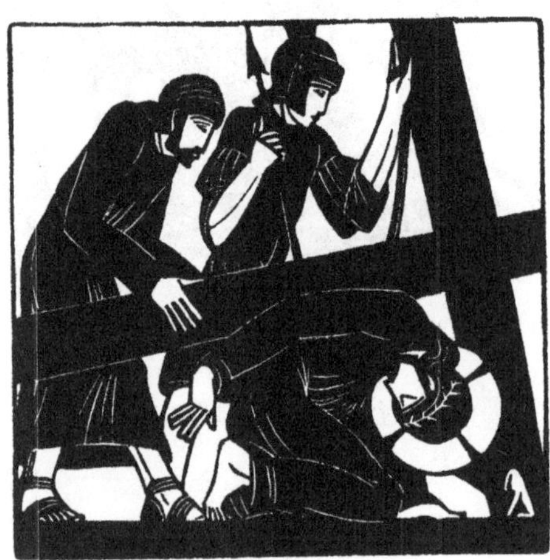

243 Jesus Falls the Third Time
1917
The Way of the Cross

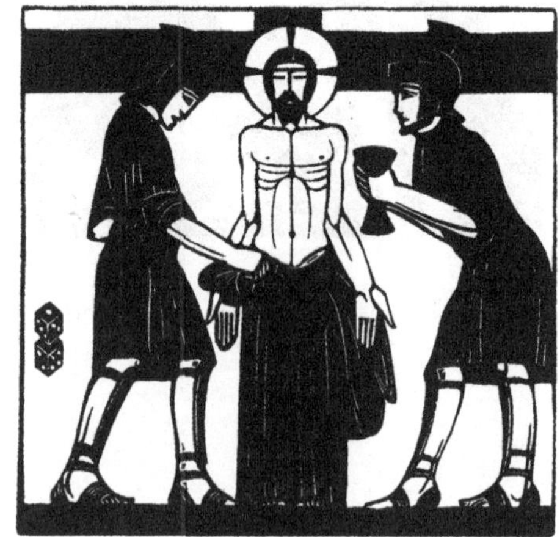

244 Jesus Is Stripped
1917
The Way of the Cross

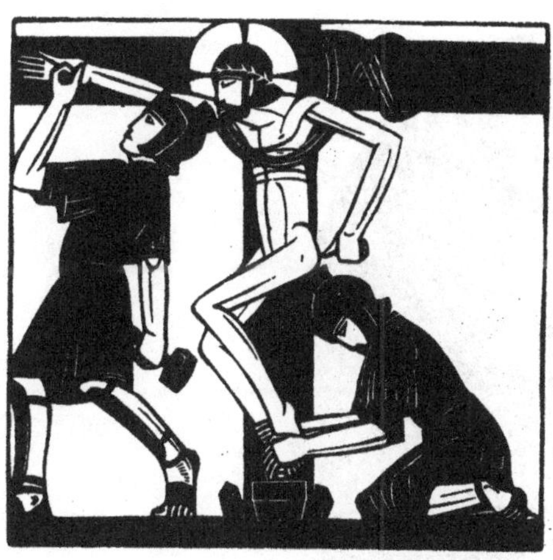

245 Jesus Is Nailed to the Cross
1917
The Way of the Cross

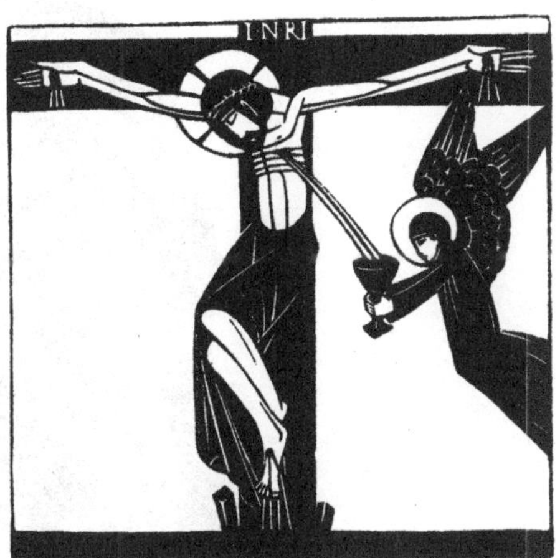

246 Jesus Dies Upon the Cross
1917
The Way of the Cross

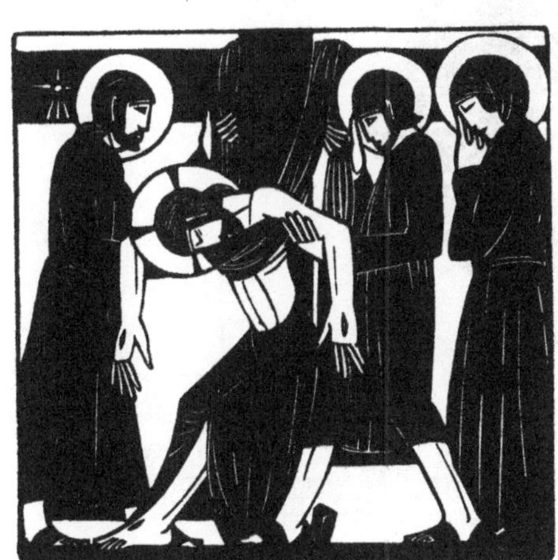

247 The Body of Jesus
Is Taken Down
from the Cross
1917
The Way of the Cross

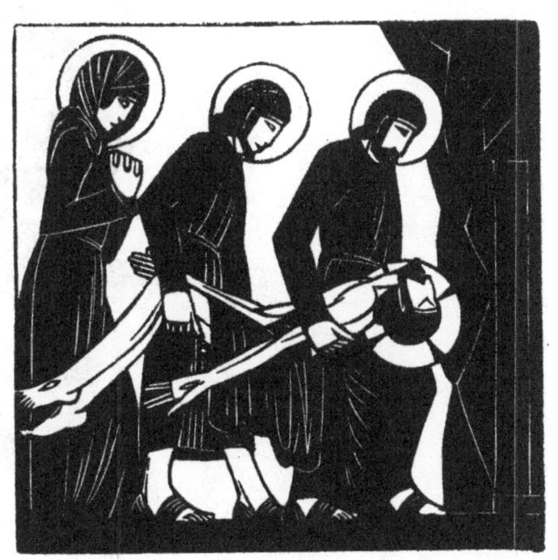

248 The Body of Jesus
Is Laid in the Tomb
1917
The Way of the Cross

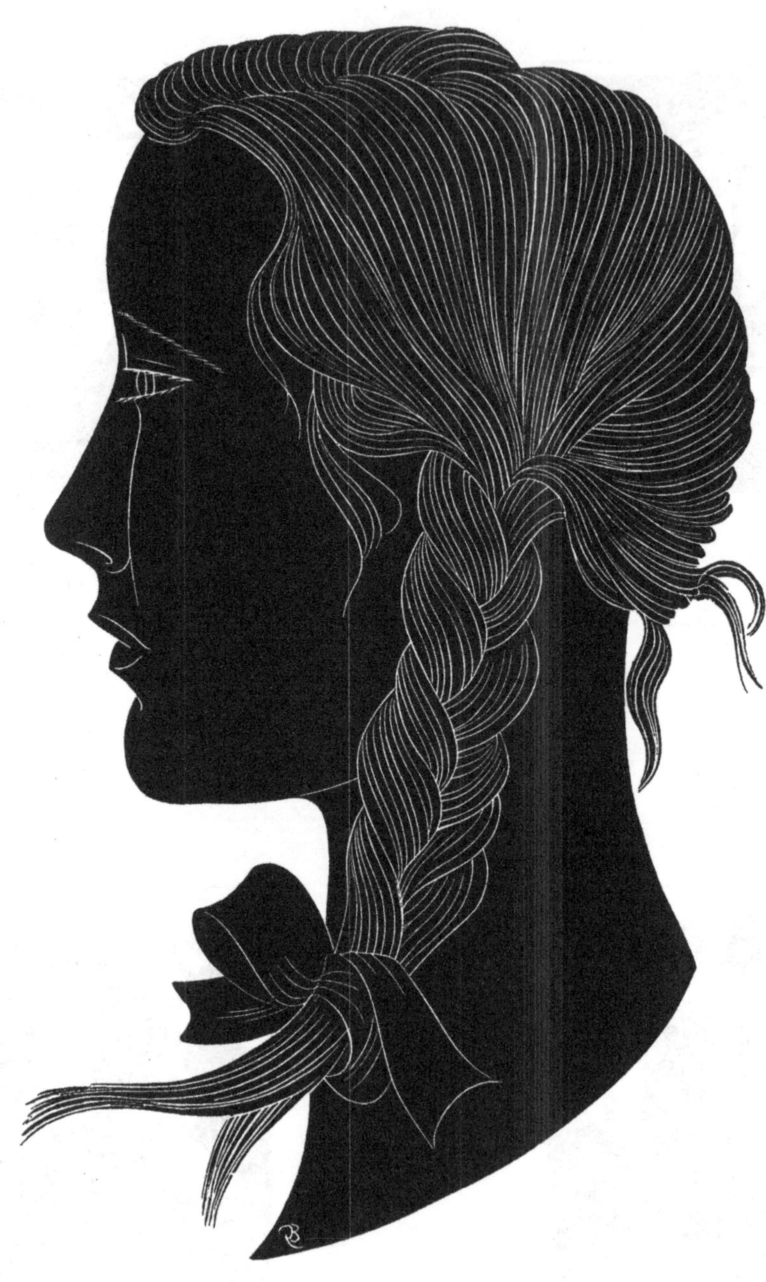

249 The Plait
(Portrait of Petra)
1922

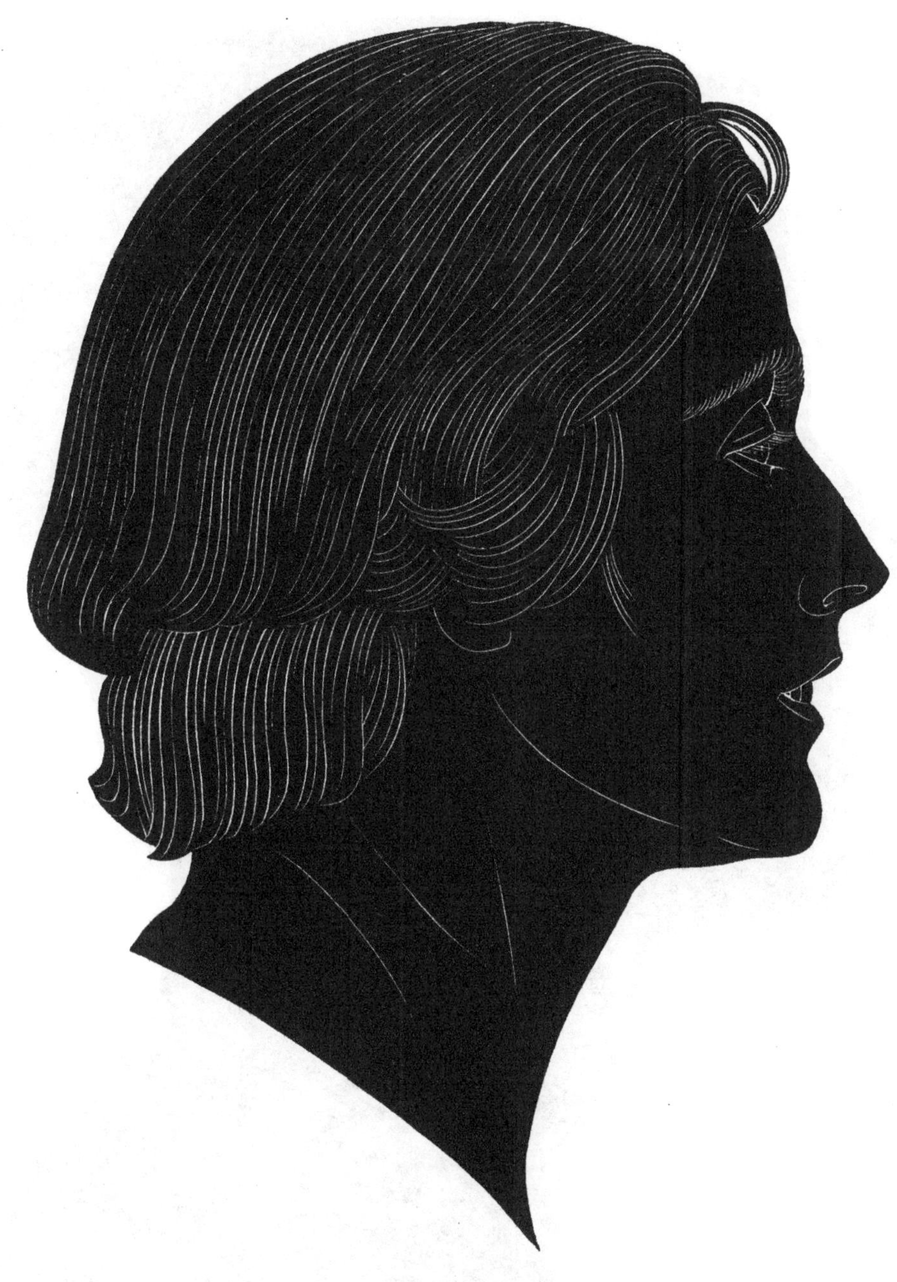

250 Clare
(Portrait of Mrs. H. D. C. Pepler)
1922

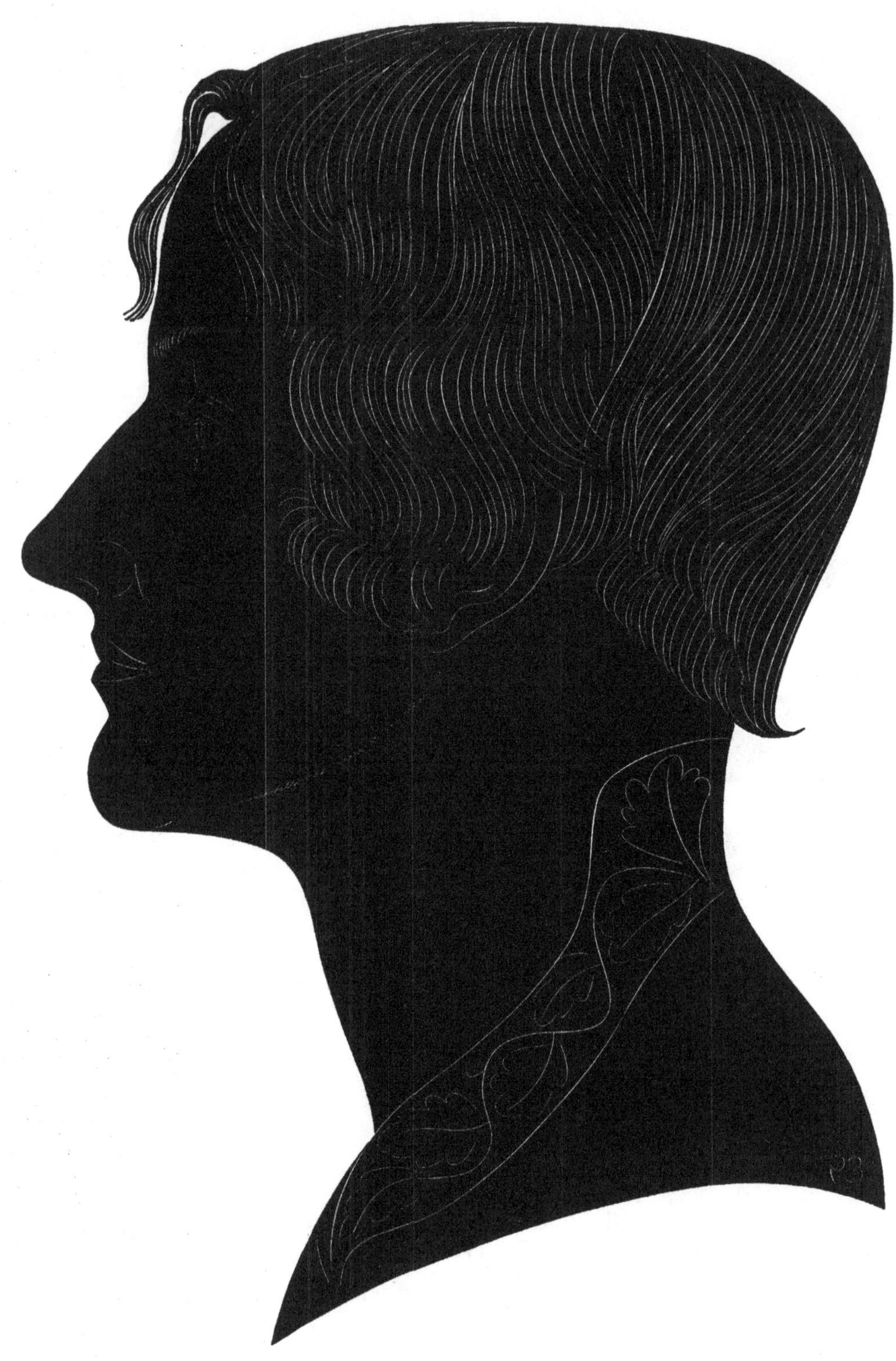

251 Mrs Beatrice Warde
(2nd state)
1926